AF530677

HUMAN RIGHTS: THE GLOBAL PERSPECTIVE

HUMAN RIGHTS
THE GLOBAL PERSPECTIVE

M.H.Syed

4831/24, Ansari Road
Darya Ganj
New Delhi-110 002
Phone: 3260807
Fax: 3274173
E-mail: essess@del3.vsnl.net.in

HUMAN RIGHTS: THE GLOBAL PERSPECTIVE

First Published, 2003

ISBN 81-88583-07-03

Published by:
Reference Press
4831/24, Ansari Road,
Darya Ganj,
New Delhi - 110002.
Phone: 3260807
Fax: 3274173
E-mail: essess@del3.vsnl.net.in

Printed in India at:
Mehra Offset Press, Delhi.

Contents

Preface

Today, Human Rights are no strange phenomenon. In fact, now, the human rights idea is universal. Not only that, it has virtually been accepted by all Nations, States and Societies, all over the world. Over a period of time, the concept of human rights has assumed importance at the global level.

The respect for Human Rights only, makes freedom meaningful and really effective. Still, the protection of human rights is a constant battle, which can not result into success, until and unless every person gets involved in it. The society is not to be neutral, but it has to essentially take a side, supporting the struggle going on in all countries of the world particularly, the developing world.

In our society, each individual has his or her responsibility towards this noble cause and intellectuals and acedemics are bound to contribute much and do a lot in this direction by way of expressing sympathy with the activists of Human Rights, in real terms.

This work is the result of a painstaking research and toilsome work for several years on the part of the author, who took the accomplishment of this book as a mission.

This book – comprehensive, authentic and exhaustive in itself – is a valuable addition to the stacks, full of works on the subject. It fills a vacuum on the basis of its merits in totality. It must be an essential possession of every scholar, social worker, politician, bureaucrat and of course, human right activist in India and abroad. Further, it must be beneficial for students in all faculties and the general readers as well.

Hopefully this modest effort would succeed in creating a stir and in making people aware of the significance and importance of the issue. The people who matter and the masses, as well should feel concerned about the matter. If that much happens, the under signed would feel honoured and encouraged to nurse his ambitious endeavours further and continue his research pursuits.

M.H. Syed

ONE

Introduction

In the modern world, the human rights idea is universally, accepted by virtually all states and societies regardless of historical, cultural, ideological, economic, or other differences. It is international, the subject of international diplomacy, law, and institutions. It is philosophically respectable, even to opposed philosophical persuasions. The universalization of human rights is a political fact.

The Universal Declaration of Human Rights adopted by the General Assembly in 1948 has been accepted by virtually all of today's 150 states; even those, notably the European Communist states, which had abstained when the Declaration was approved, have now accepted it formally in the Final Act of the Conference on Security and Cooperation. Every state has adhered to at least one human rights agreement; and more than a third of the world's states have accepted the comprehensive agreements, the International Covenant on Civil and Political Rights, and the International Covenant on Economic, Social, and Cultural Rights, with more states joining every year.

The universal acceptance of the idea of human rights and its general content may be only formal and superficial, in some cases even hypocritical, but no government dissents from the ideology of human rights today or offers an alternative to it. The steady internationalization of human rights is equally impressive. Before the Second World War, how a state treated its own inhabitants was its own business, a matter of "domestic jurisdiction," not of "international concern."

Today it is the stuff of daily diplomacy among states.

Numerous international organizations deal with it regularly, and it is never absent from the agenda of every organ and agency of the United Nations and of major regional organizations. There are dozens of international human rights agreements, and some of them have been adhered to by more than one hundred states. New international bodies-commissions, committees, and courts—occupy themselves with human rights daily. The contemporary philosophical respectability of human rights is itself remarkable.

The idea of limitations on government, on majorities-even on the "public good" in favour of individual autonomy, dignity, and need, has taken root and no present political system, no contemporary political theory, rejects it. Earlier philosophical objections have subsided or have become irrelevant. Eighteenth century notions of natural rights suffered the onslaughts of legal positivism in the nineteenth and early twentieth centuries, but human rights now are attended by resurgent "neo-natural-rights" theories, and are finding a prominent place in contemporary political, ethical, and moral philosophy, now again preoccupied with "justice," "liberty," "equality," and "rights."

Today, it is human rights that claim the mantle of natural law, not as in the past—slavery or the divine right of kings, not the inferiority of women, of particular races or of the poor. The establishment of human rights in national law and in international law has disarmed legal positivists as well. It is human rights that are positive national and international law, not the antihuman laws of Hitler or some other jurisprudence of terror.

And it is individual civil-political rights as well as economic, social and cultural rights that are the law, not unmitigated collectivism or *laissez-faire*. The idea of human rights is not an abstraction; it has specific content. What the world has accepted are the civil, political, economic, social, and cultural rights set forth in the Universal Declaration and the international covenants. They include rights of freedom from mistreatment and undue governmental intrusion, as well as rights to governmental support for the economic and social welfare of every human being.

Although specific, the rights are flexible enough to rise above differences among political systems; they are consistent with different degrees and forms of free enterprise as well as with socialism. Debates about conflicts or priorities between rights only confirm rather than depreciate any of the rights declared in the Declaration or protected by the covenants.

Relation with International Law

Concern by some governments with the condition of individuals in other countries is not new. Centuries ago, princes and popes interceded for coreligionists and others in various countries. The nineteenth century saw a number of "humanitarian interventions" by big powers, through diplomacy and sometimes through force, to protest, end, or prevent massacres, pogroms, and other atrocities. These, however, were personal expressions of "*noblesse oblige*," or extraordinary reactions to egregious events; they were sharp deviations from the international political system's assumption that, in principle, how a state treated its own citizens was its own business. Surely there was no serious disposition to render the treatment of the individual human being in his own country a subject of international diplomacy and law.

Human rights did not become the concern of international politics or law until after the Second World War, but individual welfare was not wholly beyond the ken of the international system at an earlier date even before then. International law and human rights were linked in the history of ideas, both having antecedents in natural law and in Roman law, and common progenitors in Grotius, Vattel, and Locke. In fact, international law earlier included some of what we would today as human rights obligations; for example, treaty provisions in which parties undertook to tolerate heterodox religious worship and not to impose civil disabilities on religious dissenters.

Customary international law, too, has long imposed on states a responsibility not to deny justice to aliens. In the last century, nations sought to mitigate the horrors of war by developing law to forbid particularly cruel weapons, and to protect prisoners of war and civilian populations during war. Following the First World War, the dominant powers required several states to adhere to "Minority treaties," in which they assumed obligations to respect the rights of ethnic, national, linguistic, religious, or other minorities among their inhabitants.

The League of Nations Covenant provided that the mandate system established for dependent areas should be governed by the principle that "the well being and development of such peoples form a sacred trust of civilization," and imposed "conditions which will guarantee freedom of conscience and religion" and other rights. Members of the League undertook "to secure just treatment of the native inhabitants of territories under their control"; mandatory powers were required to promote the welfare and rights of the inhabitants of mandated territories. The years following the First World War also saw a major development in the law of human rights, a development that is often overlooked and commonly underestimated: the International Labour Office, now the International Labour Organisation (ILO), launched a series of conventions setting minimum standards for labour and other social conditions. This early international law of human rights, however, was limited in scope and focus, and while it had humanitarian consequences, its motivation was largely political rather than idealistic.

Christian princes had gone to war on behalf of coreligionists in other countries, and religious tolerance was a condition of peace in religiously divided, war-weary Europe; agreements for mutual tolerance made possible the establishment of the secular state and the rise of modern international law. Powerful states exporting people, goods, and capital to other countries in the age of mercantilism insisted on law that would protect the interests which these represented.

Denial of justice to an alien was an offense to the state whose nationality he bore and jeopardized its economic and political interests. (Aliens who were "stateless," who had no nationality, had no remedy for denial of justice, since no state was offended by such denials.) States insisted on an international standard of justice (rooted in natural law) for their nationals abroad even when these states did not recognize that standard for their citizens at home. Humanitarian laws regulating the conduct of war were reciprocal undertakings defending a state's soldiery and population against the enemy.

Minority treaties were required of some states, not universal norms applicable to the big and the powerful as well. The mandate provisions were seen by many as essentially hortatory, a small rhetorical price for continuing "imperialism" instead of granting the territories self-determination and self-government. The ILO conventions were capitalism's defense against the specter of spreading socialism, and states, moreover, had direct interests in the conditions of labour in countries with which they competed in a common market. Broader law came in the wake of Hitler. The international human rights movement was born in, and out of the Second World War.

The proclaimed aims of that war included the establishment of individual rights and the "Four Freedoms" for everyone in every country, and that aim also inspired the planning for the postwar world. To begin with, the victors imposed human rights obligations on the vanquished in peace treaties, and included human rights violations in the Nuremberg Charter and prosecutions. Occupying powers presided at the incorporation of human rights safeguards into new constitutions and laws for West Germany, Japan, and Austria.

The UN Charter ushered in a new international concern for human rights everywhere. The Charter replaced the League of Nations' concentration on the rights of minorities in selected countries with heed to the rights of all individuals everywhere. The new commitment to "self-determination," together with universal human rights, it was apparently thought, would eliminate the minorities problem: some minorities would become independent by self-determination; the rest would find their rights protected equally with majorities by universal commitment to human rights for all. The Preamble of the UN Charter reaffirms "faith in fundamental human rights, in the dignity and worth of the human person, in the equal rights of men and women," and declares the determination of peoples "to promote social progress and better standards of life in larger freedom." The purposes of the UN include international cooperation "in promoting and encouraging respect for human rights and for fundamental freedoms for all without distinction as to race, sex, language, or religion".

Human rights are among the responsibilities for study and recommendation of the General Assembly (Article 13) and the Economic and Social Council (Article 62(2)), and a commission on human rights is expressly required (Article 68). Members pledged themselves to cooperate with the UN organization for the achievement of its human rights purposes. The various UN bodies have devoted years of arduous effort to promoting human rights. Human rights have been on every agenda of every body and have become a staple of UN activity.

A universal declaration of human rights was prepared and adopted. Even particular human rights violations have received attention, early as in the case of Russian wives of non-Russians and the treatment of Indians in South Africa, more recently in Chile and elsewhere. Some violations, e.g., apartheid in South Africa are perennially on the UN agenda. Other violations in other places—the treatment of Soviet Jews, allegations of torture in Chile—were the subject of extended international debate over many years. Despite resistance, it was established that within the meaning of Article 2(7) of the Charter, UN preoccupation with human rights was not forbidden intervention.

The prevailing view was that UN consideration was not intervention, and, more importantly, that human rights are an international, not a domestic concern.

The New Law

The UN Charter ushered in a new international law of human rights. The new law buried the old dogma that the individual is not a "subject" of international politics and law and that a government's behaviour toward its own nationals is a matter of domestic, not international, concern. It penetrated national frontiers and the veil of sovereignty. It removed the exclusive identification of an individual with his government.

It gave the individual a part in international politics and rights in international law, independently of his government. It also gave the individual protectors other than his government, indeed protectors and remedies against his government. The international law of human rights differs from other international laws in its motivations and impulses as well. Generally, international law is made, international obligations are undertaken, to serve common or reciprocal national interests; early human rights laws, too, we have seen, largely served states' political or economic purposes.

The move to a comprehensive human rights law also sought to appeal to national and transnational interests, perhaps in an effort to de-emphasize its radical nature. Human rights, it was urged, are related to international peace, for states that violate human rights at home are not trustworthy in international relations, and violations of those rights afford occasions, temptations, and pretexts for interventions or war.

The international human rights law also had a different kind of political motivation: states that had minority treaties or human rights provisions in peace treaties imposed on them resented being singled out and sought to universalise their undertakings. But whatever reasons (or rationalisations) were provided to mask it, the fact is that the new comprehensive international human rights law generally serves no patent, particular national interest. It is essentially ideological, idealistic, humanitarian; its true and deep purpose is to improve the lot of individual men and women everywhere, particularly where national institutions and nonlegal international forces are not adequate—a unique and revolutionary purpose for international law. The international law of human rights parallels and supplements national law, superseding and supplying the deficiencies of national constitutions and laws; but it does not replace, and indeed depends on, national institutions.

The constituency in every society that supports human rights law is different from the constituency that supports, say, international trade agreements, or military alliances, or peaceful settlements, or even international organization and cooperation. The pressures on a government to adhere to international human rights law are also different from those to adhere to other laws, and indeed, a state's adherence to human rights conventions is far less important if in fact it behaves at home, toward its own, consistently with their terms. In other respects, too, international law and politics see human rights in the context of the international political system.

Although human rights are universal, they are the claims of an individual upon his society, not on other societies. Although the society in which one lives may be crucial to life and dignity, although a right to change one's society might well be deemed fundamental, the individual does not have an absolute right to join another society and seek his rights there. Even those who are oppressed at home do not yet have an international human right to asylum elsewhere; those who are starving at home do not have an internationally recognized human right to be taken in by the more affluent societies or to be fed by them. Like other international laws, human rights law is made by treaty or convention; there is also customary human rights law made by national practice with a developing sense of legal obligation.

The declarations and resolutions of UN organs and other international bodies on human rights may have greater weight in achieving international law here than on other matters, since they purport to express the conscience of mankind on a matter of conscience. And though all law-making is a political process, humanitarian law has its own politics in both making and enforcing law.

The history of the development of the covenants is described fully by Vratislav Pechota (essay 2). It is relevant here to address the antecedents of that development. In themselves, the normative human rights provisions of the UN Charter are general and preliminary: essentially, by Articles 55 and 56, member states pledge themselves to take joint and separate action in cooperation with the United Nations to achieve respect for human rights.

Human rights are not defined or specified in the Charter, and there is no clear undertaking by every state not to commit one or another violation. The institutions, procedures, and programs for inducing national respect for rights, for monitoring the condition of human rights in different countries, and for preventing, deterring, or ending violation, are not provided. But the words of the Charter are words of legal obligation and surely the pledge of Article 56 is violated if a member state itself persists in committing gross violations of rights universally recognized as fundamental. No doubt, however, the members of the UN themselves recognized that the Charter law was insufficient. Immediately they proceeded to prepare and promulgate the Universal Declaration of Human Rights, making specific the general Charter references to human rights and freedoms for all.

The Declaration is a remarkable juncture of political, civil and economic-social rights, with equality and freedom from discrimination, a principal and recurrent theme. It declares the rights to life, liberty, and security of person, to fair criminal process, to freedom of conscience, thought, expression, association, and privacy; the right to seek and enjoy asylum, to leave one's country and return to it; rights to marriage and family, and rights of property. It declares the will of the people to be the basis of the authority of government, and provides for universal suffrage and bona fide elections. It speaks of the right to work and leisure, health care, and education. The Universal Declaration was not generally conceived as law but as "a common standard of achievement" for all to aspire to; hence its approval without dissent.

Some thought that the United Nations should rest on the Declaration and concentrate on encouraging states to raise their national norms and conform their national behaviour to its standards. Instead, governments moved to convert the Declaration into binding legal norms. The process was very, very long. In some part this was due to the ever-increasing number of states, all of which joined in the process and slowed the negotiations. In part, delay was due to the differences between a declaration and a binding covenant.

Some states that had been prepared to declare a general principle wished it carefully defined and circumscribed if it were to be clearly a legal obligation with legal consequences, for though no state was compelled to adhere to any draft covenant that might emerge, most states wanted something they might be able to adopt if it became desirable; they were reluctant, moreover, to have a covenant adopted as the international norm in whose light their behaviour would appear to be wanting.

The process was also extended because there were strong pressures on the other hand to develop and elaborate the generalities of the Declaration and give them more specific content so that they would afford greater protection. The Declaration, moreover, had not provided for its implementation, while many sessions were spent debating and elaborating means to enforce the new emerging legal undertakings. In substantial part, it took eighteen years to convert the Declaration into convention because it was necessary to accommodate, bridge, submerge, and conceal deep divisions and differences, especially between democratic-libertarian and socialist-revolutionary states; differences in fundamental conceptions about the relation of society to the individual, about his rights and duties, about priorities and preferences among them. Western states fought for, and obtained, a division into two covenants, the Covenant on Civil and Political Rights and the Covenant on Economic, Social, and Cultural Rights.

The two covenants recognize the difference in the character of rights in various subtle ways. For example, the Covenant on Civil and Political Rights is drafted in terms of the individual's rights: e.g., "Every human being has the inherent right to life"; "No one shall be held in slavery"; "All persons shall be equal before the courts and tribunals." The Covenant on Economic, Social, and Cultural Rights, on the other hand, speaks only to the states, not the individual: "The States Parties to the present Covenant recognize the right to work"; "The States Parties . . . undertake to ensure . . . the right of everyone to form trade unions"; "The States Parties . . . recognize the right of everyone to education." There was wide agreement and clear recognition that the means required to induce compliance with social-economic undertakings were different from those required for civil-political rights. But the Covenant on Economic, Social, and Cultural Rights is law, not merely exhortation and aspiration.

The rights it recognizes are as "human," universal, and fundamental as are those of the Civil and Political Rights Covenant. The obligation for a state party is "to take steps ... to the maximum of its available resources, with a view to achieving progressively the full realization" of these rights, and fulfillment may require national planning and major programs, and international assistance. But these limitations do not derogate from the legal character of the obligations. Other delays resulted from sharp differences over the inclusion or scope of particular rights.

Most of the states were concerned, or were more concerned, with values reflecting their struggle against colonialism but not included in the Universal Declaration and not previously part of the accepted human rights ideology. They insisted that both Covenants include the right of all peoples to self-determination as well as to "economic self-determination," to "sovereignty" over their resources. Western states resisted, arguing that both are at best rights of a "people," not of any individual, and surely not-like human rights generally-rights of individual is against their own society. They argued, too, that the content of these norms was highly uncertain and controversial.

The argument did not prevail, and identical provisions on self-determination now head both covenants. Also included in the Covenant on Civil and Political Rights were other, less controversial, rights not mentioned in the Declaration—freedom from imprisonment for debt, rights of children, and rights of minorities (Articles 11, 24, 27). That Covenant also prohibits propaganda for war and incitement to national, racial, or religious hatred (Article 20). Some rights included in the Declaration were substantially elaborated.

On the other hand, the right to enjoy private property, included in the Declaration, was finally omitted from the covenants. Much time was also spent in the attempt to bridge the demand of some states for effective means to enforce the covenants and the insistence of others on the "sovereignty" of states and resistance to international scrutiny and "intrusion." In sum, the international law of human rights developed by the two covenants parallels the Universal Declaration. It provides protections like those in the constitutions and laws of enlightened democratic-liberal countries as well as the promises of socialist and "welfare" constitutions.

During, and since the negotiation of these two major covenants, the UN system also promoted specialized declarations and conventions—on genocide, on the status of refugees and stateless persons, on the rights of women, and on the elimination of all forms of racial discrimination. These emphasize, extend, and supplement the protections afforded by the principal covenants. They have also made it possible to "extract" legal obligations on these particular subjects from governments not prepared to adhere to all the obligations of the general covenants. How much law various covenants and conventions have made depends, of course, on the number of adherences to them.

January 1, 1981, the Genocide Convention had 85 parties, the Convention on the Elimination of All Forms of Racial Discrimination 108, the Convention on Political Rights of Women 86, and the Convention on the Status of Refugees 81. Late in 1975, the Covenant on Civil and Political Rights and the Covenant on Economic, Social, and Cultural Rights obtained the adherences necessary to bring them into effect, and adherences have continued to trickle in. (As of January 1, 1981, the former had 65, the latter 66 adherences.) As to each of these conventions, some adherences are subject to reservations of greater or lesser significance. It matters, of course, whether covenants are accepted by populous nations or by those with small populations; whether the states that adhere are more or less disposed to comply with their undertakings; and whether some who have not adhered might nonetheless practice what the conventions require.

International human rights instruments do not legislate human rights; they "recognize" them and build upon that recognition. Human rights was an eighteenth century idea, rooted in notions of natural law and natural rights, and woven of several strands: original autonomy of the individual, converted in society to popular sovereignty; government by social compact of the people and subject to the continued consent of the governed; government for limited purposes only; the rights reserved for the individual even against the people's representatives in government.

The international human rights movement took these eighteenth-century ideas of individual autonomy and freedom and combined them with nineteenth and twentieth-century ideas of socialism and the welfare state. International human rights, however, reflect no single, comprehensive theory of the relation of the individual to society (other than what is implied in the very concept of rights). That there are "fundamental human rights" was a declared article of faith, "reaffirmed" by "the peoples of the United Nations" in the UN Charter.

The Universal Declaration of Human Rights, striving for a pronouncement that would appeal to diverse political systems governing diverse peoples, built on that faith and shunned philosophical exploration. Because of that faith—and of political and ideological forces—governments accepted the concept of human rights, agreed that they were appropriate for international concern, cooperated to define them, assumed international obligations to respect them, and submitted to some international scrutiny as to their compliance with these obligations. Those who built international human rights perhaps also saw these rights as "natural," but in a contemporary sense: human rights correspond to the nature of man and of human society, to his psychology and its sociology:

- rights "derive from the inherent dignity of the human person";
- "recognition ... of the equal and inalienable rights of all members of the human family, is the foundation of freedom, justice and peace in the world";
- respect for, and observance of, human rights will help create "conditions of stability and well-being which are necessary for peaceful and friendly relations among nations."

We are not told what theory justifies "human dignity" as the source of rights, or how the needs of human dignity are determined. We are not told what conception of justice is reflected in human rights, or how preserving human rights will promote peace in the world. International human rights are recognized as inherent, but it is not necessarily assumed that man is in principle autonomous, or that rights antecede government.

The international instruments nod to popular sovereignty, but there is no other hint of social compact or of continuing consent of the governed. Respect for retained rights is not a condition of government, or a basis of its legitimacy; violation of rights does not warrant undoing government by revolution. International human rights imply rights for the individual against society, but they are not seen as against the interests of society.

Rather, it is believed, a good society is one in which individual rights flourish, and the promotion and protection of individual rights is a public good. Any apparent conflict between the individual and society, between individual rights and a more general public good, is only temporary and superficial; in the longer, deeper view, the society is better if the individual's rights are respected. Like the eighteenth century idea of rights, international human rights also, inevitably, implicate the purposes for which governments are created.

Rights against government imply limitations on government, but there is no *a priori* assumption that in general government is for limited purposes only. To the contrary, born after various socialisms were established and spreading, and after commitment to welfare economics and the welfare state was nearly universal, international human rights imply a conception of government as designed for many purposes and seasons.

The rights deemed to be fundamental include not only civil and political rights which government must not invade, but also rights to economic and social well-being which government must actively provide or promote. The rights declared and enumerated imply a government that is activist, intervening, that is committed to economic-social planning for the society which would redound as economic-social rights to the individual.

Societal Rights

Human rights are rights which the individual has, or should have, in his society. If societies respected these rights adequately, there would be no need for international law and institutions to help protect them. International human rights law and institutions are designed to induce states to remedy the inadequacies of their national laws and institutions so that human rights will be respected and vindicated.

The individual must pursue his rights through his own laws and institutions. Even when these fail him, international law and institutions cannot provide those rights; they can only press the state to provide them. International human rights obligations are met when, and only when, national laws and institutions meet the minimum international standards and give effect to the minimum of human rights. International human rights agreements are international agreements like all others. They create rights and duties between states parties to the agreement; they may create also rights in third parties, whether states or individuals.

Failure to honour these undertakings brings the same consequences as for other international agreements: other parties can demand compliance and seek reparations, and may resort to any tribunal which has jurisdiction over such claims between these parties. Some agreements also provide for special remedies before particular bodies. The United Nations Charter made human rights a legitimate subject for discussion and recommendation by the Assembly and its sub-organs. Human rights may also properly come into the ken of the Security Council when it implicates peace and security, e.g., in South Africa. By discussing human rights the General Assembly does not intervene in matters "which are essentially within the domestic jurisdiction of any state" (Article 2(a)). Intervention, strictly, means dictatorial interference by force, and there have been no UN military interventions in support of human rights; discussion and recommendation are not intervention. Human rights, moreover, are a matter of international concern, not essentially within any state's domestic jurisdiction.

Enforcement measures by the Security Council are in any event exempted from Article 2(7). Article 2(7) speaks only of intervention by the UN, not by member states, but most challenges to activities by states on behalf of human rights as "intervention" are equally unfounded. Peaceful objections by states to human rights violations by other states are not interventions. Generally, human rights are no longer within a state's domestic jurisdiction. That which is governed by international law or agreement is *ipso facto* and by definition a matter of international concern, not a matter of any state's domestic jurisdiction.

Certainly, any state that adheres to an international human rights agreement has made the subject of that agreement a matter of international concern. It has submitted its performance to scrutiny and to appropriate, peaceful reaction by other parties, and to any special procedures or machinery provided by the agreement for its implementation.

International Legal Rights

The international instruments speak of human rights, but they do not purport to create them; they recognize their preexistence in some other moral or legal order. They confirm the concept of human rights and give it status and value in the international system. Like other international agreements, the international human rights agreements create rights and obligations among the states parties to the agreement: every party is obligated to every other state to carry out its undertakings; every other state has the right to have the obligation carried out. But these are the legal rights of states, not the human rights of the individual. If states are the promisors and promisees, however, the authentic beneficiaries are the individual inhabitants whose "human rights" the state promises to respect.

Whether the international agreements also create international legal rights for the individual is debatable. Some have strongly denied it. Others argue that as third-party beneficiaries, and the true beneficiaries, individuals have rights under international law, even when they have no direct remedy but must rely on states and international bodies to vindicate their rights. And some instruments for example the Optional Protocol to the International Covenant on Civil and Political Rights, the Convention on the Elimination of All Forms of Racial Discrimination, and the European and the American Conventions on Human Rights also provide some remedy for the individual to pursue his international legal rights by international legal remedies.

Enforcement: National and International

Human rights are rights to be enjoyed by individuals in their own societies and implemented and enforced under their laws and institutions. International undertakings are designed to help assure that national societies in fact respect the human rights of their inhabitants. International instruments require states to enact legislation and otherwise ensure that the rights are respected. In some legal systems international human rights obligations may be "self-executing" and will be given effect by officials and courts without domestic legislation.

The international system also provides "enforcement machinery." Such international instrumentalities, however, do not operate directly to grant the individual his rights; they work on the state and are designed to induce the state to carry out its obligations. Even when the individual is given some kind of an international remedy, for example, the right to "communicate" to the Human Rights Committee pursuant to the Optional Protocol to the Covenant, the communication does not produce an international mandate conferring the right; it serves only to trigger an international process to induce the state to desist from violation or to provide a remedy for past violations.

Limitations

The freedom of expression, in the classic reference, does not permit one falsely to cry "fire" in a crowded theatre; the most libertarian societies do not permit slander; all countries impose some limits on freedom of movement in some circumstances to protect national security or public order. In the rights jurisprudence of the United States these permissible limitations are not expressed in the Constitution, although sometimes read into general phrases: search and seizure is forbidden only if "unreasonable," punishment only if "cruel and unusual," infringements on liberty only if they deny "due process of law." The Kramers of the Covenant sought to define the permissible scope of limitations as strictly as possible, although inevitably in general phrases.

For example, the freedom of movement within a country or the right to leave it "shall not be subject to any restrictions except those which are provided by law, are necessary to protect national security, public order (order public), public health or morals, or the rights and freedoms of others, and are consistent with the other rights recognized" in the Covenant (Article 12(3)). Or, "the Press and the public may be excluded from all or part of a trial for reasons of morals, public order (*ordure public*) or national security in a democratic society, or when the interest of the private lives of the parties so requires, or to the extent strictly necessary in the opinion of the court in special circumstances where publicity would prejudice the interests of justice" (Article 14(1)).

One can debate the merits of these and other limitations or their particular formulations, but few would question that in principle some such limitations are inevitable and probably desirable. The limitations themselves, however, are governed by law, not by the whim of the state. Whether a particular limitation on a right is permissible under the Covenant is a question of international law, and the state's action can be scrutinized and challenged as a violation of the Covenant (see Alexander Kiss, essay 12).

The Covenant

Like all international human rights agreements the Covenant does not eliminate the essential dependence of individual human rights on national laws and institutions.

The Covenant requires states to respect the individual's rights and to "ensure" them, and the state can do that only through its own laws and institutions. Indeed, the Covenant expressly requires states to "adopt such legislative or other measures" as are necessary to give effect to rights recognized by the Covenant.

The extent of that obligation and its implications for states with different legal systems are considered by Oscar Schachter in essay 13. The Covenant's method of enforcement is described by A. H. Robertson in essay 14. There is a tendency to deprecate and depreciate it, since it is based largely on voluntary reporting, which at best tends to be self-serving and not likely to reveal violations. No doubt more intensive monitoring would be more effective. But the fact that a state has to report inevitably has some influence to induce better compliance. Further inducement will result if the Human Rights Committee develops the practice of scrutinizing these reports, asking for more information, and challenging reported claims on the basis of external evidence.

A public report by a state, moreover, will be read by other governments, and by organizations and individuals both within and outside the reporting state, and their criticism of these reports will serve to improve the state's behaviour. If states parties can be persuaded to assert their rights as parties to challenge violations, if more states accept the optional provisions under which the Human Rights Committee can receive complaints from other states (Article 41) or from private persons or organizations (under the Protocol) the remedial and deterrent influence of the Covenant will be further enhanced.

Reservations

Unlike some other international agreements, the Covenant does not expressly bar reservations generally or to particular clauses. In view of the character of the Covenant, one may assume that there was no intention to bar reservations; it is desirable to have states adhere to as much of the Covenant as possible, even if they insist on excluding some particular provision. But any state may object to a reservation by another state and may even reject a treaty relation with the reserving state as regards the Covenant as a whole. Also, there can be no reservation "incompatible with the object and purpose" of the Covenant. Major reservations that contradict the basic spirit of the Covenant would be out of order even if other parties were prepared to acquiesce in them. Surely, for a hypothetical example, South Africa could not purport to ratify the Covenant but reserve the right to maintain apartheid. Even as regards particular provisions, it would seem improper for a state to reserve a major exception permitting it to violate an important right in an important way against an important segment of its population.

Even if most states acquiesced, a single objecting state might challenge the propriety of a reservation under the Vienna Convention and impugn the claim of the reserving state to be a party to the Convention. It has been suggested that those articles of the Covenant which are not subject to derogation in time of emergency ought not to be – perhaps a fortiori – subject to reservation generally. That argument is plausible, with some limitations.

- A state may wish to make a reservation to the nonderogation clause itself, and if the reservation is not "total," it might not be a reservation that defeats the object and purpose of the Covenant.
- Some clauses are not subject to derogation not because of their fundamental importance but because they are of a character to which public emergency is irrelevant and surely not strictly required," for example imprisonment for contract debt (Article 11).

That such a clause is nonderogable, then, is no sign that it should also be not subject to reservation. Even articles that are not subject to derogation for reasons of their importance, moreover, might be treated differently for reservation purposes. The exemption from derogation is stated in terms of whole articles of the Covenant and might be deemed to exempt the entire article. But while a reservation to any of those articles as a whole may well be unacceptable as inconsistent with the object and purpose of the Covenant, a reservation to some single aspect of it might pass. Thus, for example, the right to life (Article 6) is not subject to derogation and should not be subject to reservation as a whole, But it might not be inconsistent with the object and purpose of the Covenant for a state to reserve, say, a right to impose capital punishment on persons over 17 (rather than 18) years of age. In principle, "nonderogability" should be strong but not conclusive evidence that a reservation is inconsistent with the object and purpose of the Covenant.

Declarations

Historically, spiritually, and conceptually the Covenant-like its sibling the Covenant on Economic, Social, and Cultural Rights—is a child of the Declaration and that ancestry is not irrelevant to the Covenant's meaning. Since the Declaration has been universally accepted, it is plausible to argue that it be seen as a guide to what is in the Covenant, rather than as having been rejected and replaced by it. Thus, for one example, the presence in the Declaration of Article 17 recognizing a right to own property and not to be arbitrarily deprived of it lends support to the view that such a right is intended to be protected also by the Covenant, if only by implication from Article 5(2) 23.

The transformation of the Declaration into two covenants has significance for the meaning of both of them. While each Covenant rests on its own bottom, the existence of an obligation in one Covenant may suggest that it was not intended to be implied also in the other. That a provision is designated a civil-political right and included in that Covenant may also be relevant to its interpretation. Neither the covenants nor the

Universal Declaration were wholly original documents. Both drew heavily on earlier national instruments-the Declaration of Independence and the Constitution of the United States, the French Declaration of the Rights of Man and of the Citizen-and they incorporated concepts from a universe of ideas that had become a common heritage.

The provision in the Universal Declaration that all human beings are born free and equal in dignity and rights, or that everyone has the right to life, liberty, and security of the person, echo the older national declarations; the accumulated meanings of their language over two hundred years cannot be irrelevant to the interpretation of that article in the Universal Declaration. Equal protection of the law, borrowed by the Universal Declaration (Article 7) and the Covenant (Article 26), brings a freight of meaning from the U.S. Constitution.

The phrase "public order," translated from ordre public, with the original French term inserted even in the English text of the Covenant, is clearly intended to incorporate the jurisprudence of that concept in French and other civil law. Even common terms like "national security" come into international documents with national meanings, and one is entitled to, indeed one must, go to national laws and practices to determine its meaning-and its limits. The Declaration and the covenants are comprehensive human rights agreements designed to be complete lexicons of rights. But even while these were developing, the UN was promoting other agreements on specific rights for some categories of persons.

The Convention on Genocide was adopted at the same time as the Declaration. Later the Convention on the Elimination of All Forms of Racial Discrimination, the Convention on Political Rights of Women, the Convention on the Status of Refugees, and others, supplemented the covenants, expanding on particular rights and providing additional implementation machinery. While in some respects the special agreements add new obligations and are binding therefore only on parties to those agreements, in other respects they may spell out obligations already implied in the Covenant and are available therefore as sources for interpretation of the Covenant. The Declaration and the covenants grew up while regional human rights agreements were also developing, in sight and knowledge of each other, dealing with the same problems, in the same universe, with some of the same participants. Inevitably, they drew on and reacted to each other, even when one rejected or avoided what another chose.

Different agreements may have different texts as well as different contexts, but common phrases suggest common meanings, and practice. Under accepted or authoritative interpretations of the European Convention and later the American Convention, they are not irrelevant to interpretation of the International Covenant.

Human Rights and Political Ideology

The Universal Declaration was written by diverse authors representing different ideologies. It expresses commitment to "democracy" but is consistent with different brands of democracy and with various degrees of economic free enterprise as with different kinds of socialism—provided the parties accept commitment to individual rights and respect the particular rights enumerated, as properly construed in accordance with their spirit and purpose. The variety of governments that have adhered to the Covenant suggests that they at least thought their political economic systems were consistent with respect for the rights enumerated. And in fact no system claims that it must, or has the right to, violate any of those rights. Issues arise particularly as regards the right of every person "to take part in the conduct of public affairs, directly or through freely chosen representatives," and "to vote and to be elected at genuine periodic elections which shall be by universal and equal suffrage and shall be held by secret ballot, guaranteeing the free expression of the will of the electors." (In the Declaration, these rights follow the assertion that "the will of the people shall be the basis of the authority of government." 24) western societies tend to believe that only parliamentary multi-party democracy satisfies that requirement, not the party rule of Communist or other single party states, or military or other dictatorships ruling by decree for extended, indefinite periods.

Many such systems, however, claim that the requirements of popular sovereignty and authentic vote are satisfied by occasional plebiscites and that a vote is genuine even if the individual has no choice between candidates, since he can vote "no" to the single-party slate. In today's world, authentic parliamentary democracy is not common. The Communist states surely show no signs of modifying their system (which they claim to be more democratic than Western parliamentary systems); surely they consider their system "nonnegotiable," not anyone else's business, not a subject for discussion whether in relation to human rights or in any other context. If there is to be a universal human rights ideology, if there are to be international human rights agreements including both Communist and Western states, in the hope of protecting other civil and political rights, the West will have to acquiesce in the view that the Communist system is not intrinsically inconsistent with the Declaration and the Covenant, even while the West may hope and work for movement towards greater political freedom in Communist countries. Other ideological differences are another matter. Accepting the Communist political system in principle does not mean that one should accept Communist interpretations or applications that are inconsistent with the very idea of individual rights or with the essential scope of a particular right.

Freedom of expression, for example, can be limited for reasons of national security and public order (Article 19(b). That does not permit extravagant claims of the needs of national security. Nor does it permit identifying that specific, narrow exception, or the equally specific and narrow exception for "public order," with the "needs of Socialism" or the "revolution." That would essentially deny individual rights in the name of an overriding public good as a state perceived it. Similarly, limitations on other freedoms, for example, the right to leave or return to one's country, can be limited only as "necessary to protect national security, public order or public morals," not for other reasons of national or international policy or politics.

Difficult Interpretation

Some issues of interpretation suggest themselves to any reader of the Covenant, and were foreseeable when the Covenant was concluded. States identified others when they adhered, deeming it desirable to articulate reservations or understandings. Since the Covenant has been in effect and in operation, parties have been reflecting their understanding of various provisions when they report on their compliance to the Human Rights Committee, suggesting some readings which the Committee and other readers of the reports have questioned. Some issues have arisen under similar provisions in other documents. It is not possible to anticipate or hypothesize all issues; the principal ones are identified in this volume in the essays dealing with various rights. One set of issues that may raise particular difficulties deserve special attention: those arising out of conflicts between rights.

The Covenant does not deal with possible conflicts between rights in general. In one particular case, the Covenant in effect resolves a conflict between rights: despite the provision that the state must respect the freedom of expression (Article 19(2)), the Covenant requires every party to prohibit war propaganda or any advocacy of national, racial, or religious hatred (Article 20). Similarly, Article 19(3) expressly provides that the freedom of expression may be subject to restriction necessary "for respect of the rights or reputation of others." Those provisions do not indicate which rights or freedoms of others may be protected at the expense of the freedom of association or expression, but they might well authorize states to prefer other recognized human rights, e.g., the right of privacy or the right of an accused to a fair trial (see Article 14(1)), and curtail the freedom of expression or association as "necessary" to safeguard those other rights. In other cases, the Covenant does not consider the possibility of conflict and provides no guidance as to permissible resolution.

A state might argue that since it cannot literally carry out conflicting provisions, it is free to choose between them. But usually conflict will be between a principal right and some peripheral application of another, and it may be possible to derive from the Covenant some evidence as to the choice permitted to the state. In any event, if a state may be entitled to choose between individual human rights enshrined in the Covenant, it ought not be able to prefer other rights and interests which it might create by its own law for its own purposes. It is not possible to anticipate all the issues that may arise under the Covenant. But good faith in applying the Covenant in the spirit in which it was conceived, and for the purpose for which it was created, should resolve most issues.

The important and controlling considerations are: that the Covenant is a bill of rights for the individual even against his own society, even when it acts in what it sees as the public good: that derogations from and limitations upon rights are exceptional and to be sparingly and strictly invoked. Especially because the individual is at the mercy of his government and it is the government that decides in the first instance what his rights are, it is of supreme importance that all recognize that a government's interpretation or application is not final but is subject to scrutiny by other states parties by the Human Rights Committee and other international bodies.

TWO

Through the Ages

International concern with human rights is a phenomenon of comparatively recent origin. Although it is possible to point to a number of treaties or international agreements affecting humanitarian issues before the Second World War, it is only with the entry into force of the United Nations Charter in 1945, that it is possible to speak of the advent of systematic human rights protection within the international system. None the less, it is clear that the international protection of human rights has its antecedents in domestic efforts to secure legal and dignified history, and are intimately connected with revolutionary activity directed towards the establishment of constitutional systems based on democratic legitimacy and the rule of law. Even today, the protection of human rights at both the national and international level are intimately connected, if not symbiotic. All international instruments require states' domestic constitutional systems to provide adequate redress for those whose rights have been violated. It is only when those state's own internal protective systems falter or where in extreme cases, they are non-existent, that international mechanisms for securing human rights come into play. In a sense, therefore, international mechanisms operate to reinforce protection of human rights and to provide redress when the domestic system fails or is found wanting.

Domestic Origins

Although some scholars have been be able to trace a rudimentary concept of human rights back to the Stoic philosophy of classical times via the natural law jurisprudence of Grotious and the *ius naturale* of Roman law, it seems evident that the origins of the modern concept are to be found in the English, American and French revolutions of the seventeenth and eighteenth centuries.

British Experience

While Magna Carta (1215) is often erroneously seen as the origins of the liberties of English citizens (it was, in reality, simply a compromise on the distribution of powers between King John and his nobles, the language of which only later assumed the wider significance which is attributed to it today), it was not until the Bill of Rights (1689) that rules directed towards the protection of individual rights or liberties emerged. But even this development must be seen in context. The Bill of Rights, which is described in its long title as 'An Act Declaring the Rights and Liberties of the Subject and Setting the Succession of the Crown', was the outcome of the seventeenth-century struggle of Parliament against the arbitrary rule of the Stuart monarchs. Passed after the enforced abdication of James II and the accession to the throne of William III and May II following the 'Glorious Revolution' of 1688, the Bill, which expressed itself to be declaratory of existing law and not creative of new law, subjected the monarchy to the power of Parliament by declaring illegal the claimed suspending and dispensing powers of the Crown. It also forbade the levying of taxes or the maintenance of standing army in peacetime by Crown without Parliamentary consent.

In Marxist analysis, the Glorious Revolution of 1688 and the Bill of Rights which institutionalized it, was a bourgeois revolution: it simply confirmed the ascendancy of the gentry and merchant class over the monarchy. For the most part, therefore, the Bill represented a constitutional settlement which protected the sectional interests of one group. Whig historians, however, saw the Bill as the triumph of liberty over despotism and the protection of Englishmen (women had little say in the matter) from absolutist and arbitrary government. There is merit in both these views, for the Bill of Rights not only secured the interests of the bourgeoisie, but it also dealt with certain matters having the characteristics of 'human rights', although they were not referred to as such at the time. In particular, the Bill provided the excessive bail ought not to be required, nor excessive fines imposed, nor cruel and unusual punishment inflicted'. It further provided the 'jurors ought to be duly empanelled and returned' and that all grants and promises of fines and forfeitures of particular persons before conviction are illegal and void'. While the 'human rights' elements of the Bill of Rights might appear to be slight and biased in favour of a particular class of citizens, nevertheless the whole context of the instrument was of fundamental importance, since it sought to replace the vagaries and excesses of arbitrary monarchical absolutism with parliamentary constitutional legitimacy. The Glorious Revolution was also significant because it provided a precedent that rulers could be removed by popular will if they failed to observe the requirements of constitutional legitimacy. In the view of the eighteenth century English political philosopher John Locke, who sought to discover a theoretical basis for the constitutional revolutions of the seventeenth and eighteenth centuries, bad government violated the social contract which rulers enjoyed with the governed and empowered the latter to rid themselves of the former.

American Experience

The experience of the English Revolution and the various philosophical and theoretical attempts to justify it were; not lost on the leaders of Britain's rebellious North American colonies in the latter part of the eighteenth century. Seeking to disengage the colonies from British rule following dissatisfaction over the levels of taxation and lack of representation in the British Parliament, the American Founding Fathers sought justification in the social contract; and natural rights theories of Locke and the French philosophes. In the American Declaration of Independence (1776), drafted by Thomas Jefferson, these ideas find particularly clear and felicitous expression:

> We hold these truths to be self-evident, that all men are created equal, that they are endowed by their creator with certain rights, that among these are Life, Liberty and the pursuit of Happiness - That to secure these rights, Governments are instituted among Men, deriving their just powers from the consent of the governed. That whenever any form of government becomes destructive of these ends, it is the right of the People to alter or abolish it.

While the high sounding ideals of the protection of life, liberty and the pursuit of happiness were sufficient for a declaration of independence, they were clearly inadequate as a catalogue of individual rights, which the state was obliged to protect. The Virginia Declaration of Rights, which was drafted by George Mason and which pre-dated the Declaration of independence by a month, included specific liberties that were to be protected from state interference. These included freedom of the press, the free exercise of religion and the obligation that no person should be deprived of their liberty except by the law of the land of the judgment of their peers. The drafters of the US Constitution, influenced by Mason's Virginia Declaration, included the protection of these minimum rights. It was not until 1791, however, that the US adopted a Bill of Rights containing a list of guaranteed individual rights. This was effected by a number of amendments to the constitution. Among the more well-known amendments are the First, which protects freedom of religion, freedom of the press, freedom of expression and the right of assembly; the Fourth, which protects individuals against unreasonable search and seizure; and the Fifth, establishing the rule against self-incrimination and the right to due process of law. Subsequent amendments of the Constitution have extended the Bill of Rights, (for example, the Thirteenth adopted after the Civil War forbade the practice of slavery), but no rights have ever been removed or abridged by Congress.

In many ways, the eighteenth-century post independence constitutional settlement of the US established the model to be used in subsequent revolutionary struggles. Nowhere was this more apparent than France, where the US experience directly influenced the revolution against the ancient regime.

French Experience

Although the French Revolution and the American struggle for independence had many common features, they differed in one crucial aspect. Whereas the rebellious colonies had simply sought to establish themselves as an independent sovereign nation, the French revolutionaries were concerned with the demolition of an old, absolutist system of government and the establishment of a new democratic order. This, of course, posed the same question of legitimacy which had been raised by the English Revolution a century earlier when the English had rid themselves of their monarch by enforced abdication. The theoretical solution to this problem identified by the French, taking the lead from American notions of popular legitimacy, was that of self-determination. The central proposition of this concept was therefore to be by the people of a nation lay with its people. Government was therefore to be—by the people, for the people, and any government which was not responsive to its citizens' demands could be changed by expression of the popular will.

The settlement following the French Revolution also reflects the social contract and natural rights theory of Locke and the French philosophes, Montesquieu and Rousseau. The Declaration of the Rights of Man and the Citizen (1789) made it perfectly apparent that government is a necessary evil, and that as little of it as possible is desirable. According to the Declaration, true happiness is to be found in individual liberty which is the product of the 'natural, unalienable and sacred rights of man'. Thus, while the Declaration states that certain individual rights are protected-the right to due process, the presumption of innocence, the freedom to hold opinions and religious beliefs, and the freedom to communicate ideas and opinions-it prefaces these with a clear libertarian philosophy. Article 2 of the Declaration provides that 'the aim of every political association is the preservation of the natural and imprescriptible rights of man. These rights are Liberty, Property, Safety and Resistance to Oppression'. Article 4 goes on to say:

> Liberty consists in being able to do anything that does not harm others: thus the exercise of the natural rights of every man has no bounds other than those that ensure to the other members of society the enjoyment of these same rights. These bounds may be determined only by Law.

A number of recurring themes and concepts in human rights law originate from the American and French Revolutions. Foremost among these is that rights are by nature inherent, universal and inalienable: they belong to individuals simply because they are human beings and not because they are the subjects of a state's law. Second, that the protection of rights is best afforded within a democratic framework. The concept of political self-determination formulated by the drafters of the French Declaration made it clear that the effective protection of rights was to be found only within the bounds of democratic legitimacy. Third, that the limits to the exercise of rights could be determined or abrogated only by law. This might be seen as part of the concept of the rule of law which requires that rights should be protected by law, and that in abrogating or diminishing individual rights a government is obliged to conform to constitutional legal requirements. It also requires governments to act according to law, and that the law upon which the government seeks to act should be neither oppressive, arbitrary or discriminatory. Of course, one should not forget that the revolution which gave birth to these high sounding ideals and principles also gave birth to the Terror and the guillotine. Indeed, it was for these very reasons that the political philosophers Burke, Hume, Mill, Bentham and Austin rejected the notion of natural rights as being nothing more than unverifiable metaphysical phenomena.

Whatever the theoretical or doctrinal debates over the bases for the English, American and French Revolutions, it is clear that each, in its own way, contributed towards the developments of forms of liberal democracy in which certain rights were regarded as paramount in protecting individuals from the state's in-built tendency to authoritarianism. What was significant about the protected rights was that they were individualistic and libertarian in character, they were predominantly 'freedoms from' rather than 'rights to'. In modern parlance, these would be called civil and political rights, since they dealt primarily with an individual's relationship to the organs of the state. Such was the power of these revolutionary ideas, that there are few modern written constitutions which do not claim to protect these individual rights.

'New' Rights

Civil and political rights are not, however, the only rights which are protected by modern constitutions and contemporary international law. A variety of economic, social, cultural and other rights are also the subjects of various forms of protection. Karel Vasak has sought to classify the historical development of human rights according to the French revolutionary slogan 'Liberty, Equality and Fratenity'. Each of these, he argues, corresponds, more or less, to the development of distinct categories or generations of rights. Liberty, or first-generation rights, are represented by civil and political rights; the right of individuals to be free from arbitrary interference by the state. Equality, or second-generation rights, correspond to the protection of economic, social and cultural rights; the right to the creation of the conditions by the state which will allow every individual to develop their maximum potential.

These second-generation 'rights to' require the state to put in place programmes for the full realization of the rights. Economic, social and cultural rights are some times seen as a socialist legacy or as derivative rights not worthy of the name, but such rights were protected in the domestic constitutions of the Soviet Union, Mexico and Germany in the early part of the twentieth century and since then have been included in a number of other domestic constitutions and explicitly recognized by international law. Fraternity, third-generation rights or rights of solidarity, are the newest and most controversial category of rights. These are asserted by developing states which wish to see the creation of an international legal and economic order that will guarantee the right to development, to disaster relief assistance, to peace and to a good environment. Clearly, the implementation of such rights—if rights they be—depends upon international cooperation and not simply internal constitutional measures.

From this brief historical exposition, it will be apparent that the notion of human rights has made a transition from exclusive with the protection of the individual from state absolutism to the creation of social and economic conditions calculated to allow the individual to develop to the maximum of his or her potential. As Szabo puts it, the purpose of human rights is to 'defend by institutionalized means the rights of human beings against abuses of power committed by the organs of the State and, at the same time, to promote the multidimensional development of the human personality'. It will also be apparent that the notion of the human rights is not static but dynamic, and that there may well be considerable debate about whether certain interests are worthy to be classified as rights in the proper sense—whatever that might be. The dialectic process by which it is determined that some claims or interests are predictable and others are not, is of crucial importance if it is believed that rights have a quality that is fundamentally different to other rules of law. This is an issue which will be addressed in detail in the next chapter.

The Individual in the International System

Although the origins of human rights can be traced back to the revolutionary constitutionalism of the seventeenth and eighteenth centuries, it was not until the end of the Second World War that the international community began to manifest an interest in the promotion and protection of such rights through the medium of international law. In addition to the absence of the necessary political will to undertake the appropriate action, the structure of international law itself was one of the main impediments to progress in the field. At that time, international law was simply a law which regulated relations between states. States were the sole subjects of the international legal system; other entities, including individuals, were merely objects of the system. States might adopt rules for the benefit of individuals, but such rules conferred neither substantive rights on those individuals nor were they enforceable by any procedural mechanisms. Individuals, as citizens of the state, were subject to the complete authority of their government, and other states, in general, had no legal right to intervene to protect them should they be maltreated.

The position of aliens in a foreign state, was, however, slightly different. The state of which an alien was a national might, under certain conditions, be entitled to bring a claim under international law against a delinquent host state. This would usually occur where an alien had suffered arbitrary treatment at the hands of state agents, such as the police, and had not been afforded an appropriate remedy in the state in question. Western states also argued that there should be an international minimum standard to treatment applicable to all aliens travelling abroad against which state conduct could be judged. Developing states, however, rejected this notion, claiming that an alien in a foreign country could not expect a better standard of treatment than that which a state meted out to its own nationals. It is arguable, however, that the minimum standard and equality of treatment dispute has been overtaken by developments in international human rights law. The main purpose of such state claims was not necessarily to seek redress for the injured citizen; rather, it was to vindicate the rights to the state which had been indirectly injured through the mistreatment of its own national.

Humanitarian Intervention

Notwithstanding the position of aliens in international law, the general proposition remains that before the entry into force of the UN Charter, individuals remained essentially at the disposal of their rulers. An alleged exception to this was the so-called right of humanitarian intervention. Under this 'right', states could intervene militarily in order to protect the population or a portion of the population in another state if the ruler of that state treated his or her people in such a way to 'deny their fundamental human rights and to shock the conscience of mankind'. It is doubtful whether such a right existed – although it has been asserted recently by the US and Vietnam as a justification for military incursions into foreign states – but even if it had, it was largely abused by powerful states seeking to expand their political influence. None the less, a claimed right of humanitarian intervention was invoked by a number of the Great Powers during the nineteenth century to prevent the Ottoman Empire from persecuting minorities in the Middle East and the Balkans.

Abolition of Slavery

There were, however, certain humanitarian developments which occurred in international law during the nineteenth and early centuries. Foremost among these was, perhaps, the abolition of the slave trade. Although the economics of slavery in the late eighteenth and early nineteenth centuries made the practice commercially less attractive to European states than it had been previously, its abolition was also motivated by humanitarian concerns. The practice of slavery was first condemned in the Paris Peace Treaty (1814), between Britain and France, but within the space of 50 years the General Act of the Berlin Conference providing for the European colonization of Africa declared that 'trading in slaves is forbidden in conformity with the principles of international law'. International action against slavery and the slave trade has continued throughout the twentieth century. The League of Nations adopted the Convention to Suppress the Slave Trade and Slavery in 1926 and prohibited the practice of slavery within the former German and Turkish colonies under the League's mandate system at the end of the First World War. The 1926 Convention still remains the basic international document prohibiting the practice of slavery, although it was amended by a protocol (an addendum to the treaty) in 1953 and supplemented in 1956 to deal with problems of defining the acts which constitute slavery in the modern world.

Red Cross

The other major achievement in international humanitarian law in the second half of the nineteenth century was the formation of the International Committee of the Red Cross (1863) and that organization's sponsorship of two international conventions to protect the victims of war and the treatment of prisoners of war. The work of the Red Cross has continued throughout two world wars and beyond, and it has sponsored a number of conventions dealing not simply with the status and treatment of combatants, but also with the treatment of civilian populations during times of war and limiting the methods by which wars may be waged. Although of considerable importance, consideration of humanitarian law in time of military conflicts falls outside the scope of this work, which is concerned solely with human rights in time of peace.

International Labour Organization (ILO)

Early twentieth-century efforts in the humanitarian field are largely associated with the post-First World War international settlement. The International Labour

Organization, created by the Treaty of Versailles (1919), was a response to the Allied Powers' concerns about social justice and standards of treatment of industrial workers which had largely been prompted by the Bolshevik Revolution of 1917. The ILO, which became a specialized agency of the UN in 1946, may be seen as the precursor of systems for the protection of economic, social and cultural rights. The ILO has sponsored over 150 conventions dealing with, inter alia, conditions of work, remuneration, child and forced labour, the provision of holidays and social security, discrimination and trade union rights. Its work continues today and the organization ranks among the more important human rights institutions, although its work seldom attracts the attention it deserves.

League of Nations

The League of Nations, an international organization established after the First World War to provide a system for ensuring peace and security, and facilitating international cooperation, made no provision for the protection of human rights. Nevertheless, the League's founding document, the Covenant, committed the member states to work towards certain humanitarian objectives such as establishing human working conditions for individuals, the prohibition of traffic in women and children, the prevention and control of disease and the just treatment of native and colonial peoples. The creation of the mandate system under the League, by which the former colonies of the defeated Axis Powers of Germany and Turkey were placed under the tutelage of the victorious powers, was, perhaps, one of the major humanitarian achievements of the organization. Under this system, 'a sacred trust of civilization' was placed upon the administering states to bring the mandated territories to self-government. While the paternalistic language of the Covenant might be viewed with distaste today, nevertheless the administering powers were required to ensure the absence of racial or religious discrimination in the territories under their guidance. In fact, few of the mandates achieved independence before the Second World War, and two of the territories – Palestine and Namibia-created international problems of considerable longevity. The mandates which had not achieved independence before the Second World War were subsequently transferred to the Trusteeship system under the UN Charter.

Protection Treaties

Mention should also be made here of various treaties concluded after the First World War, since many of these contained provisions for the protection of minorities. While the post-war peace settlement attempted to respect the principle of self-determination based on the concept of national cohesion, it became clear that the re-establishment of Poland and the creation of successor states to the old Austro-Hungarian Empire meant that state boundaries would inevitably create divisions among certain peoples and consign them to live as ethnic, linguistic or religious minorities in the new states. A number of treaties were therefore concluded between the Allied Powers and these states in order to secure the protection of the civil and political rights of the minorities. Specific minority protection treaties were concluded with Poland, Czechoslovakia, Romania and Greece, while provisions on the protection of minorities were included in the peace treaties with Austria, Hungary and Turkey. In addition to those treaties, certain states made declarations concerning the protection of minorities within their states as a condition of becoming members of the League of Nations; these were Finland, Albania, Latavia, Lithuania, Estonia and Iraq. The League of Nations also exercised a supervisory function in respect of these 'obligations of international concern'. A procedure was established whereby minority groups which considered that rights were being violated could bring the matter to the attention of the Council of the League. The Council could then refer the matter to an ad-hoc Minorities Committee for conciliation and to attempt a friendly settlement between the parties. If a settlement was not forthcoming, the full Council could determine the matter itself or remit it to the Permanent Court of International Justice for determination.

It is clear that the minorities protection treaties were not concerned with the question of individual rights but rather with the rights of groups. The main purpose of the treaties was to ensure the equal treatment of the ethnic, religious or linguistic minorities in the states in question and to allow the peoples constituting these group to preserve and develop their own distinct identities within the framework of the nation state. It will also be apparent from the states with which treaties were concluded that the existence of minorities within them has proved fertile ground for dispute throughout the twentieth century. While the minority protection treaties did not amount to human rights treaties in the classic individualistic and libertarian mould, none the less they were of substantial significance in that they provide a basis within the context of the League of Nations of a right of petition under international law by a group of private individuals. It is possible to discern here the germ of the right to individual petition to a supervisory and protective international institution under international law.

United Nations

Despite the advances made in the sphere of humanitarian law and in the protection of economic, social and cultural rights during the nineteenth and early twentieth centuries, it was not until after the cataclysmic events of the Second World War that international human rights law began to develop in a coherent and recognizable way. The atrocities of the Nazis against their own people in Germany and against those conquered territories created such revulsion that, even before the conclusion of the war, the Allies determined that the post-war settlement should include a commitment to the protection of human rights. This they saw as a necessary prerequisite to the creation of a just and stable international order under the auspices of the planned United Nations Organizations. No longer should a state be able to argue that the way in which it treated its own citizens is simply a matter of exclusive domestic concern, but the treatment of those individuals, should, where appropriate national protection of rights was deficient, become the concern of the international community. The irony here was that while the Soviet Union denounced the Nazi genocide, Stalin himself had, before the war, systematically violated the rights of his own people, disposing of an estimated five million political opponents and enforcing collectivization on large number of peasants. The Soviet Union could also legitimately argue here that the matter was entirely within its domestic jurisdiction. None the less, the Charter of the International Military Tribunal at Nuremberg, which had been created by the Allied Powers, including the Soviet Union, to try Nazi war criminals on the basis of international law existing at the outset of the Second World War, declared the crimes against humanity were crimes under international law. While the tribunal's judgement may have been flawed in that assertion, it nevertheless established the basic principle that how a state treated its own citizens was now a legitimate matter of international concern.

UN Charter and the Universal Declaration

Although Article 2(7) of the UN Charter reaffirmed the principle of non-intervention by the Organization in matters essentially within the domestic jurisdiction of the member states, thus appearing to preclude international intervention in the human rights field, it also contained several specific references to human rights. The Preamble to the Charter reaffirmed the faith of the 'peoples of the United Nations' in fundamental human rights, in the dignity and worth of the human person and in 'the equal rights of men and women'. The language of reaffirmation is interesting, since it appears to presuppose the existence of human rights prior to the entry into force of the Charter which, at least in the sense of positive law, would have seemed at that time to be a dubious claim. The Charter also included as one of its purposes in Article 1 'promoting respect for human rights and fundamental freedoms for all'. The promotion of human rights by the UN was also reinforced, by Article 55, and under Article 56 the member states pledged themselves to take joint and separate action in cooperation with the UN for the achievement of this and other objectives under Article 55. A number of other provisions in the Charter concerning various institutional competencies also referred to human rights as a general category. Although the UN Charter therefore appeared to acknowledge the prior existence of phenomena known as human rights, it contained no list of such rights, nor did it refer to a source for discovering exactly what the rights were. There had been a proposal to incorporate a list of rights in the Charter during its drafting, but this had been defeated. The absence of a catalogue of human rights was nevertheless viewed as a defect and a move to draft, in the words to US President Truman, 'an international bill of rights' was undertaken within one year of the entry into force of the Charter.

The work of drafting the 'international bill of rights' was assigned to the Commission of Human Rights (CHR), a subsidiary organ of the UN's Economic and Social Council (ECOSOC). The Commission, which was composed of government representatives, decided that the catalogue of human rights should take the form of a resolution of the UN General Assembly, since it was unlikely that any consensus could be achieved on incorporation of the rights into the Charter or that support for a legally binding human rights treaty would be forthcoming. The major advantage of a declaration in the form of resolution was that it would not be legally binding but would, in the words of Eleanor Roosevelt, the chairman of the CHR, proclaim 'a common standard of achievement for all peoples and all nation's. The Universal Declaration in its final form contained a list of civil and political rights and economic, social and cultural rights to which all persons were entitled without discrimination. Significantly, however, the Declaration did not contain any institution or mechanism for ensuring that the rights were observed. Although the Declaration was originally adopted in a non-legally binding form, subsequent practice has transformed it into an instrument of considerable juridical potency, although its precise legal status is still the subject of some debate.

International Covenants

As it was recognized by the UN General Assembly at the outset that the Universal Declaration was not intended to create legally binding obligations on the member states, it mandated the CHR to complete the drafting of an internationally binding treaty which would not only transform the rights referred to in the Declaration into positive law, but would also provide institutions and mechanisms for supervision and enforcement. Unfortunately, this task proved to be more difficult than originally envisaged, since a dispute arose between members of the Commission about the relationship between civil and political rights, on the one hand and economic and social rights, on the other, and also over the appropriate means of implementation, supervision and protection. It was finally decided that instead of a single treaty or covenant being drafted to protect both categories of rights, two covenants would be prepared, each devoted to the different groups of rights. The two separate covenants, the International Covenant on Civil and Political Rights (ICCPR) and the International Covenant on Economic and Social Rights (ICESCR), were opened for signature in 1966, but did not enter into force—that is become effective—until a full decade later in 1976. The salient difference between the covenants is that while Article 2 of the ICCPR provides that the protected rights will be respected and ensured immediately, Article 2 of the ICESCR simply provides that states should 'recognize' the rights contained in the Covenant and should implement them progressively in accordance with specific programmes. It is also of particular significance that while the ICCPR establishes the Human Rights Committee (HRC) to supervise implementation of the Covenant and to provide by means of an optional protocol a mechanism by which individuals may petition the HRC, the ICESCR simply consigns the function of supervision to a political body of the UN, i.e. ECOSOC.

UN Special Conventions

Notwithstanding the difficulties of establishing the 'universal' system for promoting and protecting human rights, the UN also undertook programmes to draft legally binding instruments to deal with specific aspects of human rights. These have included treaties on the prevention and punishment of genocide. The prohibition of sexual and religious discrimination, the suppression and punishment of apartheid, the prohibition of the practice of torture, international cooperation on matters relating to refugees and statelessness and, most recently, a specific convention on the rights of the child. Brief mention should also be made here of a number of institutional measures and initiatives taken by UN in order to promote and protect human rights.. ECOSOC in particular has established procedures under Resolutions 1235 and 1503 by which gross and consistent violations of human rights by particuiar states may be investigated.

UN and Decolonization

Of fundamental importance in the overall development of the UN's concern with human rights has been its practice in the field of decolonization. As indicated earlier, a number of the mandates created the League of Nations after the First World War had not proceeded to self-government before the outbreaks of the Second World War. The UN Charter therefore provided for the transfer of the mandates to a trusteeship systems under which the territories would be administered and prepared for independence. One of the basic objectives of the trusteeship system was stated in Article 76(1)(c) of the

Charter to be encouragement of respect for human rights and fundamental freedoms for all. This is supervised by the UN through the medium of the Trusteeship Council. There is now only one trust territory left in the world – the Pacific Islands Territory – which is administered by the USA.

It was not only the former mandates which became subject to UN supervision under of the Charter. States with colonies or non-self governing territories (NSGTs) were placed under an obligation to have paramount regard for the well-being of the peoples within the territories and to facilitate their development. Administering states were placed under an obligation to report to the Secretary General of the UN of the advances made in their colonies. While Chapter XI did not place an obligation on administering states to grant independence to their colonies, none the less subsequent developments in the 1960s greatly increased the momentum of decolonization. General Assembly Resolution 1541(XV), clarifying the reporting obligations of administering states, was adopted together with Resolution 1514(XV), the Declaration on the Granting of Independence to Colonial Countries and Peoples. This resolution called for the immediate decolonization of all NSGTs through the exercise by the people in such territories of the right of self-determination. No pretext, such as lack of economic or educational preparedness, was to be permitted to retard the process. Although the UN Charter referred to the principle of self-determination, it certainly did not refer to a right of self-determination. It is, however, now generally accepted that such a right exists in international law, and that view is reinforced by General Assembly Resolution 2625, the Declaration on Principles of International Law Concerning Friendly Relations and Cooperation Among States in Accordance with the Charter of the United Nations, which is regarded as a convenient statement of customary international law, and a common Article 1 to both international covenants which provide that all peoples have the right to self-determination. The underlying rational for inclusion of this right, which is clearly a collective right, is that a people which is under alien dominating through the institution of colonialism is not free, thus any notion of the enjoyment of individual or other rights within that context is meaningless. Whether the right to self-determination extends beyond a right to decolonization or to the right to minority secession is an open question, although a reading of Resolution 2625 would seem to support this where the minority in question is subject to discriminatory treatment by the government of the state. Certainly, the effects of large-scale decolonization by the former colonial powers has had a massive impact on the structure of international society. New states, largely in the developing world, have transformed the context of international political and legal debate by an insistence on the restructuring of the international system to respond to their needs. It is largely from these developing states that third-generation rights have emerged.

Helsinki Process

An international development that occurred during the period of *detente* between the West and Communist blocs during the early 1970s, and which deserves mention, was the Conference on Security and Cooperation in Europe, otherwise, known as the Helsinki Process, since the Conference was convened in the Finnish capital of that name in 1973. Although the primary function of the Helsinki Process was to establish a framework for the development of peace and security in Europe, it also resulted in formal consideration of human rights issues. While the Soviet Union was concerned to have its western borders recognized, the West sought to exact human rights commitments from the Eastern bloc in exchange. The Final Act of the Conference, which, significantly, was stated to be non-binding, declared the participating governments determination to respect and put into practice respect for human rights and fundamental freedoms including the freedom of thought, conscience, religion or belief. They also resolved that they would respect the rights of peoples and their right to self-determination. Although the Final Act was clearly not a legally binding instrument, it did contribute in a significant way to state practice in the field of human rights, since it was declaratory of accepted human rights norms. In this way, it might be said to have contributed to customary international law in the human rights field. Of considerable importance in the Helsinki Process was the fact that the Final Act of the Conference provided for assessment of the commitments established by a series of review conferences. This created the institutional structure whereby the declared intentions of the parties, including observance of respect for human rights, could be measured. The Helsinki Process continued in Madrid and more recently Paris (1990). At the latter meeting, the 'Charter of Paris for a New Europe' was adopted in which it was declared by the 34 participating states that:

> Human rights and fundamental freedoms are the birthright of all human beings, are inalienable and guaranteed by law. Their protection and promotion is the first responsibility of government. Respect for them is an essential safeguard against an over-mighty state.

There then followed a commitment to democratic government and political, pluralism and a list of individual civil and political rights to which all are entitled without discrimination. Although the Paris Charter is, again, not legally binding, it nevertheless reaffirms the juridical significance of the state rights under international law. It also marks the fact that the former Communist bloc states have demonstrated their commitment to the liberal-democratic ideal.

Regional Systems

There are at present three regional human rights systems. These are the European human rights system, the inter-American human rights system and the Organization of African Unity's Charter of Human and Peoples' Rights. There have been proposals for the establishment of an Islamic human rights treaty, the most recent being the Cairo Declaration in 1990 by the Organization of the Islamic Conference, but as yet no concrete results have occurred. A regional human rights treaty for South-East Asia and the Pacific has also been proposed, but this emanated from LAWASIA, a private lawyers' group and has, as yet, had no discernible impact on the governments of the region.

European System

Of the three systems currently in existence, the European Convention on Human Rights and Fundamental Freedoms (1950) is the most developed in terms of its longevity and the quantity of its jurisprudence. Created by the Council of Europe (an international institution designed to facilitate European cooperation; which should not be confused with the European Community), the European Convention was designed to fulfil a three-fold purpose; first, to strengthen democracy and commitment to the rule of law by the member states, second, to sound an alarm against incipient totalitarianism; and, third, to act as a bulwark against the perceived threat of encroaching communism. While the Convention has performed these functions tolerably well, the experience of the Greek Coup and its aftermath in 1967 demonstrated the limits of the Convention's effectiveness. Here, a military coup by a *junta* of army colonels resulted in totalitarian government and the large-scale denial of human rights. In particular, political opponents of the junta were arbitrarily imprisoned and subjected to torture. Despite its denunciation of the Convention and its withdrawal from the Council of Europe, Greece remained responsible under the Convention for its actions. Although this caused difficulty and considerable embarrassment for Greece in the conduct of its international relations, it provided little protection for those whose rights had been violated. None the less, in the 1970s, the newly democratized states of Greece, Spain and Portugal ratified the

European Convention as a means of strengthening their democratic processes.

The main achievement of the European Convention, however, has been to provide a mechanism by which individuals who believe that their rights have been violated by their states can petition the European Commission in an attempt to secure redress. As will be seen subsequently, the Commission's main function is to secure a friendly settlement between the individual and his or her state, but if this is not forthcoming the matter may be remitted to the European.Court of Human Rights, whose rulings and awards of damages are, binding on the state. Through this mechanism, substantial numbers of individuals have secured redress for both major and comparatively minor violations of their rights.

The European Convention and its ten protocols are concerned primarily with the protection of civil and .political rights, although Protocol 1 does seek to protect the right to private property. Protection of economic and social rights in Europe is sought to be achieved by the procedures established by the European Social Charter (1961). This instrument, which was also adopted by the Council of Europe, is intended to be complementary to the European Convention. Like ICESCR, it is drafted in a way that makes it clear that the realization of economic and social rights is to be achieved progressively. Supervision under the Social Charter is to be achieved simply by a state reporting system to the Council of Europe by a Committee of Independent Experts. While it might have been reasonable to expect that Europe would have been much dynamic than other regions of the world in implementing fully economic, social, and cultural rights, this has not proved to be so, and the Charter has been something of a disappointment.

Inter-American System

The inter-American human rights system is distinctive since it is formed by two separate but clearly interrelated mechanisms of protection. First, all member states of the Organization of American States (OAS), a regional organization whose objectives are similar to those of the UN, are committed to human rights obligations under the OAS Charter. Like the UN Charter, the OAS Charter, which was adopted in 1948, does not contain a list of protectable rights. Nevertheless, through the processes of amendment of the OAS Charter and institutional adaptation, the American Declaration of the Rights and Duties of Man (1948), which may be regarded as the analogue of the Universal Declaration, has been recognized by the Inter-American Court of Human Rights in an advisory ruling as an authoritative interpretation of the OAS Charter which is binding on all OAS member states. Furthermore, the Inter-American Commission on Human Rights is obliged by its Statute to apply the American Declaration when dealing with human rights issues under its country report, on site investigation or individual petition procedures.

The second pillar to the inter-American human rights system is the American Convention of Human Rights, otherwise known as the Pact to San Jose (1969). This is modelled on the European Convention, but since it was drafted at a later date, its framers were able to take account of some of the defects of the European Convention and correct; them. The American Convention, like its European counterpart, is concerned almost exclusively with civil and political rights, although a protocol, the Pact of San Salvador (1989), has added a list of economic, social and cultural rights which are to be implemented progressively by the states parties. A novel feature of the Protocol is that it creates a right of individual petition to the Inter-American Commission in cases where the right to join a trade union or the right to education is denied.

As with the European Convention, supervision of the rights protected by the American Convention is to be achieved through a commission and a court. The Commission screens all individual applications to ensure they comply with the Convention's admissibility requirements and, in the case of admissibility,

A Continual Process

From this brief historical excursus, it is perhaps apparent that both instruments and institutions for the protection of human rights on a universal and regional basis have developed exponentially since the end of the Second World War. There now exists a confusing plethora of treaties, conventions, covenants, charters and declarations dealing with human rights and related humanitarian issues. The proliferation of competent institutions under these instruments is no less confusing. Furthermore, a great many activities in the human rights field take place at a bureaucratic level, largely through the modification of existing institutions and institutional procedures, which are hardly apparent to the majority of casual observers. Much of the remainder of this book will therefore be devoted to a systematic analysis of the existing instruments and institutions concerned with human rights protection, and it will also attempt to illuminate the less accessible areas of international bureaucratic activity in the field.

Before this task; can be undertaken, there are two important preliminary matters which must be considered. First, considerable reference has been made so far to various groups of rights, especially the two major categories of civil and political rights and economic, social and cultural rights, without any attempt to define what they are . Furthermore, it might be said that the term 'rights' itself demands some analytical enquiry in an attempt to determine exactly what is being considered in this book. Second, since the protection of human rights is in the last resort a matter for international law, it is desirable that some description of the nature, problems and attributes of that legal system are considered. Both these issues will be analysed in the following chapters.

THREE

Fundamental Issues

The root of humanitarian disasters, refugee flows or mass exoduses often stems directly from violations of human rights. Addressing the cause is as essential to preventing humanitarian tragedies similar to those experienced in Rwanda or in the countries of the former Yugoslavia as it is to the search for comprehensive solutions. A continuum between human rights law and humanitarian law is necessary; protection of the victim should be the overriding concern of the United Nations and its agencies and programmes. Since 1948, the UN has developed a comprehensive body of international standards and norms for the promotion and protection of human rights, the major instrument being the international bill of human rights. In 1970, the General Assembly adopted a number of resolutions which recognized that fundamental human rights as accepted in international law and international instruments continue to apply in situations of armed conflict.

While the first World Conference on Human Rights held in Tehran in 1968 did not explicitly refer to humanitarian law in its proclamation, it affirmed that humanitarian principles must prevail during periods of armed conflict. The Vienna Declaration and Programme of Action, the concluding document of the 1993 World Conference on Human Rights, called on all States and parties to armed conflicts to adhere strictly to humanitarian law as well as to minimum standards for protection of human rights as laid down in international conventions. The Conference also recognized the gross violation of human rights as one of the major factors leading to the displacement of people and expressed grave concern over continuing violations of human rights in all parts of the world -in disregard of international standards - and the lack of adequate and effective remedies for the victims.

Human rights and humanitarian law, once clearly distinguishable segments of international law, are increasingly being viewed in an integrated and holistic manner, where the individual has a continuum of protection under human rights law as well as that provided under humanitarian law, as warranted by the specific circumstances.

The Office of the UN High Commissioner for Human Rights (OHCHR), as an institution devoted to the promotion and protection of all human rights, emphasizes the value of early warning and preventive action aimed at deterring human rights violations and defusing situations with the potential for humanitarian disasters. The information and findings of UN human rights experts (special rapporteurs, special representatives, experts of human rights treaty-based bodies), complemented by those submitted by UN human rights field offices, represent a valuable contribution to an early warning mechanism of the UN in this area.

OHCHR recognizes that the wealth of information at its disposal needs to be systematically organized and analyzed if it is to be an effective and useful tool. The objectives are to strengthen the early warning capacity of the UN in the humanitarian field, enhance the substantive exchanges between OHCHR, the Office for the Coordination of Humanitarian Affairs (OCHA) and other Departments and Programmes, and to integrate human rights concerns before crises arise, thus guaranteeing effective cooperation both in terms of preparedness and response.

Human Rights training should be considered part of the overall training background of all UN humanitarian staff. The Office of the High Commissioner is developing a human rights manual for all UN staff members which will be available soon. The manual will cooperate with the Complex Emergency Training Initiative (CETI) as well as with the UN staff college in Turin on the question of initiatives aimed at familiarizing all UN staff with international human rights standards.

As possible immediate steps, contacts should be established with the Office of Human Resources Management (OHRM) and the UN Staff College Project with a view to integrating human rights into the courses held at Headquarters and at the College. Training of UN humanitarian staff in the field, as well as staff at Headquarters and new recruits, in human rights standards, monitoring methodology, technical cooperation procedures and other topics, should be given priority attention. A mechanism could be established so that all newly recruited staff undergo appropriate human rights training. In the case of field staff, one or more officers could be appointed as trainers and delegated the responsibility for providing on-site training to all field staff, based on OHCHR training materials.

In regard to the human rights aspects of UN humanitarian operations, it is important to learn from past experience and to attempt to integrate human rights concerns whenever possible, to include human rights experts in large-scale humanitarian operations, and to emphasize the protection and promotion of human rights, including the creation of viable national human rights institutions capable of preventing the recurrence of similar humanitarian crises.

When a humanitarian operation is considered, the human rights dimension should be part of the planning, requiring close cooperation between OCHA, the UN High Commissioner for Refugees (UNHCR) and OHCHR. While the need and opportunity for inclusion of human rights field officers or advisers within humanitarian operations will vary, an explicit human rights strategy would be pivotal to the planning of major humanitarian efforts. The strategy could be of an advisory nature and/or cover training and institution-building issues.

Humanitarian staff, particularly in the field, should be fully conversant with human rights standards and procedures.

The effectiveness of the UN machinery and mechanisms in the field of human rights would be enhanced through more consistent use of these procedures by humanitarian workers, resulting in a greater degree of protection for individuals and other vulnerable groups. Procedures on how this information would be handled could be discussed in-depth between OHCHR and the various humanitarian actors so as to preserve their mandates, independence and specific missions.

OHCHR'S, global project for internally displaced persons (IDPs), in the context of its technical cooperation programme, is a good example of humanitarian and human rights interfacing. According to the Representative of the Secretary-General on IDPs, internally displaced persons are: "Persons or groups of persons who have been forced or obliged to flee or to leave their homes or places of habitual residence, in particular as a result of or in order to avoid the effects of armed conflict, situations of generalized violence, violations of human rights or natural or human-made disasters, and who have not crossed an internationally recognized State border".

Internal displacement constitutes one of the greatest challenges confronting the international community. Unlike refugees, whom IDPs greatly outnumber, there exists no single agency to assume responsibility for the promotion and protection of the rights of IDPs. A Representative on IDPs was appointed by the Secretary-General at the request of the Commission on Human Rights in 1992, his mandate supported by OHCHR. The Representative's mandate is concentrated on three main areas:

– developing an appropriate normative framework for meeting the protection, assistance, reintegration and development needs of IDPs: significant progress has been made in this direction over the past few months with the formulation by the RSG of Guiding Principles on Internal Displacement. The Guiding Principles consolidate in one document the rights and guarantees relevant to the protection of persons

> from forced displacement and to their protection and assistance during displacement as well as during return or resettlement and reintegration. They are intended to provide practical guidance not only to the RSG but also to States and other authorities, intergovernmental organizations, NGOs and all other groups and persons with a role to play in addressing the needs of IDPs.

Ensuring the rights of IDPs worldwide to protection and assistance presents the international community with one of the most daunting challenges of our time. Under its technical cooperation programme, OHCHR's global project for IDPs, relying on effective institutional arrangements, will be implemented jointly with the Representative of the Secretary-General (RSG) on IDPs, with the objective of making the rights of some 25 million IDPs a reality.

The broad scope of priority activities to be put in place will guarantee the widest possible distribution of the Guiding Principles on Internal Displacement as well as other related materials – a Training Manual and Fact Sheets are examples – in the official UN languages and, as appropriate, local languages; field offices will rely on the Guiding Principles for the technical guidance essential in their monitoring and reporting functions. Educational and training activities will be provided primarily at the national level, in response to requests from Member States. Workshops on IDP-related issues will be attended by the RSG and his support staff. Interagency needs assessment missions will utilize staff seconded for that purpose. The project will also ensure a focus on IDP activities by the treaty bodies and the mechanisms of the Commission on Human Rights in Geneva.

- fostering effective institutional arrangements for addressing these needs; and
- focusing attention on specific situations of internal displacement with the aim of ensuring that they are effectively addressed. The Secretary-General

> recognizes that addressing the plight of IDPs is a priority for the international community. Over the past few years OHCHR, in addition to supporting the work of the Representative, has become increasingly involved with IDPs in its own right.

OHCHR is developing a global project for internally displaced persons (IDPs) in the context of its technical cooperation programme. The aim of the project is to meet the growing operational requirements of the Representative, particularly in the areas of promotion, education, training, and strengthening of national capacities. The objective is to provide the necessary resource requirements to meet the commitments undertaken by OHCHR on behalf of IDPs. The project also identifies possible future activities of OHCHR which could be initiated on behalf of IDPs, on condition that sufficient institutional capacity for mandated tasks and other commitments is first ensured. It will provide a framework for action by OHCHR and the Representative of the Secretary-General on the basis of individual requests from member states for activities at the national level or occasionally in a regional or sub-regional context.

As long as crimes of torture, rape and murder go unpunished, we cannot hope to prevent their recurrence. Those who contemplate indiscriminately attacking civilians, or forcing them out of their homes simply on account of their ethnicity or religion, must know that there is a price to pay for such actions. This justifies the pertinence of UN efforts to date to demand accountability—the establishment of the ad hoc criminal tribunals for former Yugoslavia and Rwanda is a case in point. Mary Robinson, High Commissioner for Human Rights, addressed the Diplomatic Conference in Rome concerning the finalization and adoption of the statute for a permanent ICC.

We look forward to cooperating closely and developing an effective modus operandi with the ICC in due course.

Indeed, the relationship of the ICC and UN human rights and humanitarian actors and institutions is a subject which elicits considerable interest. Discussion and analysis will complement OHCHR's ongoing efforts to facilitate access to the information available from treaty bodies and mechanisms of the Commission on Human Rights, to quantify and measure human rights progress (or lack of it) so that benchmarking becomes possible and readily available within the UN.

There is a broad space for forging effective linkages between humanitarian assistance and human rights programmes. The separate mandates and different methods of work can produce a remarkable added value if perceived as complementary and mutually supportive and if we maintain the focus of all we do to increase the extent of protection for the victims.

FOUR

Various Theories

The central concern of this study is to examine the broad array of universal and regional instruments and institutions for the protection of human rights. Already the term 'human rights' has been employed generously with little attempt to define it. From the preceding chapter, however, the reader may have glimpsed that the phenomenon known as human rights is connected not only with the protection of individuals from the exercise of state or governmental authority in certain areas of their lives, but that it is also directed towards the creation of societal conditions by the state in which individuals may develop to their fullest potential. This description may reveal what human rights are intended to achieve in a teleological sense, but it does not reveal which human rights exist or what they are. This, of course, begs the question whether it is necessary in an enquiry into the institutions and the instrumentalities of human rights protection to attempt to define the nature of the phenomena under consideration. Surely it is appropriate simply to acknowledge that there now appears to be almost universal acceptance of human rights as identifiable; concrete, legal norms?. Indeed, commentators such as Wessbrodt and Vasak state unequivocally that human rights have become a universal ideology. If this were so, it would seem that the need for theoretical enquiry into the nature of human rights begins and ends here.

Even if one were to accept uncritically the proposition put forward by Wessbrodt and Vasak, it is none the less clear that their assertions raise a number of acute problems, Some of the problems may be posed in the form of the following questions: Are all three generations of rights 'human rights' in the true sense? If they are, are they all co-equal or is there some hierarchical relationship between them? Even within the category of civil and political rights, are all rights of an equal standing or are some more important than others? What differentiates civil and political rights from other kinds of rights anyway? Are human rights different from other kinds of rights? What is the relationship of rights to other kinds of rules? Are rights defeasible? Upon whom lies the obligation to 'prove' or 'disprove the existence of a right? Can their existence be proved objectively in any event? Do different cultures really have the same understanding of human rights? Are Chinese concepts of human rights the same Western, Islamic or African concepts? What would be the consequences if the concepts were shown to be fundamentally different?

All of these questions, and many more, are of fundamental importance, since perceptions about the existence, worth and relationship of rights one to another, and to legal norms in general, produce practical consequences as far as the protection of human rights is concerned. Take, for instance, the question of whether economic, social and cultural rights are true rights or simply aspirational targets. If they are the latter, then no human being can legitimately claim that his or her government is under an absolute, indefeasible obligation to accord those rights to him or her through a programme of progressive implementation. They are merely claims to a better life to which a government may give effect if economic conditions become more favourable at some undetermined future date. If they are rights, however, the government is under a positive obligation to accord them through the appropriate implementation mechanisms. Furthermore, do these rights exist independently of their reduction to positive law in an international instrument? If they do, are they inherent to individuals and therefore to be protected despite any unilateral binding commitment by the state.

The way in which we approach questions such as these

depends upon our understanding of human rights within some form of theoretical framework. Even those who would deny that it is necessary to look beyond the positive law contained in the vast array of existing legal instruments have already implicitly adopted a theoretical stance, although they may be unaware of having done so. The function of theory, however, is to provide an analytical tool by which important questions such as those above may be posed and tentative answers offered. It permits the construction of paradigms which lend coherence and consistency to any debate about rights and a model against which putative rights may be measured. It also provides mechanisms by which it is possible to determine the precise ambit of the rights upon whose existence there may be agreement.

From the foregoing, it may be evident that two very broad categories of enquiry about human rights are implicit. The first, often referred to as analytical jurisprudence, raise questions about the nature and origin of rights and how it is possible to know that we have any rights at all. The second category of enquiry, which is sometimes called normative jurisprudence, poses questions about the specificities of rights which individuals are acknowledged to possess, and how such rights stand in relation to each other. While a substantial amount of work has been done in these fields by domestic jurists, international lawyers have concerned themselves little with such questions. International human rights theorists have tended to fall into one of two very broad schools of analytical jurisprudence - the natural and positive law schools - which we will examine shortly. It is in the field of normative jurisprudence that international theorists have been more active, but in the absence of sound analytical foundations, normative enquiry has assumed an air of unreality. This may be a reflection of the poor state of international legal theory, in general where commentators still have difficulty in adequately explaining the nature of legal obligation in international law.

It should not be thought, however, the domestic jurists

are irrelevant to our inquiry into the analytical and normative aspects of human rights. There are two reasons for this. First, the protection of human rights is primarily a matter for domestic law. As we will see later in the book that it is only when domestic law falls short of the standards imposed by international law, that international mechanisms for individual protection become engaged. Thus, what domestic commentators say about rights within domestic systems has direct relevance to international lawyers. Second, the majority of human rights instruments create institutions to supervise the systems of which they are part. Very often these institutions function either in a judicial or quasi-judicial manner. The decision makers within these bodies are therefore required to apply what might be called traditional techniques of legal reasoning to questions concerning the rights under consideration and, in a sense, to behave like judges in domestic courts and tribunals. Indeed, many of the people who staff these international institutions concerned with human rights supervision are themselves lawyers and judges trained in the craft of domestic law who bring with them all the legal theories, assumptions and methodologies of their national systems. In analysing how these people make decisions, it is therefore appropriate to apply, by analogy, the theories of domestic jurists. One needs only to examine the extensive and detailed jurisprudence of the European Court of Human Rights to see the accuracy of the assertion.

In this chapter, it is possible to do little more than provide a cursory examination of some of the major theories which are of relevance to human rights. A caveat should be entered that such a brief treatment of these theories will lead inevitably to some inaccuracies and distortions and a loss of subtlety possessed by much of the writing under consideration. This chapter should, therefore, be taken only as a route map and must in no way be considered a complete topographical guide.

Natural Law School

There can be little doubt that human rights are the rights of man as they were known as first progeny of the natural law school. As we saw in Chapter 1, the American Declaration of Independence and the French Declaration of the Rights of Man and the Citizen both had their origins in natural rights theory.

While precepts of natural law may be traced back to classical times, for present purposes it may be said that the modern school of natural law emerged in medieval times with the writings of the early Christian philosophers, foremost among whom was Saint Thomas Aquinas. The Thomistic view of natural law postulated that it was that part of God's perfect law which could be divined through the application of human reason. Part of early natural law philosophy was the idea that each person's station in life was determined by God, but that all people - whatever their status - were subject to the authority of monarchs constrained by divine rules, but that all human beings were endowed with a unique individual identity which was separate from the state. Indeed, this latter facet of natural law doctrine may be seen as containing the seen as of the natural rights idea that each person constituted an autonomous individual.

Of course, the basis of early natural law was entirely theistic, that is, it required belief in the Deity to render it coherent. The next stage in the development of natural law, however, was to sever it from its theistic origins and to make it a product of enlightened secular rational thought. This task was undertaken by Dutch jurist Hugo de Groot, who is usually known by his Latin name, Grotius, and who is generally acknowledged to be the 'father of international law'. In his treatise De lure Belli ac Pacis, Drotius argued that it was possible to rationalize the existence of natural law, which was the basis of all positive or written law, on a non-empirical basis by examining the axioms of geometry. Such a mathematical approach to the question of 'right reason' did not depend on the Deity for their validity. This rationalistic, secular approach to law appealed to post-Renaissance scholars, and from the application of Grotain 'right reason' it is possible to discern the development of individual or natural rights theory.

Throughout the seventeenth century, the Grotain view of natural law was refined and, eventually, transmuted into natural rights theory through which subjective, individual rights came to be recognized. Foremost among the proponents of natural rights doctrine was John Locke. Locke argued that all individuals were endowed by nature with the inherent rights to life, liberty and property which were their own and could not be removed or abrogated by the state. However, Locke also postulated that in order to avoid the uncertainties of life in a state of nature, mankind had entered into a social contract or voluntary association by which the exercise of their inalienable rights was transferred to the ruler of the state. Where the ruler of the state broke the social contract by violating the natural rights of the individual, subjects were free to remove the ruler and replace him or her with a government which was prepared to respect those rights.

Locke used his social contract theory to explain, and as an apology for the English Glorious Revolution of 1688. King James II, by violating the natural rights of his subjects, had forfeited his right to rule and had legitimated the consequent change in government. From the Lockean view of natural rights, two things are evident; first, the individual is an autonomous being capable of exercising choice and, second, the legitimacy of government depends not only upon the will of the people, but also upon the government's willingness and ability to protect those individual natural rights. While Lockean natural rights theory was clearly an artificial construct designed to explain the nature of man in political society, it nevertheless exercised a profound influence over political thinking in the seventeenth and eighteenth centuries. The language of both the American and French Revolutions, and the writings of

French philosophe Jean-Jacques Rousseau and German moral philosopher Immanuel Kant, demonstrate the philosophical pedigree of natural law and natural rights.

While Rousseau followed the main thrust of Locke's social contract theory, he declared that far from creating individual natural rights, natural law, conferred inalienable sovereignty on the citizens of a state as a whole. Thus, whatever rights were derived from natural law dwelt within the people as a collectivity and could be identified by reference to the 'general will'. It will be readily apparent that the general will was not an absolute quality and could either transform itself or be transformed by a persuasive leader. While Rousseau's theory was therefore derived from natural precepts. It is obvious that it could be employed to justify demagoguery and totalitarianism. Indeed, it may be argued that the Terror of the French Revolution might be traced to a perversion of the 'general will' thesis.

Kant developed his ideas from a more general appreciation of the non-empirical natural law and natural rights tradition. The basis of Kant's theory was the categorical imperative, that is, the absolute moral good which is identifiable in the exercise of the virtuous will by all rational individuals. In Kant's theory, the categorical imperative operates on three levels; first, it specified universal acts of duty on all individuals; second, it provides systematic rules for determining these duties, and third, it specifies the relationship between freedoms and duties. Underlying the categorical imperative, however, is the idea that individuals are under a duty to develop their rational capacities and to employ them for the promotion of happiness in others. While the categorical imperative might be seen to be primarily duty-based, it has, as its correlative, a system of rights. Unlike the old natural law tradition, however, such rights are not prescribed, but flow from the consequences of the Kantian duty-based system. In a society of rational; self-determining human beings, Kant postulated that freedoms or rights would emerge as a consequence of the application of the categorical imperative. Such rights may therefore be described as consequential and non-relational in that they do not depend upon each other for their existence or worth. Unfortunately, because of the non-relational nature of rights in Kant's theory, it is particularly difficult to apply to concrete situations.

Although there has been something of a revival in the post-Second World War period, natural rights theory fell into general disrepute during the nineteenth century. The major criticism directed at natural rights theory was that it was not scientifically verifiable. How was it possible to know where rights came from, what they were and what content they had? Critics pointed to the a *priori* moral or value structures and assumptions derived from the personal preferences of the various theorists and declared that natural rights could have no objective existence. As English utilitarian Jeremy Bentham argued: 'Right is the child of law; from real laws come real rights, but from imaginary law, from "laws of nature", come imaginary rights .... Natural rights is simple nonsense: natural and imprescriptible rights, rhetorical nonsense upon stilts.'

Despite these criticisms of natural law and natural rights, however, sight must not be lost of the powerful influence which they have exercised over the emergence and development of human rights. Natural rights theory has the merit of providing the basis for a system of law which is allegedly superior to the law of the state and to which appeal may be made if it appears that the latter is unjust, arbitrary or oppressive. It may even be argued that the early revolutionary constitutional documents were 'natural rights' documents, and that following the barbarous excesses both prior to and during the Second World War, a revived natural rights movement led to the drafting of the major international human rights instruments. Of course, the view might be taken that although human rights had their origin in natural law, it took a system of positive law to provide a definite and systematic statement of the actual rights which people possessed.

Law of the State

While natural law theorists derived their ideas of rights from God, reason or *a priori* moral assumptions, positivists argued that the existence and content of rights could be derived only from the laws of the state. While the approach of the natural law rights theorists was essentially non-empirical, the empirical methods adopted by the positivists reflected the scientific milieu of the 'Age of Enlightenment' of eighteenth-century Europe.

It was Scotsman David Hume who first raised the dichotomy between the naturalist and positivist schools of jurisprudence. Hume argued that inquiry into social phenomena could be divided into two distinct categories : First, the category of facts which could be proved to exist empirically and which could be demonstrated to be true or false. This was the 'is'. Second, there was the category of morality which could not be proved to exist objectively and about which people might have legitimate differences of opinion. This was the 'ought'. In Hume's view, it was only the 'is' - those matters which were empirically provable - that formed the basis of valid scientific enquiry. This had the consequence of severing the discussion of morality from the analysis of legal systems. Once this had been done, natural law appeared to be simply an argument about which moral position was; better than another. Furthermore, while natural law failed to demonstrate how a systematic legal system could be constructed from its precepts, positive law took as its starting point the existence of formal legal systems.

The apparent amoral starkness of Hume's position was given a humanitarian face by the development by Jeremy Bentham of a school of positivism known as utilitarianism. The central thesis of utilitarianism was that human existence was dominated by pleasure and pain, and that by increasing the former and diminishing the latter, the lot of mankind would be improved. The aim of utility, therefore, was to increase the overall stock of human pleasure, which could be calculated on a mathematical basis. The ultimate test of utility, therefore, was the implementation of rules which gave the greatest happiness to the greatest number of people - the maximization of felicity. It will be apparent that Bentham's utilitarianism was not amoral, but its morality was derived not from a metaphysical source; rather, its origins lay in the expression of the majority's personal preferences. Clearly this had the potential to lead to a tyranny of the majority and to the oppression of the minority in any given state. It is perhaps paradoxical, therefore, that Bentham and his followers employed utilitarianism as a potent vehicle for English flaw reform.

The main achievement of Hume and Bentham was to make law an autonomous field of scientific study separate and distinct from natural law inputs, and to pave the way for the more systematic approach of John Austin. Austin's empiricism led him to conclude that the only valid laws were the commands of the sovereign, or the ruling political power, which were accompanied by appropriate sanctions or remedies. From this position, it was possible to construct a rational system of interlocking and scientifically verifiable rules. The Austinian, legacy, however, has been, rightly or wrongly, to suggest that rights are simply those rules which the state has enacted for the protection of individuals and their property interests. In terms of Hohfeldian linguistic analysis of legal rights, it might be said that the Austinian position is that the state grants an immunity to individuals with a corresponding disability on the part of the state which prevents it from interfering with those immunities. The main criticism directed at this form of positivism are that it places no moral constraints on the rules adopted by states and individual only enjoy such rights as the state is prepared to grant them. Thus, the Nazi Nuremburg Laws on racial purity may have been immoral, but from a positivist point of view they were laws none the less, having been adopted by the government in power. Similarly, within a positivist framework, a law requiring all prisoners to be tortured would be legitimate despite its immoral quality.

The positivist position does, however, have certain advantages. It enables individuals to point to concrete norms and prescriptions that allow them to vindicate their rights. Professor H.L.A. Hart, a prominent and influential moral philosopher, has attempted to remove from positivism the less palatable aspects of its Austinian legacy. He has argued that although law and morality stand independently of each other, nevertheless the laws which a government adopts have been recognized and accepted by the community as a whole. This, therefore, provides legitimacy for the laws passed. Of course, Hart's theory is only as good as the system of government in power, so that the community standards and laws of Nazi Germany will be different to those of present-day Britain. It is also true of positivist approaches that may be possible to identify substantive rules for the protection of human rights within a legal system, but the reality of the situation may be that the social and institutional conditions are such as to deny the effective exercise of those rights.

Negating Utilitarianism

The central criticism of utilitarianism is that it sets as its priority the well being of the majority. Little thought is given to minorities or individuals within a state whose preferences are not represented by the majority and who may, in consequence, be severely disadvantaged or, in rights talk, deprived of their rights. Take, for example, the issue of homosexuality. The majority of people within a state might find the practice of homosexuality so abhorrent or abominable that would wish to prohibit it legislation. Clearly, this would satisfy the central axioms of utilitarianism by maximizing the happiness of the majority. The homosexuals, a minority whose practices would be forbidden, would be able to make no argument to gainsay the utilitarian position since, as a minority, their preferences would have to give way to the wishes of the majority. Under a different theory, the treatment meted out to the homosexuals in our fictitious state might look like discrimination, or the consideration of a minority group as having less worth than the majority. Clearly, in a pluralistic, democratic state such a position would be untenable. Because of the tendency to a tyranny of the majority inherent in utilitarian focus.

Two of the most notable critics of utilitarianism are Dworkin and Nozick; but it is only in their criticism of utilitarianism that they are united. Each author starts from a different point of departure and arrives at starkly different conclusions. Nozick's rights theory flows from his general political philosophy which demands an ontological commitment to a particular species of morality and social organization. In his theory, he postulates a group of men and women in a state of nature who combine to form the minimal state. The minimal state is not only based on certain moral precepts but is itself one of those moral precepts. To have more than a minimal state whose functions are limited to those of a 'night-watchman' would be to deprive its citizens of more liberty than necessary, which would in itself be immoral. The other moral bases of the minimal state are the right not to be killed, assaulted, robbed or defrauded; the right to acquire, retain and dispose of property; the right to performance of contracts and the right to do as one pleases so long as it does not violate the rights of others. Wrongdoing, therefore, corresponds only to violation of these rights. The role of the minimal state in such circumstances is limited to enforcement of the moral bases of the state by punishing violators, settling disputes and awarding compensation: the 'night-watchman' role. If the state were to transgress into other areas of activity such as providing welfare or redistributing wealth, it would exceed its function and become immoral by depriving citizens or their liberty to act. Nozick's main criticism of utilitarianism, therefore, is that it scarifies liberty of the individual for the sake of the majority; it takes no account of the fact that an individual's life is the only one she or he possesses.

Nozick's thesis is, of course, highly theoretical and

application to forms of liberal democratic and capitalist state organization would simply have the effect of entrenching existing social inequalities. But what Nozick is seeking to do, is to construct a theory which would maximize the liberty available to all individuals without accepting the anarchist critique that maximum individual liberty is only possible without the state. With Nozick, the state remains a necessity, but one which must hardly encroach upon its citizens' freedom of action.

The Nozick's minimalist state strikes one as theoretically harsh and potentially populated by bleakly self-interested individuals. One might consider the other major contemporary critic of the utilitarian school whose anchor is firmly set in the Anglo-American liberal tradition: Gerald Dworkin. In Dworkin's view, rights are defined as political 'trumps' held by individuals 'when, for some reason, a collective goal is not a sufficient justification for denying them what they wish as individuals, to have or to do, or not a sufficient justification for imposing some loss or injury upon them'. In other words, rights perform the same function as trump cards in a game of bridge or whist where any trump card will always possess a higher value than the highest card of any other suit. In the same way a right will always defeat a policy designed to promote general welfare unless a good argument can be adduced for it not doing so. This definition of a right clearly counters the utilitarian thrust that individual preferences must always give way to those of the majority, since it says that in some circumstances the interests of the individual must take priority over those of society as a whole.

As a definition of rights, Dworkin's approach is unobjectionable, but it tells us nothing of where rights come from, what they are or where they stand in relation to each other. To answer these questions, it is necessary to understand that they are constructed on the foundation of Dworkin's commitment to the political doctrine of liberalism, one of the central tenets of which is that governments must treat individuals within their populations with equal respect and concern. Thus, although Dworkin's theory is anti-utilitarian this respect is shown because the individual cannot be sacrificed for the benefit of overall social welfare, he none the less accepts the Benthamite utilitarian credo that everybody counts for one, but nobody counts for more than one. What he argues is that in aggregating the preferences of individuals, the utilitarians deviate from the central liberal proposition that individuals must be treated as individuals. It is therefore not the principle of one person one vote which is wrong, it is the mechanics of aggregation which are flawed. This is so, Dworkin argues, because in making decisions individuals are swayed by two types of preference; the first of which is acceptable, the second of which is not. First, individuals have personal preferences which rest on individual taste - a preference for Coke over Pepsi, for example. Such preferences are innate and do not involve preferences about other people's preferences. It is this second-preferences about other people's preferences which, Dworkin argues, distorts the utilitarian hedonic calculation. This is so because, although in theory we would wish to assign the greatest number of liberties to everyone, our choices would be constrained by external preferences; by giving preference to those people whose preferences we would wish to see satisfied. This distinction leads, in Dworkin's view to a kind of double counting in favour of those whom we would wish to have their preferences fulfilled, which in turn, leads to a violation of the principle of equal respect and concern. Since, however, external preferences - preference about preferences - cannot be excluded from the calculation, but since they clearly violate the principle of equal respect and concern, a system of rights is necessary to 'trump' potential deviations in the hedonic calculation.

Dworkin's distinction between different kinds of preferences is extremely subtle, and it is doubtful whether it can be sustained in practice. Nevertheless, it is crucial to his understanding of rights in a liberal democratic society. At this point, it is possible to discern why rights are necessary and ought to be taken seriously in Dworkin's scheme, but it still does not tell us what rights we have, that is, the analytical side of the equation. Here Dworkin argues that there is no general right to liberty as such, since this would be meaningless, but that there are rights to specific liberties such as freedom of expression, association and religion, and freedom in personal and sexual relations. From whence, however, are these specific rights derived? In Dworkin's view that all derive from the fundamental right that everybody is entitled to 'treatment as an equal', which in turn is derived from the central tenet of liberalism that everybody must be treated with equal respect and concern. In what sense, however, is the right to treatment as an equal fundamental? It is because, argues Dworkin, it is the source both of the general authority of collective goals and of the special limitations on their authority that justify more particular rights'. Thus when a right is claimed it must be demonstrable that it is supported by the fundamental right to equal treatment.

While one can take issue with Dworkin's theory of rights at a number of levels, it is none the less useful because it attempts to reconcile societal goals with individual preferences and establish a hierarchical order of rights. The major problem with Dworkin in attempting to apply his theory to the international human rights field, however, is that his thesis is applicable only to the conditions of a liberal democracy possessing strong democratic institutions. In most states where gross human rights violations occur, they are not always endowed with either that form of political system not strong democratic institutions. This does not mean that Dworkin's thesis is wrong, but simply that it is has limited application. Nevertheless, both the Council of Europe and the inter-American systems for the protection of human rights explicitly require the prior existence of forms of representative democracy within their member states. It may well be that Dworkin's theory of rights might be fruitfully adopted and adapted to explain both the existence and application of rights within these systems at least.

Consideration of anti-utilitarian jurists cannot be deemed complete without a brief examination of Rawls Theory of Justice. In this work, he argues that justice is a way of distributing the rights, duties, benefits and burdens among individuals within society. He further posits, as distinct from utilitarians, that every person is inviolable and that even the welfare of society cannot displace this inviolability:

> Justice denies that loss of freedom for some is made right by a greater good shared by others. Therefore, in a just society liberties of equal citizenship are settled; the rights secured by justice are not subject to political bargaining or to the calculus of social interest.

Like Nozick, but starkly different results, Rawls starts with the familiar social contract theory in which all persons are in an original position of equality as regards the distribution of freedom and power. Each, however, is endowed with a "veil of ignorance" about his or her own personal qualities and attributes. In this state, the rational person who is ignorant of their own potential will, in Rawls' view, chooses two principles of justice. The First Principle will be that everyone has an equal right to the most extensive total system of equal basic liberties compatible with the same system for others. The Second Principle is that social and economic inequalities are to be organized to that they are of the greatest benefit to the least advantaged and so that they provide a system of equal access to all offices and equality of opportunity. Thus, in Rawls' system, there is a general conception of fairness and equality in which all social primary goods such as liberty and opportunity, income and wealth are to be distributed equally unless an unequal distribution actually operates to the advantage of the least favoured.

Unlike Dworkin, who does not concede a general right to liberty, Rawls argues to the contrary, that liberty is the pre-eminent right and that all other rights are subsidiary to it.

Within such a system, rights may only be restricted if, first, they would strengthen the total system of liberty shared by all or, secondly, if less than equal liberty were acceptable to the citizens so deprived. What then, are the rights comprehended by the First Principle? Among these Rawls would include political liberty, freedom of expression, conscience and thought, and freedom to integrity and inviolability of the person - including the freedom to hold property. All such rights would be held equally by citizens in a just society. Rawls recognizes, however, that some citizens, although actually possessing the most extensive system of equal rights within society, might because of other factors, such as ignorance or poverty, be unable to take full advantage of their rights. Clearly, this does not affect the intrinsic value of rights possessed by individuals but it does hinder their enjoyment of those rights. In Rawls' terms, it affects the worth or value of the liberties held. How, then, is this disparity in the worth or value of liberty to be compensated for? Rawls' answer to this is by the application of the Difference Principle. This principle states that an equal distribution of resources is to be preferred unless it can be demonstrated that an unequal distribution would make both the advantaged and disadvantaged better off. Thus, this form of distributive justice should be implemented to ensure that each person enjoyed the full worth of his or her liberty.

Again it may be argued that Rawls' theory is acceptable in so far as it applies to liberal democratic societies, but that its application to other forms of political organization make it unrealistic. None the less, it is clear that even at a cursory glance Rawls' concepts could be applied to arguments in favour of the third generation right to development which demands a reallocation of the world's resources to maximize the wellbeing of those in the developing world.

New Realism

The explosion of regulatory activity in USA following President Roosevelt's economic 'New Deal' led a number of

American jurists to consider new methods of attempting to explain the functions of law within a complex, highly regulated industrial society. In this task they were aided by the input of social scientific perspectives, particularly that of the then relatively modern discipline of sociology. Foremost among the legal realists were Karl Llewellyn and Roscoe Pound. Their major concern was, to paraphrase Llewellyn, to discover what law does rather than what law is. Because of their empirical framework, the legal realists had no general theory of rights as such, but considered them as forming part and parcel of their study of the processes and interaction of policy, law and legal institutions. Within this framework, rights might emerge as the end-product of such a process of interaction, thereby reflecting the prevailing moral values of society at any given time. In this sense, the realists provided a kind of 'snapshot' of rights as a temporary manifestation of an ongoing process. Although Pound devised a prescription for the validation of human wants, human demands and social interest through the principle of social engineering, he did not identify a mechanism or method by which individual rights might be prioritized both in relation to each other and in relation to societal goals. As Shestack points out, this lack of 'goal identification' renders Pound's approach deficient in assisting normative enquiry.

None the less, a contemporary development within the realist school perhaps addresses some of the criticisms directed at Pound. This is the Yale School of International Law, whose main proponent is Myres McDougal. He and his colleagues have developed a value-explicit and policy-orientated approach to human rights based on the 'super-value' of the protection of human dignity. Like other legal realists, McDougal, Lasswell and Chen argue that demands for the satisfaction of human rights derive from a broad based international sharing of values. These values are manifested by demands relating to such social goods as respect, power, enlightenment, well-being, health, skill, affection and rectitude. All of these values contribute towards, and are validated by,. The super-value of human dignity. The objective of the value-explicit policy-orientated approach is to offer a prescription for the world community in which all the values identified are shared through the application of democratic principles.

While the Yale School might be criticized on the ground that the concept of the 'super-value' of human dignity might not mean the same thing for all cultures at all times, nevertheless it does seem to represent an idea upon which a large core of consensus might be secured, especially since the humanitarian drive for many international human rights instruments has its origins in seeking protection and redress for individuals who are the subjects of inhumane treatment. Furthermore, the identification of a common goal or goals, again, as represented by the major human rights instruments, provides evidence of a minimum of shared values within the world community. This kind of approach avoids problems of metaphysical abstractions which characterizes a substantial amount of theoretical debate about human rights, but it still does not answer the question of whether human rights are immutable or whether - and this is a dangerous argument - they simply reflect prevailing social interests.

Marxist Theory

Before leaving our consideration of the theoretical schools which might help us to think in a coherent way about rights, it is probably pertinent to mention Marxist approaches to the issue. Marx, arguing from a scientific basis, claimed that the alleged law of nature was both idealistic and a historical, and as such the claim by seventeenth-and eighteenth-century bourgeois revolutionaries to the effect that rights were both inalienable and imprescriptibie was unsustainable and indefensible. Rights, Marx argued, were simply a bourgeois concept and a product of bourgeois-capitalist society, designed to maintain and reinforce the pre-eminent position of the ruling class. None the less, Marx was prepared to concede that even within the early stages of communist revolutionary state, rights, of a particular species, might still have an important role to play in the transformation of society. In order to understand this argument, it is necessary to consider the Marxist approach to the nature of the individual within both the capitalist and the communist state.

In Marxist theory, the essence of an individual is that of a social being who uses his or her abilities to satisfy his or her needs. The fulfilment of these needs in capitalist society, where the means of production are controlled by the ruling class, is impossible since it results in the alienation of the working class. The true potential of human beings, in Marxist doctrine, can only be realized if they are enabled to return to their true nature as social beings. This, however, can only be achieved in a truly communist society where all means of production are held in common and there is an absence of class conflict. Such a communist society can only come into being, however by a revolution of the industrial proletariat. This, in turn, will transform itself into a dictatorship of the proletariat and, though historical and economic forces; lead to the withering away of the state. Until the state withers, however, the revolutionary party must occupy a vanguard position using the state and its institutions for the transformation of society. It is at this point that Marxist concepts of rights emerge. During the period of transformation there are no individual rights, since these are egoistic, bourgeois property-based 'right'; there are only legal rights, which are granted by the state and which are directed towards the transition from the communist state to communist society. These legal rights are, however, only contingent in that they are concerned simply with the mechanics of transformation. As such, these rights can only be social and economic, since they are directed towards the reduction of the means of production to common control. It is only this species of rights which contributes towards the Marxist objective of returning individuals to their status as social beings. Once the process of transformation has taken place, the need for rights disappears, since each individual will be in a free and spontaneous relationship with all other individuals. Within Marxist theory, therefore, rights are simply achieved, the tools are no longer needed and may be conveniently disposed of. Furthermore, rights have no transcendental or eternal value; they are positivistic in the sense that those rights which are deemed to exist are fixed solely by the state.

While some states such as China and North Korea still hold firm to teaching based on Marxist principles, other erstwhile communist states such as those comprising the Commonwealth of Independent States have abandoned not only Marxist economic theories, but also Marxist theories of rights. Indeed, a number of the old former communist bloc states, such as Hungary and Czechoslovakia, have become parties to human rights instruments that clearly give effect to individualistic civil and political rights. Nevertheless, the contribution of Marxist thought to the development of international instruments on social, cultural and economic rights have been pronounced and should be dismissed lightly.

Classification in International Law

It was indicated earlier in this chapter that a great deal of debate about the juridical nature of humans in international law has tended to focus on the normative relationship between various alleged categories of rights. Some commentators, such as Cranston, take the view that only civil and political rights can properly be called human rights, and that economic and social rights are simply claims against the state which it is not obliged to fulfil. Other jurists, such as Tunkin, who are more predisposed to a socialist orientation, argue that only economic and social rights have any real meaning, since civil and political rights serve to reinforce the present unequal distribution of all social and material goods and impede the process of development. Such dogmatism tends to produce unfortunate effects, since, as we shall see below, it hinders appreciation of the fact that just as not all civil and political rights are individualistic, not all economic and social rights, are collectivist in orientation. However, even within supposed categories of rights, there is debate about whether the more fundamental rights and freedoms can be separated from those which are less fundamental.

The position of the UN General Assembly is clear on this issue. It has stated on a number of occasions that 'all human rights and fundamental freedoms are indivisible and interdependent and that equal attention and urgent consideration should be given to the implementation, promotion and protection of both civil and political and economic, social and cultural rights'. This statement, however, is not particularly useful, since it does not reflect the actual position as regards the different goals and implementation programmes of the various human rights instruments which we will be considering in detail later in this book. Furthermore, it might be questioned whether such an approach is also intellectually compelling, since different societal conditions might demand the setting of different priorities with regard to different classes of human rights. This is not to argue that certain rights may be regarded as less important than others on some kind of arbitrary hierarchical scale, rather that in an imperfect world with an imperfect allocation of resources, the priorities within different states may dictate a different allocation of such resources. None the less, it is possible, both as an intellectual exercise and as a matter of practicality, to adduce weighty arguments in favour of the contention that between different classes of rights, and even within classes of rights, there is some kind of hierarchical classification of rights.

Basic Rights

Are there some rights that might be regarded as more fundamental than others? Certainly, there is some support for this view in the wide variety of international human rights instruments now in force. The UN Charter, for example, states in its Preamble that the peoples of the UN are determined 'to reaffirm faith in fundamental human rights ....', apparently indicating that these fundamental human rights enjoyed an existence prior to their recognition by the Charter and prior to their reduction to positive law by the various UN instruments. Such rights have also been described as 'supra-positive' or 'elementary' rights by Theodoor van Boven who argues that their validity 'is not dependent on their acceptance by the subjects of law but which are at the foundation of the international community.' In referring to 'supra-positive' rights, the immediate impression is that Van Boven is claiming some kind of natural law origin for his fundamental rights, but throughout his discussion there is constant reference to human rights as a manifestation of international social order, thereby implying that rights, including supra-positive rights, have a sociological basis for their existence. As he says: 'These rights lie at the foundation of the international community as presently represented in United Nations and, in a more limited sense, in other important world-wide and regional organizations." This statement would seem to suggest that fundamental rights are not static but dynamic and that other human rights may be exalted of such a status. Indeed, Van Boven claims that this has been the case for such rights involving the prohibition of race and sex discrimination, since nearly all international human rights instruments take as their point of departure the need to ensure the absence of discrimination on these grounds.

Perhaps the most compelling argument in favour of treating some rights as fundamental lies is the fact that in the ICCPR as in the European, American and African regional human rights conventions, certain rights are characterized as inviolable in that they may not be derogated from even in times of war or other national emergency. Included in this list are the right to life; freedom from torture, inhuman and degrading treatment; freedom from slavery or servitude; freedom from *ex post facto* laws and freedom of thought, conscience and religion. Other rights, however, may be derogated from; under defined conditions. This would seem to imply that there is a difference between rights which may be derogated from and those which may not, the natural conclusion being that the former are to be regarded as more fundamental than the latter. Furthermore, the UN Convention Against Torture makes it clear that there can be no justification under any circumstances for the commission of the prohibited acts in that Convention. It would therefore seem that an argument could be made that these non-derogable rights have the characteristics of *ius cogens*, that is, norms which can never be derogated from, and must, in that sense, be seen as fundamental both within the realm of international human rights law and international law in general. And if these non-derogable rights are indeed fundamental and do bear the characteristics of ius cogens, then it is possible to argue, as Van Boven does, that these rights are 'binding on States, even in the absence of any conventional obligation or of any express acceptance or comment'.

Other Rights

It may be recalled from Chapter 1 that although the UDHR included reference to all categories of rights-civil, political, economic, social and cultural-within the framework of a single instrument, it proved impossible to secure agreement between the member states of the UN upon the drafting of a legally binding document embracing all of the rights contained in the Declaration. While some states argued that all types of rights constituted an indivisible and mutually self-supporting whole, others, particularly the US and the UK, took the view that whereas civil and political rights were immediately enforceable and justiciable, economic, social and cultural rights depended upon positive, programmatic implementation. These Western states, whose political and economic structures had been heavily influenced by the revolutionary constitutionalism of the seventeenth and eighteenth centuries, argued that only first-generation rights - freedoms from state interference - were all that international law could reasonably be expected to protect as a matter of immediacy. Economic, social and cultural rights were not amenable to such immediate protection and were best fulfilled through a progressive reporting system. The ultimate drafting of two separate Covenants dealing with the two broad categories of rights would seem to support the contentions adduced by the Western states. While the ICCPR provides for immediate protection by requiring states to 'respect and ensure to all individuals within its territory and subject to its jurisdiction the rights recognized'. The ICESCR, on the other hand requires only that states 'undertake to take steps ...to the maximum of their available resources, with a view to achieving progressively the full realization of the rights recognized.' The conclusion which is drawn by some commentators, such as Craston, from this differential implementation structure, is that whereas civil and political rights are human rights properly so - called, economic and social rights, do not enjoy such a status. If this position were taken to its logical conclusion, it would also mean that these second-generation rights do not require protection or implementation because they are not 'real' rights.

It is questionable, however, whether the drafting history and the arguments about implementation of the perceived categories of rights should determine decisively whether or not one category should be regarded as 'real' rights and the other not. At the theoretical level, it might be possible to argue that the right to education (which is classified as a social right) is of a different moral order to freedom of expression (a civil right), but this is an argument about the relational value of rights and not about the existence of such rights. Of course, whether we choose to accept economic, social and cultural rights as rights properly called, will depend upon our own preferred theoretical standpoint.

It we descent to the level of pragmatism, it also becomes clear that alleged distinctions between the two categories of rights often verges upon the arbitrary. Take, for instance., the argument that civil and political rights are capable of immediate protection, whereas economic, social and cultural rights require progressive implementation. While it is undeniable that the latter group of rights will probably require the spending of a higher proportion of a state's Gross Domestic Product (GDP) on such items as education, social security and health care, it is still obvious that civil and political rights also require a reasonably substantial element of public spending in order to ensure adequate protection. The right to a fair trial, for example, requires the maintenance of an effective justice system, the provision of publicly financed defenders, the payment of interpreters for individuals whose language is not that of state in which they are being tried, the provision of adequate security systems to enable the courts to be open to the public, and so on. While the costs associated with the implementation of such a system are probably not of the order of providing comprehensive social security for individuals within a state, none the less they will not be negligible and may impose a significant burden upon the treasuries of some states.

It should also be noted that the alleged division between civil and political rights, on the one hand and economic, social and cultural rights on the other, is largely arbitrary and cannot be entirely sustained by reference to the two UN Covenants. Both Covenants, for example, deal with rights involving freedom of association and family matters which may be categorized as hybrid rights, since they exhibit characteristics of both classes of rights. If one takes a selection of provisions from the ICCPR, it is possible to discern that they are not the 'freedom from' rights, which are normally associated with that Covenant, but 'rights to', which are usually regarded as second-generation rights. Article 24(1), for example, requires state intervention in order to ensure that a child is accorded 'the right to such measures of protection as are required by his status as a minor, on the part of.. The State'. Conversely, the ICESCR has a substantial number of provisions which would appear not to require state intervention for their protection.

These are more of the 'freedom from' than the 'rights to' species and include the right to strike, the prohibition of the use of children in harmful work, and so on.

The existence of these hybrid rights makes it apparent that any classification and hierarchical ranking of rights in international law is not easy and that, indeed, it may be questionable whether there is any real utility in attempting to do so. Putting rights into particular categories tell us little about the value of a right; it simply provides fodder for moralizing or choosing a preferred political position in debates about human rights. This is not to deny that there may well be a certain utility in differentiating between the implementation measures attached to certain rights, since it permits determination of the varying degrees of state obligations with respect to all rights in general. Ultimately, however, whether rights are civil, political, economic, social or cultural in orientation makes little difference to their qualitative status as rights, but it may make a difference to the speed with which they are implemented by states.

Solidarity Rights

The emergence of third-generation or solidarity rights is closely identified with the rise of Third World nationalism and the perception of developing states that the existing international order is loaded against them. It may also be seen as a claim by developing states for fairer treatment and for the construction of a world system that will facilitate distributive justice in the broadest Rawlian sense. The basis for these claims is not, however, simply moral, but can be identified as having a legal basis in a number of existing international instruments.

The UN Charter itself places human rights in a pivotal position to assist in the creation of a peaceful international order and economic development. Article I (2) of the Charter provides that one of the purposes of the UN is 'to develop friendly relations among nations based on the principle of equal rights and self-determination of people'. Article 1(3) further provides that another purpose of organization is 'to achieve international cooperation in solving international problems of economic, social, cultural or humanitarian character, and in promoting and encouraging respect for human rights and fundamental freedoms...'. These purposes are further reinforced by the substantive provisions of the Charter, particularly Articles 55 and 56, which clearly demonstrate that the creation of suitable international conditions is a prerequisite to the full social development of all individuals.

A number of other international instruments also support the view that the international community is obliged to establish a favourable global system for securing the better participation of developing states. The common Article 1 of the two International Covenants, for example, provide for both the political and economic right to self-determination. Article 1(2) provides :

> All people may, for their own ends, freely dispose of their natural wealth and resources without any prejudice to any obligations arising out of international economic cooperation, based upon the principle of mutual benefit, and international law. In no case may a people be deprived of its own means of subsistence.

Article 2(1) of the ICESCR also provides that states parties are to 'take steps individually and through international assistance and cooperation, especially economic and technical, to the maximum of available resources, with a view of achieving progressively the rights recognized in the present Covenant by all available means'. These provisions, it is argued by some jurists, provide a clear basis; for a number of claimed solidarity rights.

What, then, are these third-generation or solidarity rights? Burns Weston identifies at least six categories of solidarity rights.

1 The right to economic, political, social and cultural self-determination.

2 The right to economic and social development.
3 The right to participate in and benefit from the Common Heritage of Mankind and other information and progress.
4 The right to peace.
5 The right to a healthy environment.
6 The right to humanitarian relief.

It is immediately apparent that these rights have two dominant characteristics: first, they are collective in nature and, second, they depend upon international cooperation for their achievement. It is also apparent that these rights build upon and develop existing categories of rights and in that sense they are, as Weston suggests, historically cumulative.

The fact that third-generation rights are collective in nature does not automatically mean that they should be thought of as less than 'real' right for that reason alone. While traditional liberal conceptions of rights emphasize their individualistic quality, it is none the less apparent that even within the category of rights which might be described as civil and political, certain rights are collective in nature. These include the right to exercise one's religion in community with others, the right of peaceful assembly and the right to freedom of association. The rights categorized as economic, social and cultural, which are contained in a variety of international instruments, are also largely collectivist in nature, but are nevertheless recognized by the parties to those instruments as positive rights. The fact, however, that the new generation of rights depends for its implementation on international cooperation leads some authors to assert that they are little more than aspirational claims which do not possess the binding quality which; is the hallmark of rights proper. Others, such as Alston, however, argue that there is no need to resort to claiming new rights which may be categorized as third generation, since by and large the problems which they seek to address are dealt by existing instruments. Alston has also argued that claims for novel rights such as the 'right to tourism' obscures the need to properly develop existing rights, and more particularly, implementation programmes. He has also argued that there should be a system of procedures for granting a kind of approved origin mark to any 'new' rights proclaimed by the General Assembly.

Proposed Solutions

As the foregoing discussion amply demonstrates, there is considerable debate about what rights are, where they come from, what their content is, how they relate to each other and how new rights might be properly identified. The proposed solutions to these questions are as numerous as the questions themselves. It is, however, the identification of the questions which is of importance, since they act as signposts towards a coherent method of thinking about human rights. What is also apparent is that debate about human rights is not static, but is part of continuing dialectic process through which progress in the field might be, and manifestly has been, made. The attention is now focused upon the rather more pragmatic issues of the system of international law by which human rights are protected and the precise nature of the international instruments which both contain in concrete form the rights to be protected and the institutions through which this is achieved.

FIVE

Universal Factor

"It seems that a man who is nothing but a man has lost the very qualities which make it possible for others to treat him as a fellow man." With this sentence, taken from the study on Imperialism which forms the second part of The Origins of Totalitarianism (1951), Hannah Arendt defines the fundamental condition of human rights: A human being has rights only if he is other than a human being. And if he is to be other than a human being, he must in addition become another human being. Then "the others" can treat him as their fellow human being. What makes human beings alike is the fact that every human being carries within him the figure of the other. The likeness that they have in common follows from the difference of each from each.

Thou shall not kill thy fellow human being—To kill a human being is not to kill an animal of the species. Homosapiens, but to kill the human community present in him as both capacity and promise. And you also kill it in yourself. To banish the stranger is to banish the community, and you banish yourself from the community thereby.

What is this figure of the other in me, on which, it is said, my right to be treated as a human being rests? It is this question which we deal with in this chapter.

"Nothing but a man," writes Hannah Arendt. That is, nothing other than an individual of the species Homosapiens. A powerful species; in the struggle for life enacted in the theatre of the world, Homosapiens have emerged victorious over all other species. And they continue, successfully, to combat them, using hygiene, sanitary arrangements, the protection of the environment, and so on. Each human being is a specimen of this species. He resembles any other member of the species, as a chimpanzee resembles a chimpanzee.

Is the figure of the other (ape) present in every ape? Apes are able to tell each other apart and to distinguish themselves from other species of animals. They can communicate amongst themselves by systems of sensory signals based on the five senses and motility. These systems constitute a sort of language which endows the animals with a sort of community in which affective states (Aristotle's pathemata) are exchanged, along with admonitions as to conduct.

This signal-based language is not wholly lacking in the human species, but its role is confined. Animals' capacity to communicate is determined by the genetic stock common to the species, and is of the order of instinct. Human beings have very few instincts. In comparison with their animal brothers, young human beings are slow to realise their capacity in the language of their fellow. And this human language is not common to the species. It functions not by bodily signals, but by signs. These arbitrary signs, combined according to rules which are also arbitrary, but which are fixed by syntactic structures, make it possible to designate any object, real or not, internal or external, as their referent, and to signify something about that object. Finally, and this is what interests us here, this signification is addressed.

It is what we today call the "pragmatic" function of human language, which governs the formation of the figure of the other. Explicitly or implicitly, every human sentence is destined to someone or something. Some answer, some response, some link or follow-up is expected. The polarisation is marked in our languages by the verbal "persons" and the personal pronouns. I am the one who is speaking now; you are the one to whom the communication is currently addressed. You are silent when I speak, but you can speak, have spoken, and will speak.

Animal communication is, we might say, homogeneous.

By contrast, the distinguishing characteristic of interlocutor is the relation of simultaneous similarity and disparity introduced between the speakers. The instances you and I cannot merge, since while the one speaks the other speaks no longer or not yet. You and I are dietetics, and as such are correlated with now, and now designates the present of speech. From it, the temporality of past and future unfold. But relative to the capacity to speak, which by definition is not confined to the present but extends to every possible interlocutor, you and I are alike. Persons capable of speech alternately occupy the instance I and you. When they say I, they are a past or future you, and when they are in the position of you, they are so because they have spoken or will speak as I.

Interlocutor thus implies that human beings cannot, as animals, merge into a community based on signals. They do so only when the impossibility of interlocutor reduced them to that meager resource. In theory, the human 'we' does not precede but results from interlocutor. In this we, the figure of the other remains clearly present to each, to the extent that the other is his possible interlocutor. The one and the other can come to an agreement, after reasoning and debate, and then establish their community by contract. This is the principle of the Greek politeia or the modern republic. The citizen is the human individual whose right to address others is recognised by those others.

It is important to distinguish the republican principle from the democratic fact. The demos is not a contractual but a natural and cultural community. The individual of the demos is recognised as such not for his right to speak, but for his birth, language and historical heritage. These individuals form a nation (in the medieval sense in which one hears nature), whose principal characteristic is the homogeneity of its constituents. Interlocution does not engender this community; between the members of the nation, language and mores function as signals of recognition. Though possessed of interlocutory capacity, the demotic individual, whether a serf or a free man, uses the language to signal emotions and actions to other specimens of the variety of Homines to which they collectively belong. This relationship to language excludes the alterity implicit in civic interlocution. The other remains alien, and does not enjoy the rights reserved to a national. The very Greeks who invented the politeia excluded barbaroi. The right of interlocution is not granted to every human being. The figure of the other is that of a threat weighing on the national community from without, which cannot help but undermine its integrity.

I oversimplify my description to bring out the essential opposition between the demotic and the civic. The difference between them is the consideration given to interlocution, which modifies the figure of the other. The people keeps the other out; the city interiorises the other. In contemporary human communities, for various reasons, these two aspects are for the most part not distinguished: more or less nation, more or less republic. For example, the institution of a European community undoubtedly draws its justification exclusively from the civic principle.

In the republic, there is a principle of Universalisation, which relates to the function, inherent in speech, of addressing the other. If a human being can speak, he is a possible interlocutor. The principle is not invalidated merely by the fact of his speaking a language foreign to the national language. Homosapiens have always spoken a multitude of languages. But they are all human languages comprising the structural characteristics I have briefly outlined. These characteristics guarantee that an unknown human language can in principle be translated into a known one. I do not wish to take up here the difficulties and enigmas of translation. The theoretical possibility of translation is quite sufficient to extend interlocution to any human individual whatsoever, regardless of natural or national idiom. Civility may become universal in fact as it promises to do by right.

The form in which civility is extended to national or

demotic communities is a serious question. History offers a profusion of different modes, linguistic as well as political and economic. These include an obligatory single language, an official language alongside which traditional languages are tolerated, compulsory multilingualism, effective multilingualism, and so on. The pattern established depends on the balance of military, political, economic and cultural power. These relations determine how interlocution extends, but they cannot curb its extension. There is no limiting the function of destination inherent in the structure of sentences: one may beg a service of a tree or a river, and issue a command to a cat. If the addressee is human, he is immediately vested with the status of interlocutor, capable, in his turn, of addressing the first speaker.

There is no *a priori* limit to the interlocutory capacity. By its association with the recursiveness and translatability of human language, it cannot help but bind all human speakers in a speech community. From this effective (de facto) power there arises what I shall term an effect of right (UN effect department droit). If any human being can be an interlocutor for other human beings, he must be able to, that is, must be enabled or allowed to. We move from the potential implied by competence to the permission implied by entitlement. We know, however, that capacity does not legitimacy make. But it is tempting to merge the two categories in the case of interlocution, both because the capacity to enter into dialogue with others is possessed equally by everyone, and because interlocution in itself implies reciprocity of speech. Reciprocity respects not only the alliterate of interlocution but the parity of the interlocutors. It thus guarantees their respective liberty and their equality before the word. These are the characteristics of justice itself. The slippage here from the fact to the right resembles the contemporary confusion of democracy and republic. But how can we avoid it?

Let us take it that the capacity to speak to others is a human right, and perhaps the most fundamental human right.

If the use of this capacity is forbidden, whether de facto, by some injustice of fate, or on principle, for example as a punishment, a harm is inflicted on the speaker thus constrained. He is set apart from the speech community of interlocutors. To no one is he any longer someone other, nor is anyone now his other. There are many ways of imposing silence. Amnesty International knows them better than anyone. Its vocation is modest but decisive. It is minimal. Amnestos meant he who is forgotten. Amnesty does not demand that the judgment be revised or that the convicted man be rehabilitated. It simply asks that the institution that has condemned him to silence forget this decree and restore the victim to the community of speakers.

Amnesty's task is in accordance with the provisions of the public law of the republican democracies. I nevertheless maintain that this legality conceals confusion between a capacity, the aptitude for speech, and legitimacy, the authority to speak. In other words, there is, strictly speaking, no natural right. It is of the essence of a right that it be merited. The same goes for the capacity to enter into dialogue. It is not true that it realises itself spontaneously. It requires care and attention, an entire learning process. It requires precisely what is called civilisation. The human being as such is no other than a member of the species Homo: an animal that can speak. It is true that its language is so constituted that it effectively contains the promise of interlocution. But if he is to bring out and respect the figure of the other that this promise bears in it, he must free himself from that in him which will not recognise the figure of the other, that is, his animal nature. Children do not spontaneously enter into dialogue. There is something in us which resists, something which does perhaps "speak," but in signals rather than according to the rules of interlocution.

Civilisation, understood here as the process of learning how to share dialogue with you, requires a moment of silence. Aristotle said: The master speaks and the pupil listens. For that moment, the status of I is forbidden to me, I am assigned the position of you for the master, at the tacit pole of destination. Tacit does not imply passive. The exaltation of interactivity as a pedagogic principle is pure demagogy. The pupil has the capacity to speak; he has to win the right to speak. To do so, he must be silent. The suspension of interlocution imposes a silence and that silence is good. It does not undermine the right to speak. It teaches the value of that right. It is the exercise necessary for excellence in speech. Like the pupil, writers, artists, scholars, and novices must enter into retreat in order to learn what they will have to say to others.

The master, whatever his title, exempts his pupils from the sharing of speech in order to tell them something that they do not know. He may even speak to them in a language that they do not understand. The master is not the figure of the general other, of you, but the figure of the other in all its separateness. He is the stranger, the foreigner. How can one dialogue with the foreigner? One would have to learn his language. This question is in some measure analogous with that of literature and the arts, testifying to something that is "present" otherwise than as interlocutory expectation: something opaque, Beckett's the "Unnamable."

The silence that the learning process of civilisation imposes is the moment of a labour of estrangement. It is a matter of speaking otherwise than is my wont and saying something other than what I know how to say. Through the alterity of the master, the strangeness of another logic is, in silence, imposed. He takes me hostage in order to make me hear and say what I do not know. Emmanuel Levinas has elaborated this theme better than anyone.

From this brief analysis, it follows that the interlocutory capacity changes into a right to speak only if the speech can say something other than the *deja dit* (what has already been said). The right to speak implies a duty to announce. If our speech announces nothing, it is doomed to repetition and to the conservation of existing meanings. The human community may spread, but it will remain the same, prostrated in the euphoria it feels at being on such very good terms with itself. It is the main function of the media today to reinforce the interlocutory consent of the community. They are boring to the extent that they teach us nothing. Interlocution is not an end in itself. It is legitimate only if, through others, the other announces to me something, which I hear but do not understand.

We should then distinguish three different levels of the "right to speak." First, the faculty of interlocution, a principle factually inherent in human language; second, the legitimation of speech, due to the fact that it announces something other, which it strives to make us understand; and last, the legitimacy of speech, the positive right to speak, which recognises in the citizen the right to address the citizen. The latter aspect merges the two former. But this confusion is good. By authorising every possible speaker to address others, their public makes it every speaker's duty to announce to those others what they do not know. It encourages announcements; it instructs. And, on the other hand, it forbids that anyone be arbitrarily deprived of speech. It discourages terror. In this way it governs silence in everyone's best interest, authorising the silence of discipline and outlawing the silence of despotism.

This picture of the republic is idyllic, but the idyll conceals something far from idyllic. The threat of being deprived of speech is not contingent; it weighs constantly on the interlocutory right. This is precisely why the republic is indispensable. The human speaker is always afraid that a "keep quiet" will debar his words. He complains of the precariousness of his membership in the speech community. Even the good silence of the writer, the monk, or the pupil contains an element of suffering. Any banishment is a harm inflicted on those who undergo it, but this harm necessarily changes to a wrong when the victim is excluded from the speech community. For the wrong is the harm to which the victim cannot testify, since he cannot be heard. And this is precisely the case of those to whom the right to speak to others is refused.

The right to impose silence which the community grants itself as a sanction is always dangerous. The death sentence evidently does an irremediable wrong to the condemned man, even if he is guilty of a heinous crime. But in relation to our present topic, death is not necessarily the wrong done to him. There are, as the Greeks put it, "beautiful deaths," of which the citizens continue to speak long afterward. It happens that a speaker is more eloquent dead than alive, and does not therefore die for the community. So we must reverse the relation: it is the wrong, which is the cause of death, since it implies the exclusion of the speaker from the speech community. The community will not even speak of this exclusion since the victim will be unable to report it and cannot therefore defend himself of appeal.

Those who escaped extermination in the camps are aware of this. Restored to the community, they can describe and narrate what the administration of death was. But how can they communicate the abjection to which they were reduced? It was first and foremost the severing of communication. How can one communicate by means of interlocution the terror of what it means no longer to be destined to anyone or anything? They were not spoken to, they were treated. They were not enemies. The SS or Kapos who called them dogs, pigs, or vermin did not treat them as animals but as refuse. It is the destiny of refuse to be incinerated. The ordeal of being forgotten is unforgettable. It reveals a truth about our relationship to language that is stifled and repressed by the serene belief in dialogue. Abjection is not merely when we are missing from speech, but when we lack language to excess. Our debt to announcement can never be acquitted. The other in language, the other that language is, does not say what must be said. It keeps silent. Does it even wait? Excluded from the speech community, the camp victims were rejected into the poverty, the misery of this secret. In that misery resides the true dignity of speech. Clearly, the ordeal of being forgotten cannot be expressed in the sharing of speech, which is, *exhypothesi*, ignorant of it. Neither I nor you, the deportee is present in the language of his lords and in that of the deportees themselves only as the third person, who is to be eliminated. He is superfluous, as any speaker is superfluous in relation to the other. But precisely for that reason, absolutely responsible for himself.

The abjection suffered in the camps horribly illustrates the threat of exclusion, which weighs on all interlocution. On the school playground, the child to whom the others say, "We're not playing with you" experiences this unspeakable suffering. He suffers a wrong equivalent, on its own scale, to a crime against humanity. Even those who submit themselves to such separation in order to exalt the annunciatory power of language run the risk of abjection. True, they forswear the company of others only in order to listen more intently to the foreign master. But this enslavement to the other is perceived as a suspicious dependence on a power alien to the interlocutory community, as a sort of betrayal. The Latin sacer (sacred) expressed the ambivalence of the abject: human refuse excluded from the interests of the speech community, yet a sign, perhaps, in which the other has left its mark and deserving of respectful fear.

In his analysis of the sublime effect, Edmund Burke termed horror the state of mind of a person whose participation in speech is threatened. The power which exceeds the capacity of interlocution resembles night. Though we seek to tame it by dialogue, it does not have the figure of the you. It may be well or ill disposed. We cannot understand it. It may be God, it may be Animal, it may be Satan. In silence we strive to translate its voice in order to announce it to the community of speakers. In this way we seek to make our relation to the other dialectical. But the strangeness of the other seems to escape any totalisation. The effort of translation must be endlessly renewed. It is precisely when we think we have reduced the abject or the sacred to transparent meanings that it becomes most opaque and returns to us from without like an accident. The discontent from which contemporary societies are suffering, the post-modern affliction, is this foreclosure of the other. It is the reverse of the triumphant identification with the other, which affects modern republics at their birth. Saint-Just enacted a law in the name of the other, and instituted the first totalitarian reign of terror.

Wiser than the dialecticians, the Jacobins, and the deciders, Freud acknowledged that abjection was not an episode but a situation constitutive of the human relation to interlocution. As children, we are kept on the margins of interlocution, and condemned to exile. The situation of infantia is that of the incomplete human being who does not yet speak. The child is spoken to and spoken of, but is not an interlocutor even though he is plunged into the interlocutory community. The statements that concern him have no value for him except as signals or gestures; they are difficult for him to decipher because they are arbitrary, and he has little instinct. He is affected by them, but has no language in which to articulate his own affective states. These reside within him unconsciously, in forgetfulness, which is always present. They do not enter the temporality associated with the instances of destination you and I. They loom up in the course of the individual life history in apparently unmotivated ways. They block interlocution. With them, the inevitable wrong and abjection of infantia erupt into adult relations.

From our native prematurity a mute distress results. It is to this distress that we owe our capacity to question everything around us. But we also owe to it our need to be welcomed, the request that we be authorised to enter the speech community. In interlocution a drama is played out between me and you; it is the drama of authorisation. The question of assertion that we address to others is invariably coupled with an entreaty: Deliver me from my abandonment, allow me to belong among you. This entreaty allows a wide variety of modalities: friendship, hatred, love, and even indifference. But in it resides the foundation of the right to speak. For it is this right that assures me that my request will be heard, and that I will not be rejected into the abjection of infantia. Yet at the same time, I have to announce to you the opaque otherness that I have experienced, and still am experiencing, as a child.

The law says, Thou shalt not kill. Which means, you shall not refuse to others the role of interlocutor. But the law that forbids the crime of abjection nonetheless evokes its abiding threat or temptation. Interlocutor is authorised only by respect for the other, in my words and in yours.

The Evaluation

Whether moral decisions are evaluated by universal standards or by those of local traditions, moral conflicts are always contextual. Kant's categorical imperative is absolutely universalistic, but its test cases are concrete and particular. One should, for example, return a deposit even when the depositor alone was aware of the arrangement and has since died. In the same way, when I now raise the question of how we can deal with evil, I do so in a specific context. The moral conflicts I shall discuss are those that occur in the aftermath of the collapse of totalitarian regimes and of military and other dictatorships. The question is whether the eyils perpetrated under murderous political regimes can, should, or will be punished; whether those responsible for murder, kidnapping, and mass incarceration and discrimination, can, will, or should be made to pay for what they have done.

"Paying" here, means paying a part rather than the whole price for their acts. Even when the indictment is for common murder, the consensus against capital punishment in political cases is very strong, and this is also true in those countries where capital punishment has not been abolished. Hannah Arendt's grave meditations on the justification of capital punishment in the Eichmann case are therefore irrelevant in the current context. The alternative to be faced is not that of life or death, but of prosecution or inaction.

Whether the perpetrators of such crimes will be

prosecuted is not itself a theoretical question. In all probability some will be prosecuted, but a majority will not. Thus we are confined to two issues: whether there are legal grounds in the existing constitutions (or laws equivalent to constitutions) for the prosecution of these persons; and whether they should be prosecuted, that is, whether there is a moral obligation to prosecute them.

Each combination of "can" and "should" in relation to these question represents a moral standpoint. Political considerations or their own life histories make people incline to one or another of the combinations. In what follows, I address some of the merits and demerits of the arguments and evaluate some of our general intuitions on this subject.

The available options can be defined in terms of six possible combinations of a legal and a moral position. The combinations will become clearer as we proceed. (A) There should be no prosecution at all, nor can there be. (B) There should be no prosecution though there is no obstacle to prosecution. (C) The perpetrators should be prosecuted, but cannot be. (D) They should and can be prosecuted. (E) They should be prosecuted for historical justice to be done. Finally, (F) They should pay for their crimes; they should be prosecuted and yet, at the same time, they should not be prosecuted.

The Justice

In whichever of the four combinations it occurs, the formula that perpetrators of heinous crimes "should be punished" implies that "justice should be done." The other formula, according to which "they should not be punished," can imply one of three things. It can imply, most radically, that "justice should not be done." It can imply resignation: "There is no justice in this matter anyway." Or it can imply a positive moral standpoint: "it would be unjust to punish them."

Let us consider the first formula, according to which justice should be done. In thus subscribing to the injunction that "perpetrators of heinous crimes should be punished," we take responsibility for the punishment of the perpetrators. We do so regardless of whether they can (legally) be punished, and of whether they will in fact be punished. We take that responsibility even if we go on to say "and yet they cannot be punished." We are responsible for their punishment because, irrespective of the ultimate course of events, our injunction is an act equivalent to signing the decree of their punishment. Signing is an act of taking responsibility. Signing and taking responsibility are not acts to be approached lightly. Even in one's capacity as an ordinary citizen, one should take one's responsibility no less seriously than would an appointed judge, a member of a jury, or a member of a political body—of an executive or legislative body.

Those who subscribe to the "ought" sentence, "perpetrators of heinous crimes ought be punished" must consider which crimes are heinous and which persons are to be identified as their perpetrators.

In identifying the perpetrators of politically motivated or conditioned crimes, we can avail ourselves of more than forty years of discussion of the Nuremberg trials. The conclusions of this discussion are fairly clear. If like Honecker, one gives the order "shoot to kill" in regard to innocent persons the soldier who obeys that order is not. Certainly, the soldier too is responsible for the death of the persons he has shot. One is the author of one's own deeds, good or bad. But one is not necessarily the author of the conditions under which they were committed. In this political context, the accused is guilty of a crime if he or she is not only the author of the crime, but also of the circumstances under which that crime was ordered or encouraged.

Who is to decide which heinous crimes must be punished for justice to be done? Under the present conditions, only the population of the country where those crimes were committed has, or can claim to have, the authority to decide. There can be no question of international jurisdiction. (German jurisdiction over the crimes committed in former East Germany is not a counter example. Germany is in the same position as post-war France, which regarded Vichy as a part of the French State.) Yet the unreflective intuition of the population is unreliable, for it is divided along generational lines. In regimes of long standing, different generations have different life experiences, and in a long era of enforced silence, crimes unmentioned because unmentionable will tend to be forgotten. The politics of repression are the politics of psychological repression; even the guilty begin to forget their guilt. But the suffering of the mourner is not mitigated by the lapse of time. Enforced silence rather deepens the wound. Only now can victims and the families of victims cry out for justice and revenge.

If one subscribes to the sentence "perpetrators of heinous crimes should be punished," one also needs a yardstick more reliable than the intuition of the members of a specific community. Yet it is precisely this intuition that one must rely on, for no one other than the members of this community is entitled to determine which crimes are so heinous as to call for punishment. This remains true even if it is decided that legal action cannot be taken.

Since decision here is a matter of judgement, one stratagem for evaluating our intuition is to replace the current cases with analogous ones from history. Those analogous stories should be of a kind we have been familiar with since primary school.

The procedure I recommend here is not a mental experiment, but an exercise in becoming aware of our judgmental intuitions. Let us take well-known historical examples of treason, confiscation of wealth, instigation of civil war, political assassination, and mass extermination—whether or not the latter was committed under forms of legality. Whenever the intuitive consensus is in favour of punishment, the judgement will apply to contemporary cases too. By considering many historical examples, we find out something about our intuitions. For example, in cases of treason, confiscation of wealth, instigation of civil war, or political assassination, our judgement may be divided. A profusion of historical texts exists of which we may base our interpretations and reinterpretations. Sometimes we are uncertain whether the deeds in question were crimes at all. They may also be viewed as virtuous deeds. The prophet Jeremiah committed treason, Judith assassinated Holofernes. And even in those cases where we do intuit a crime, it does not follow that we regard the perpetrator as criminal. Even if we take the execution of Mary Stuart to be a judicial murder, we do not intuitively condemn Elizabeth the First as a murderess. But mass murder, be it an act of collective political proscription (as happened under Sulla), or an act of collective terrorism against the "religious alien" (as happened to the Protestants during the St. Bartholomew's Night Massacre) is not open to a forgiving understanding and interpretation. Such acts are unanimously condemned as evil, at least in the context of the European tradition of the last few centuries and rightly so, for they are the visible faces of evil.

Turning now to the question of historical justice: when we subscribe to the sentiment that justice should be done—irrespective of whether it will be done—it is historical justice of which we speak. The "should" refers to the exclusively moral motivation behind the insistence on historical justice. But history includes the further. In enforcing historical justice, we may not consider the pragmatic consequences of our judgement, but we must take into account the moral judgement of future generations. For this reason only genuinely heinous crimes should be punished, for only in such cases can we be certain that all morally competent future generations will subscribe to our verdict and not interpret the act we punish in a different fight. It is an entirely different matter whether future interpreters will consider the perpetrators in the same psychological light as we do, whether they will reinterpret the personhood of the perpetrators. Psychological or phenomenological hermeneutics does not concern the moral judgements of events. Opinions may differ about Hitler's personality, but no morally competent person can ever justify

Auschwitz. In short, when we demand that heinous crimes ought to be punished in order for historical justice to be done, we are claiming that all morally competent future generations would consent to the historical justice of our judgement. Whether, in punishing, we punish anything other than the manifestations of evil, is an empirical question, and one which has nothing to do with historical justice. Or if it does, we cannot know this. But it is clear that, for historical crimes, there can be no statute of limitations, precisely because they are heinous in the sense that we have just defined.

Heinous Crimes

The heinous crimes that should be punished for the spirit of historical justice to prevail are those which count as manifestations of evil. But nothing has, as yet, been said about evil. I hope that my theoretical interpretation of evil will illuminate our problem without shifting the focus of our inquiry. I discern evil in the acts in which others discern it; it is my account of evil that is distinctive.

Evil is not an accumulated or excessive moral badness distinguished from all other categories of badness by quantity. Evil is qualitatively different from the morally bad. This qualitative difference has become explicit in modern times, although it had already been discovered by particularly discerning moralists such as certain Jewish prophets and Greek philosophers. The knowledge of moral evil emerges through reflection. Where there is no freedom to choose principles of action, there can be badness but not evil. Moral evil requires a fairly sophisticated and consistent system of self-justification. A bad character chooses to commit injustice rather than suffer it; he makes an exception for himself. He does not, however, invent principles that make the wrong right. A bad character succumbs to base passions such as envy, and behaves in a cowardly fashion. Yet he can feel remorse and may indulge in gestures of disorderly repentance. Our model of evil, by way of contrast, is Satan, not because he does the wrong things, but because he induces others to do the wrong things by persuading them that evil is right. Plato's Thrasymachos or Calicoes are devilish, not because they are bad characters, but because they make a strong case for maxims that confuse our capacity to distinguish between good and evil. As Kant pointed out, evil resides in evil maxims, not in desires or weakness of character.

In modernity, where traditional morals have become attenuated, evil maxims easily gain the upper hand. Totalitarianism in particular is morally founded on evil maxims. These evil maxims form the basis of the discourse initiated in a totalitarian regime, a discourse into which the proverbial "man on the street" is drawn. The citizens begin to speak the language of totalitarianism and as a result come to take for granted acts which a year before they would not have accepted, and the endorsement of which would have been entirely out of character. Only through internalising this discourse can they come to believe that they have an obligation to denounce their parents to the police or to confess to crimes that they never committed.

I once compared totalitarianism to a disease. Normal people – people neither especially good nor especially bad – are exposed to the disease, take the contagion, and become alienated from their previous selves. If one catches the virus of evil, one becomes evil, even if there had been no original evil in one's character. Devils are in fact rare phenomena. Evil characters, if we compare their numbers to those of the wrongdoers who have caught the virus and become evil under its influence, are few and far between.

After the demise of totalitarianism, it is not difficult to distinguish between the originally evil and those who became evil through secondary infection. The former originates the evil maxims, stick to their principles to the last, their consciences unruffled, and ascribe the defeat or failure of their principles to the weakness of their followers. The followers, by contrast, can get confused, rewrite their pasts, forget the evil they have committed and remember only the evils they have suffered;

they can slough off their totalitarian self. This is how evil could seem banal to Hannah Arendt. But evil is not banal, even if evil persons become banal after the demise of their power base. The soul is not healed just because the epidemic has passed. The pathetically banal soul does not even feel guilty; he or she feels only the remorse of having bet on the wrong horse. Pangs of conscience or repentance are rare.

There is, moreover, a difference between initial and continuous totalitarianism. In the original or initial state, evil has a high density and visibility; it is demonic. What is merely bad is normally repulsive, but a certain power of attraction emanates from moral evil as such. Evil maxims on the one hand align themselves with the underworld of the human soul, and on the other don the garb of high sophistication. Evil in this form is sorcery; it terrifies, demands submission. But in the continuous phase of totalitarianism (we refer here to communist totalitarianism, since Nazism was defeated in its first phase), the density and visibility of evil diminish, and its epidemic effect dies away. The principal victims of the regime were immune from the virus in any case. Others were morally immune and never succumbed. In this later phase, they are joined by those who were only slightly infected, who now shrug off their infection and may even attack evil on its home territory. Since the demon is always associated with (totalitarian) power, the slackening of the regime in the continuous phase necessarily has a therapeutic effect.

The collapse of totalitarianism brings the epidemic to an end. Evil maxims are still around, as they always will be while there are maxims to choose and freedom to choose them. But for the time being the bearers of evil maxims seem to have been marginalised.

This specificity of evil, that it is not necessarily a permanent resident of the souls it inhabits, but may enter a soul and subsequently leave it, obviously complicates the issue of retribution. Let us take an example. We know that X was the author of a heinous crime, and we believe that heinous crimes should be punished in order for historic justice to be done. But perhaps the X of today is not the X who committed the crime; perhaps the virus of evil that inhabited his soul has departed leaving only the empty husk of an elderly body and a banal soul. Puccini's Tosca looks at the dead Scarpia and exclaims "and before this man all Rome trembled!" One could repeat her exclamation with reference to many a person alive today. But those who trembled had, at the time, good reason to do so. Scarpia was an evil, treacherous, political murderer—and there are Scarpia who walk amongst us today, enjoying both their lives and the benefits of their crimes. Should they be allowed to do so with impunity?

Manifestation of Evil

At the outset, I specified six combinations of two elements, one of them moral, the other legal. These were the six major recommendations for dealing with the unique issues of justice raised by the collapse of totalitarian and other criminal dictatorial regimes. I then identified two categories of crime, the historical and the heinous. Finally, I identified heinous crimes as manifestations of evil. In returning to these six combinations, I shall now consider only the case of evil. The granting of general amnesties or the application of the statute of limitations to functionaries and high officials of the former regimes presents no grave moral problem in my view. On the contrary, there are good reasons for behaving in this way. The only exception I make is where such officials or functionaries were perpetrators of evil.

Let us now turn to the arguments against punishing the perpetrators of evil. There are several arguments intended to show that not even those guilty of the most heinous crimes should be indicted. 1 shall consider this point by point. I shall not, however, take into account the view of unreconstructed Stalinists, for in their view, no crimes were committed, and if any were committed, they occurred only as the side effects of an otherwise commendable course of action. Besides, these people have no arguments to offer in the standard language or morals or politics, from which their discourse as much as their actions have excluded them.

In the judgement "perpetrators of heinous crimes should not be punished," "punishment" can refer either to legal punishment alone, that is, to indictment, or to moral punishment.

First proposition: Perpetrators of heinous crimes should not be indicted but only morally censured.

To this I answer: One cannot morally punish a person who is removed from normal moral discourse, who does not experience pangs of conscience, or who has already forgotten his crimes. One cannot morally punish a person who despises morals as "petty bourgeois" or as utterly irrelevant.

Modern society is not a homogeneous community. Evil or infected persons can avoid moral censure by choosing to live among those who are morally like themselves. In this community, public censure is dismissed, and the prospect of divine punishment mocked as superstition.

Perpetrators of heinous crimes in a totalitarian regime cannot subsequently be morally punished unless they feel remorse. But if they feel anything approaching adequate remorse, they have already been morally punished, and need no second moral punishment.

Thus, we see that the recommendation that perpetrators of heinous crimes should only be morally punished is inconsistent, for in either of the two case we have raised, those who are only morally punished are not punished at all.

Second proposition: Those guilty of heinous crimes should not be punished at all.

Under this heading there is a single purely moral argument. There are, however, various admixtures of pragmatic and moral reasons that can be adduced in its favour. The purely moral reason is religious, even if it is on occasion found in the mouths of unbelievers. It is the precept love your enemies, forgive those who have wronged you.

But even if I succeed in loving my enemies, should I also love those who have wronged my neighbour beyond repair? Those who have wronged me I can perhaps forgive. There is no need to open secret police files. And if they are opened, and the name of the person who denounced me comes to light, I can perhaps forgive him or her. But one cannot forgive the murder of other people's children, nor should one. One has no moral right to forgive in the name of the dead or of the mourners. For there is logic in the Christian commandment; you should forgive those who have wronged you because the principle is of justice, as distinct from revenge. But others should not forgive on your behalf, nor should you forgive on others' behalf, or there would be no justice. If you forgive in the name of others, you can forgive yourself in their name for the evil you perpetrate, and this is an immoral principle.

All the pragmatic arguments in favour of not punishing the guilty in this case boil down to the desire to turn over a new leaf. There are two versions of the argument.

First version: Too much blood has been shed; let us put an end to bloodletting. Everything that has happened until now should be forgotten. We should not poison our souls with the desire for revenge. Revenge calls forth further revenge and there is no end to it.

Second version: National reconciliation requires that the past be buried. For this we need everyone's skill and cooperation. It is useless to concern ourselves with the past, we must look ahead, to the future.

In the first formulation, pragmatic and moral considerations are combined. In the second, the moral motivation is negligible.

Let us first consider the "new leaf argument. The moral considerations in this position are consequentialist. One might equally maintain that a people could only turn to a new and clean page of history after having meted out punishment for heinous crimes; this would not be a consequentialist position. Even if one believes that historical justice must be done for any page of history to be clean, it is not in order to cleanse the pages of history that crimes are punished. The motive for the act of retribution is to restore the balance of justice as far as humanly possible.

In the argument under scrutiny, however, retribution is suspended and the act of justice deliberately forgone because of the fear that this act will itself lead to injustices, indeed to a series of injustices. This fear is not unfounded. Every gesture of retribution carries in it the risk of escalation. It is not an insignificant possibility that the morally right may result in the morally wrong.

Although acknowledging these consequentialist points, we should note that there are also consequentialist arguments in favour of punishment. Among them are the following: There can be no turning over a clean leaf without catharsis, and there can be no catharsis if we simply sweep crimes under the carpet. The idyllic new page of history will not after all be clean. The decision not to prosecute the offenders does not cause hatred, resentment, and personal grievances to be forgotten: they simply resurface at the next suitable occasion.

Those who oppose punishment on moral grounds often do so on the basis of a deterrent theory of punishment. Punishment is no longer necessary, it is argued, because the perpetrators of heinous crimes are no longer in a position to commit such crimes. They cannot repeat their crimes. And no one else can either. In contemporary Argentina, no one can any longer cause people to disappear by kidnap, torture and murder, as happened in the past. In newly unified Germany, no one can give the order that those who cross the border should be shot. Thus, it no long serves any deterrent function to punish those who committed these heinous crimes.

Let us assume, for the sake of simplicity, what I do not acknowledge in fact, that the main principle of punishment is deterrence. Imagine the situation where veteran mass murderers continue to live in the same conditions as everyone else, or, for that matter, in better ones. What kind of morality would this example suggest to present and future politicians? It would convey a simple message: whatever they do, however criminal their acts, they will get away with them, provided only that they rule for a sufficiently long time and take pains to hide their crimes under forms of legality. People will be so anxious to turn over a new leaf that the crimes of their rulers will go unpunished in the future as they did in the past. This is what the present and future politicians will conclude.

It is possible that no political crimes could today be of the same magnitude as those of the past. But the principle remains: there are crimes on a smaller scale which can still make people miserable, and one never knows what opportunities for evil will arise in the future. If one accepts the principle of deterrence, the negative formulation "we need not punish where there is no reason to deter" must be balanced by the positive formulation "if we wish to deter, we must punish."

The policy adopted in Spain in the aftermath of the Franco regime may serve as a model for the successful combination of moral and pragmatic considerations. A clean page in the history of Spain was opened and the consequences were morally and pragmatically benign. But it should also be said that the context was unique. The Spanish solution can serve as an example only in countries where decisions take place in a somewhat similar context. The purely moral injunction "love your enemies, forgive those who have wronged you" takes on an aura of truth in the context of the Spanish Civil War, in which both sides committed heinous crimes. Symbolically and in very truth, men and women had to forgive the sins of those who had wronged them, their families and friends. In the ex-communist States, and in post-totalitarian States, the situation is quite different, and the example of Spain not therefore applicable.

Let me turn briefly to a second version of the "new leaf of history" argument. In this version, it is argued that the past should be forgotten in order that the future can begin. This is a technological argument; it treats historical periods as if they were machines. The obsolete appliances have to be thrown away and replaced by new ones. However commendable in the field of technology, this attitude is wholly out of place in relation to a nation's history, which is no less about remembering and hanging on to the past than it is about the projection of the future. A nagging awareness of the past creates the third dimension of history, the dimension of meaning that gives life to any projection of the future, however radical the break with the past. A future that is fabricated *ex nihilo* rests on unsound foundations; there is nothing to underpin it. There can, in short, be no notional reconciliation if one forgets the very events that set the nation at odds.

Punishment in the Next World

"Perpetrators of heinous crimes should be punished, for no counterargument has so far convinced us of the contrary." Anyone subscribing to this verdict thereby signs the decree of punishment, whether or not the punishment will in fact be carried out. To sign it is to be led by the belief that it is wrong to let heinous crimes go unpunished, that justice should be done. The blood of the victims cries out to heaven for punishment to be administered in the next world, but no less to ourselves and to posterity for punishment in this world.

Three persons say in unison: the perpetrators should be punished. The first adds: alas, they cannot be. The second insists: since they should be punished, they can be punished. The third raises her hands in perplexity: they should be punished, and yet, at the same time, they should not. These are the lasts of the three combinations that we introduced, and I shall analyse them one by one.

The first position is this: justice requires that we prosecute the perpetrators of heinous crimes, but the legal system does not permit it. Prosecution would, to take an example, require retroactive legislation. Compromises are, alas, necessary in political life, and in this case, justice cannot be done.

The second position denies the relevance of this "cannot."

Whatever we should do, we must be able to do. No legal system, not even a brand new one with its origins in democracy, can be allowed to stand in the way of justice. If there is a consensus that heinous crimes have been committed, the perpetrators have to answer for them. There is no place for legalism here, the argument runs, first and foremost because the brand new laws should not run counter to our moral intuitions. As Judith Shklar has rightly said: there is a continuum between moral and legal considerations.

The argument, we should but we cannot, is based on principles of legal positivism on two counts. First, it disallows the suspension of our own laws—laws such as the statute of limitations—in certain extraordinary cases, such as the punishment of heinous crimes, and second, it treats the pseudolaws of totalitarian regimes as if they were real ones. But not everything written on a piece of paper and passed as law by a bunch of murderers, their accomplices, and the agents of their institutions, bullied into obedience, qualifies as law. Thousands of trainloads of Kulaks were "lawfully" driven to the taiga and left to starve to death there with their children. The legitimate Prime Minister of Hungary was tried and executed according to laws extant. Where laws were produced according to whim, political convenience, and the dictates of political revenge, there were no laws. We conclude that the position "they should be punished, but cannot be" is a lopsided one; its two components are not equally stable. Morality is on the side of those insisting on punishment, but the legal aspects of the argument are treated as little more than a pragmatic consideration, at very best a token on the altar of national, historical reconciliation. And where morality collides with pragmatic considerations, the old Kantian recipe is still valid; the moral "ought" would have priority. What one ought to do, one can do. That is, despite all pragmatic arguments to the contrary, the morally approved course of action should go ahead. Let us then have a new round of Nuremberg Trials. The Nuremberg Trials are our example, and the example is there to be imitated.

We turn now to the last position. It states that heinous crimes should be punished—and simultaneously insists that its perpetrators should not be punished. This position sounds absurd and paradoxical, but it is neither. It locates a moral conflict. All moral conflicts, like moral choices, are contextual. The context for this position is the same as that for the other two positions. It arises in States where the constitution does not provide for the prosecution of those guilty of heinous crimes.

The moral argument for this position can be summed up as follows: positions one and two both state that a moral ought (justice should be done) is confronted with a mainly legal and pragmatic consideration, which brings into focus certain secondary moral issues. The two positions diverged on one count. For the first position (justice should and cannot be done), the obstacles to justice could not be obviated. For the second (justice should and therefore could be done) the obstacles could be removed. But the second position is essentially wrongheaded, for the suspension of the law for particular cases is not just legally but morally wrong. The maxim that the law should be suspended in particular cases is an evil maxim. Philosophers who locate evil in evil maxims have always counted arguments in favour of its suspension as evil. It was because he could not condone such arguments that Socrates suffered an unjust death rather than attempt to escape the laws of his country, and that Kant made such a strong case not against tyrannised but against the trial of Louis XVI. And it is also wrong to believe that the maxim cannot be evil simply because no evil consequences have flowed from it in certain cases. It is commonplace that good results may flow from bad intentions or designs, but no commonplace makes good of bad or bad of good.

The maxim that perpetrators of heinous crimes should be punished is transcontextual. Evil should be punished everywhere, under all circumstances, and no less, therefore, in the context we here consider. To this maxim there is no exception. Self-punishment, in the form of repentance or penitence, does not constitute an exception. But if a person can be punished only by suspension of the law, he should not be punished, because the maxim that recommends suspension of the law is itself evil. This does not, of course, affect the principle that evil should be punished. Evil should not go unpunished, but neither should one act upon evil maxims, whatever good consequences may follow. Thus, the conclusion: perpetrators of heinous crimes should and at the same time should not be punished. No paradox here, just a moral conflict in context.

If we confront the advocates of the third position with the Nuremberg Trials, they will answer that the context in which they must reach a verdict is entirely different. This is not because the Nazi crimes were of a different degree of heinousness; evil is evil, evil is always infinite, and we can say with Nicholas of Cusa that in an infinite triangle all sides would always be equal, for all of them would be infinite. But a particularity of the Nazi crimes tried in Nuremberg is that they were committed against many different peoples, so that no existing law could possibly have applied to them. For evil to be punished, recourse to the fictitious laws of nature was necessary, and this meets with our own intuitive—and retrospective—approval. If there is a procedure based on fictitious natural law, it is the consensus of moral intuition that must guide us in establishing the tightness of the principle. And the arguments we have set out show that there is no consensus at all as to whether people who have committed heinous crimes should now be punished. When intuition is so disparate in its conclusion, we have no moral justification for recourse to the fictitious laws of nature which must by definition reflect moral intuition.

Three Positions

In our discussion of evil, we concluded that those guilty of heinous crimes should be punished, for justice must be done. The discussion was conducted in the abstract, irrespective of context. All three positions remain thoroughly problematic. If the first is accepted, heinous crimes remain unpunished. Petty thieves will go to prison in countries where mass murderers will enjoy a peaceful old age.

If the second position is accepted, a procedure that feeds on moral legitimacy will be pushed forward in the absence of any such legitimacy. If there should be a second edition of the Nuremberg Trials without the support of consensual moral intuition, it will cast a retrospective shadow on the Nuremberg Trials themselves. They can remain an exemplary act of justice only on condition they are not copied. The Nuremberg Trials act as the embodiment of the regulative idea, the "ought" sentence according to which those guilty of heinous crimes ought to be punished. Their context remains forever unique.

The first two positions do have a certain value as recommendations. They at least tell you what to do. The third position, by contrast, is not a recommendation at all; it merely formulates a moral conflict. Where a moral choice is confronted with a pragmatic or consequentialist consideration, the categorical imperative or one of its variants can cut the Gordian knot. But where two moral choices confront one another, no categorical imperative is available. One chooses one principle, and thereby infringes the other; or if one chooses neither, one infringes both. Yet it is impossible to choose both at once—this is the definition of a moral conflict.

One might say here, with Derrida, that justice is always incalculable, that it requires that one calculate the incalculable, that it addresses itself to singularity, that, in deciding, we should give ourselves up to the impossible decision; that we should, while taking account of rules and laws, nevertheless decide. Yet everything that can hamper men and women in the process of decision is here present in the extreme, for there are no laws and no rules, not even the prospect of guidance, to orient those who decide. No new law will be founded, or ancient law revived, by their decision. All that will transpire is the impossibility of founding such laws. On the one hand, the argument runs, those who decide will incur guilt whatever course they fasten on. And on the other, choose we must, at least in the inner fastness of our souls.

But the question whether those guilty of heinous crimes should be punished is, in this way, evacuated of its political and social content, and no longer calls for a straightforward answer even when it is asked in a specific context. The question is simply thrown back to the person who asks it: you choose, you sign, it is your responsibility, only be aware that you choose between two evils. It emerges that the double formula "those guilty of heinous crimes should be punished and at the same time should not be punished," this gesture of throwing the ball back into the court, of informing the decision-makers that moral conflict cannot be resolved but only cut off by the leap of choice, is a confession of defeat. It concedes our impotence in the confrontation with evil.

A False Conclusion

Something must have gone wrong at the outset, for the conclusion is not merely disquieting but downright false. We know from experience that evil can in fact be resisted that many men and women have resisted evil in dark times. And evil must indeed by resisted while it is in power. But in our context, where the dilemma of punishing evil arises, evil has fallen from power. Evil, as we have seen, is intimately related to power, it thrives on the confidence that its power is irresistible, whether this power is political, social, or psychological. There is no evil without power. Resistance to evil, on the other hand, is found in persons combining two characteristics: good maxims and excellent character. Good maxims immunise them to the attraction of evil; they do not become infected during the epidemic. They know where right ends and wrong begins. Their character makes them stand up to evil and oppose it, and they would rather suffer than commit injustice. In resisting evil, they display courage and decency. Contrast this with the qualities needed to subscribe to the verdict that those guilty of heinous crimes should be punished. No courage and decency is needed here. Quite different moral characters can subscribe to the judgement, not least those cowards who hid in the dark while evil was still in power. We thus conclude that what I called our impotence in facing evil are not the manifestations of general human fragility, but a predicament that follows from the very character of evil.

Let me recapitulate the core of our predicament. There are evil persons in the world; they originate evil maxims, they are demonic. But the radius of their influence is generally insignificant. Thus, for many contingent reasons, social, political, and others, the influence of evil maxims suddenly spreads, mobilising the worst psychological drives and recruiting to its cause the subtlest intellectual apparatus. The epidemic flourishes, evil gains the upper hand and begins to operate on a grand scale, leaving behind it human hecatombs, misery and devastation. And then, if there is still a "then," the epidemic recedes, and the evil maxims are replaced by disappointment or cynicism. If a totalitarian regime lasts long enough, the worst of the malefactors are already in their graves, beyond the reach of human retribution.

The obstacles to punishment we have discussed so far have been pragmatic and legalistic. But there is another possible obstacle to punishment. The perpetrators cannot be punished, because the main culprits, the initiators of all the evils, are now beyond the reach of human retribution. And those who created the initial conditions in which heinous crimes were committed are the true perpetrators. A handful of them are alive, but most of them are dead. Can justice still be done?

A repeat of the Nuremberg Trials, we have argued, is morally impossible, given the absence of moral consensus about its desirability. The so-called laws of nature are only the projections of our general moral intuition. In the absence of this consensual intuition, the laws of nature are a mere anachronism. But why is there no moral consensus about the desirability of new Nuremberg Trials?

The Nazis were in power for little more than ten years, characterised by the escalation of evil. It was possible to bring to justice all the perpetrators of Nazi crimes, with the exception of Hitler, Himmler, and Goebbels, who escaped through suicide. Soviet totalitarianism, in contrast, lasted between forty and seventy-five years. After the years of escalation of evil, there was a cyclic diminution of its energy. The regime was the same, heinous crimes were still committed, and the suffering of the victims was no less than it had been at the height of the terror. But the diminishing energy of evil led to a kind of canalisation. New generations grew up, and many terrible deeds were simply forgotten. To reawaken memories is not, for the most part, welcome. The moral issue here is not whether this oblivion is a good or a bad thing. It is simply that under these conditions, even if there were a consensus about which crimes were so heinous as to require punishment, no moral consensus about new Nuremberg Trials could possibly emerge.

If evil maxims can establish a power base that lasts long enough, perpetrators of evil will, in all probability, never be punished. Those who commit the most execrable crimes will get away with it. This is why we are impotent against evil. Good can resist evil while evil lasts, but becomes impotent against it after evil's demise.

Evil is active while it holds power, but once its power is gone, evil is just an empty shell, the physical body of a person who was once evil. Can evil be punished while it lasts, while it is evil incarnate? The answer is no, evil cannot be punished, but is self-destructive. It turns against itself. Self-destruction is the inevitable logic of evil however long it is in power, however long it lasts.

The perpetrators of heinous crimes should be punished because justice should be done. The times were out of joint, and we must set them straight. But it is of secondary importance whether the surviving perpetrators of crimes are actually punished. The Claudius with whom we have to deal has already lost both crown and queen. But there are no clean new pages in the book of history, and there is no cleansing to be attained at the price of forgetting. On the contrary, like Horatio "speaking to the yet unknowing world," we should tell and retell the story of those "carnal, bloody, and unnatural acts," those "accidental judgements, casual slaughters," and "deaths put on by cunning and forced cause," perpetrated by the hand of evil, in the twentieth century, in our own house, and on such a scale as was never dreamt of in Horatio's, or even Hamlet's philosophy.

SIX

Relationship with International Law

International human rights law is a branch of public international law, that is, the law which has been developed to regulate relations between entities having international personality, such as states, international organizations and possibly individuals. In order to understand the functioning of the various institutions charged with the supervision of human rights, it is necessary to have a basic appreciation of the salient aspects of the international legal systems. In the human rights context, international law possesses a dual quality, since it creates both the obstacles to effective human rights protection and provides the means for overcoming such obstacles.

Independence

This has been described by Brownlie as 'the constitutional doctrine of the law of nations'. It is also sometimes regarded as synonymous with the term 'independence'. In essence, it represents the totality of a state's rights in the conduct of its external relations and in the ordering of its internal affairs. This does not mean, however, that states are completely free to exercise their sovereignty or independence on both the external and internal planes, since they are subject to various limitations imposed on their activities by international law.

The main feature of the sovereign state is that it is entitled to exercise exclusive governmental control over its territory and persons therein subject to any contrary rules of international law. It is important to note, however, that states, being the pre-eminent subjects of the international legal systems, and the creators of law within that system, have the primary task of participating in the formulation of rules by which their conduct is limited.

One particular consequence of state sovereignty which should be noted here is that since all states are sovereign equals, a state is not bound to submit itself to international adjudication unless it has first signified its consent that it is prepared to do so. Thus, the popular notion that a state can be taken to the International Court of Justice (ICJ) or the European Court of Human Rights (ECHR) for an infraction of the law by another state almost at whim, does not reckon with the impediment of the necessity to produce the delinquent state's consent that it be required to submit to such a course of action.

Friendly Relations

The rule against intervention is the necessary corollary to the doctrine of state sovereignty. If a state has the right to exclusive jurisdiction over its internal affairs, then it would clearly run counter to this to permit other states to intervene in those affairs. But what exactly is intervention? There has been considerable debate about this. Intervention clearly means something stronger than simple meddling or interference in the way the government of a state orders its internal affairs. It would for, example, have to be more than a critical comment on the pursuit of some domestic policy by another state. Lauterpacht, for instance, stated that in order to constitute intervention, an act must amount to a dictatorial interference in the affairs of another state without lawful justification. A more precise way of putting this might be that it must amount to an attempt by one state to perform state-like functions within the territory of another state. This view is reinforced by the language of the 1970 UN General Assembly Declaration on Principles of International Law concerning friendly relations and cooperation among State in accordance with the Charter of the United Nations, which states:

No state or group of States has the right to intervene

directly or indirectly, for any reason whatever in the internal or external affairs of any other State. Consequently, armed intervention and all other forms of interference or attempted threats against the personality of the State or against its political, economic or cultural elements, are in violation of international law.

This formula, although contained in General Assembly resolution which is technically not legally binding, has been relied upon to such an extent since 1970 that it is now regarded as a precise statement of the rule of non-intervention in customary international law.

The combined effect of the doctrine of sovereignty would seem to preclude the taking of any meaningful action by the international community in the context of human rights abuses by states. If persons within states are subject to the local laws, then surely other states cannot come to their aid if those local laws appear to violate human rights, since this would infringe the sovereignty of the other state and constitute an intervention in its internal affairs. This view would also seem to be confirmed by Article 2(7) of the UN Charter, which provides that the organization is prohibited from intervening in matters essentially within the domestic jurisdiction of any state.

As we have seen, however, sovereignty is not absolute, but it is itself limited by international law. Thus, once human rights have been elevated to a matter of international rather than national concern, states may no longer plead that human rights are a matter essentially within their domestic jurisdiction. It then becomes legitimate for states to make diplomatic protest about human rights violations and to institute sanctions against deliquent state. Some commentators have even argued, as a variation of the nineteenth-century doctrine of humanitarian intervention, that military force may be used against states which violate human rights, since one of the purposes of the UN is to promote and protect such rights. Such an argument runs counter to the major thrust of the UN Charter, which is to facilitate peaceful settlement of disputes and to outlaw the use of force in international relations, and it has also been explicitly rejected by the ICJ in Nicaragua v United States of America. It is not difficult to see that any modern notion of 'humanitarian intervention' would be bedevilled by the same subjectivity and potentially self-serving designs of militarily powerful nations as was the case in the nineteenth century.

Position of Individual

As we saw earlier in this book that before 1945 the individual was simply an object of the law within the international legal system. Individuals were characterized in terms of nationality, that is, the bond which created legal ties between them and their state. States were therefore not generally constrained by international rules concerning the treatment of their own nationals, but they were, as we have also seen, obliged to treat the nationals of other states in accordance with certain international standards if they were not to violate international law. But even here, the individual was merely the vehicle by which an international claim originated; it was the state which suffered the wrong through the maltreatment of its national. Within the international legal system, therefore, individuals were characterized as objects and not subjects of the law. Rules might be made for the benefit of individuals, but they did not confer substantive rights that could be enforced by procedural mechanisms which might be initiated by those same individuals. Exceptionally, however, the Permanent Court of International Justice recognized in the Danzing Railway Officials Case that certain rights created by the treaty could, where such an intention was expressly stated, permit individuals to enforce those rights in the domestic, or as they are known by international lawyers, municipal courts of the states parties. This, however, was a different matter to conferring procedural rights to individuals for enforcement of positive rights by an international tribunal.

In the post-Second World War era, the position of the

individual has changed considerably. No longer are individuals seen as rightless objects of international law with no procedural capacity, rather, they are seen as the bearers of rights and correlative duties within the context of the international legal system. To some extent, therefore, they may be classified as limited subjects of international law. Although it had long been recognized that individuals were under a duty not to commit acts of piracy or war crimes under international law, it was not until the judgment of the International Military Tribunal at Nuremburg that it became fully established that international law placed direct obligations on individuals not to commit crimes against humanity, and the superior orders were no defence to the commission of those crimes. As the Nuremburg Tribunal itself observed: 'Crimes against international law are committed by men, not by abstract entities, and only by punishing individuals who commit such crimes can the provisions of international law be enforced.'

Now under international law, individuals may be held personally responsible for war crimes, genocide, torture and furthering apartheid. It is irrelevant that these individuals were following orders by implementing the policies of the state. By making individuals responsible under international law for their acts demystifies the claims that such international crimes are simply an expression of the 'collective will' of the state.

Local Remedies

The post-Second World War period is also significant in the development of the individual as a partial subject of international law, not only because of the clear articulation of human rights in an increasing number of legally binding instruments, but also because of the conferring of procedural capacity upon individuals to enforce their rights before a variety of international tribunals. Individuals may now, under certain conditions, initiate proceedings before UN, European, American and African institutions.

While the methods by which individuals may bring applications, petitions or communications, as they are variously known, before the appropriate universal or regional institutions to secure remedies for the alleged violations of human rights will be considered in the appropriate places in subsequent chapters, it is worth remarking here that there is one factor which is common to all such procedures: individuals must in all cases attempt to secure redress of their grievances internally. This is known as the exhaustion of local remedies rule and is of fundamental importance in international human rights law.

The local remedies rule has its origin in the law of state responsibility or the law which governs the circumstances consequences of a violation of international law by states. Violation of the law by a state may be direct as, for example, when a state breaches a treaty, or indirect, such as when a host state fails to afford appropriate redress to an alien who has been injured by the agents of the state. It is in the latter circumstances in which the local remedies rule operates. Until an individual attempts to exhaust all available local remedies, the state of which he or she is a national is prevented from taking up or espousing the claim at the international level. As noted above, when a state decides to espouse a claim, it does so for itself and not on behalf of the individual, since it is the state which is injured through the wrongful treatment of one of its nationals. In a sense, the identity of the individual is irrelevant, as long as he or she is a national of the claimant state.

In its traditional international law guise, the rule has both theoretical and pragmatic bases. First, it is designed to ensure respect for the sovereignty of other states by not casting premature aspersions on the ability of that state's institutions to afford appropriate redress to the individual in question. As the International Court of Justice said in the Interhandel Case:

> ...the rule requiring the exhaustion of domestic remedies as a condition of the presentation of an international claim is founded upon the principle that the responsible

State must first have an opportunity to redress by its own means within the framework of its own domestic legal system the wrong alleged to be done to the individual.

Second, the rule is designed to prevent the proliferation of international claims by aggrieved individuals. Before a claim can be pursued on the international plane, therefore, individuals must attempt to exhaust all effective remedies whether they be judicial, arbitral or administrative. Remedies which are ineffective or illusory need not be pursued. Furthermore, if it is obvious that there are no remedies to exhaust or that the provision of a remedy is likely to be unduly tardy, the need to comply with the rule is obviated.

In its human rights guise, the local rule remedies rule operates in a slightly different context. Here, concern is not with the rule as a precondition to a state pursuing its own claim against another state on the international plane, rather it is with the rule as a precondition to the admissibility of a claim by an individual before an international tribunal against his or her own state. The rationale for the rule is, however, substantially the same: the state must be given the opportunity to redress by means of its own legal procedures any wrong claimed to have been done to the individual concerned before international mechanisms of protection are engaged. A review of all of the international instruments which provide a right of individual application will demonstrate that exhaustion of local remedies by the applicants is a necessary prerequisite to securing legal standing. What the instruments do not disclose, however, is the attitude taken by the various competent institutions to the interpretation of the provision. Each institution has developed its own approach on such issues as upon whom the obligation lies to prove exhaustion and, indeed, what constitutes exhaustion. Although these matters will be dealt with in detail later, it is appropriate to note here that the requirement to demonstrate the exhaustion of local remedies is much more rigorous in the European Convention system than it is under the universal and inter-American systems. Possibly the major reason for this is that while the social and political conditions in the Council of Europe States are generally conducive to the protection of human rights, in the Americas and certain parts of the world covered by the universal system, they are not. The enforced disappearances of large numbers of individuals within Latin and Central American states in the recent past tends to demonstrate this point.

Framing the Law

As human rights law is a branch of international law, the means of its creation are identical to that of international law in general. Thus, in order to determine the origins of human rights law, it is necessary to examine the traditional sources of international law. Here, Article 38 of the Statute of the International Court of Justice is generally accepted as the authoritative statement of such sources. It provides

The Court, whose function is to decide in accordance with international law such disputes as are submitted to it, shall apply:

(a) international conventions, whether general or particular, establishing rules expressly recognized by the contesting states;
(b) international custom as evidence of a general practice accepted as law;
(c) the general principles of law recognized by civilised nations;
(d) subject to the provisions of Article 59 (which provides that the previous decisions of the ICJ have no binding force except in the decided case itself) judicial decisions and the teaching of the most highly qualified publicists of the various nations, as subsidiary means for the determination of rules of law.

Before briefly examining each of these sources of law, it is appropriate to point out that since the international legal system is a decentralized and horizontally integrated legal system having no central legislature, rules are created largely by agreement or emerge through the process of interaction between states. Thus, the law-creating processes of international system have much in common with gemeinschaft societies, although it is doubtful whether the international system is able to demonstrate the cohesion of such societies.

Conventions and Treaties

The principal method of making international law in the modern world is by way of convention or treaty is essentially an agreement between two or more states establishing legally binding rules in a particular area. Article 2(1)(a) of the Vienna Convention of the Law of Treaties 1969 defines a treaty for the purposes of that Convention as 'an international agreement concluded between States in written form whatever its particular designation'. While there is a requirement that a treaty be in writing, the definition makes it clear that it is the form of the instrument which is important, not its title. Treaties are given a variety of names-conventions, charters, covenants, protocols, and so on, but their essential quality is that they are consensual agreements between two or more states under international law. A treaty between two states is generally known as a bilateral, contractual or particular treaty, whereas a treaty between more than two states is known as a multilateral or general treaty, since it seeks to establish rules for a significant number of states parties. Multilateral treaties are also sometimes referred to as international legislation, but this is misleading given the absence of any legislature in the international system. Such a designation simply seeks to convey the idea that a large number of states are party to a particular treaty and conform to the same rules. Treaties have one major advantage over other methods of international law creation: they are accessible and the rules established are more or less clear.

It will already be apparent that the greater part of international human rights law is contained in multilateral treaties. And while it is true that these treaties comprise an accurate index of the individual rights that are protected and the obligations that are assumed by the states which have become parties of the relevant instruments, there are also a number of other matters which must be considered. First, multilateral treaties often allow states to condition their obligations by the entry of reservations. A reservation is defined by Article 2(1)(d) of the Vienna Convention as 'a unilateral statement, however phrased or named, made by a State .... whereby it purports to exclude or modify the legal effect of certain provisions of the treaty in their application to that state'. This does not mean that a state may modify its obligations at will. Treaties will often lay down the precise extent to which reservations may be entered. Article 75 of the American Convention on Human Rights provides, for example, that : 'This Convention shall be subject to reservations only in conformity with the provisions of the Vienna Convention on the Law of Treaties ....' Even where a treaty is silent on the question of reservations, both the Vienna Convention and customary international law demand that a reservation must, if it is to be lawful, be compatible with the object and purpose of the Convention. Thus, for example, an attempt to derogate by way of a reservation from a right in a human rights treaty which is expressed to be absolutely non-derogable, would clearly not be compatible with the object and purpose of such a treaty.

Second, the notion of derogations from certain treaty provisions is one of the distinctive hallmarks of human rights instruments. In nearly all instruments states may, by unilateral declaration, derogate from their obligations under certain clearly prescribed conditions. Such derogations are not only rigorously defined within the particular instruments, but they are also subject to supervision by the institution charged with responsibility for protecting the rights in question. Certain rights, such as freedom from torture, are classified as non-derogable under any circumstances.

A third point to note is that whereas the fundamental breach of a treaty will usually result in the termination of obligations under such an instrument, this is not so in the case of human rights treaties. Article 60(5) of the Vienna Convention provides that the rules concerning termination 'do not apply to provisions relating to the protection of human persons contained in treaties of a humanitarian character'. The rationale behind this rule is clear – if a state could simply discharge its obligations under a human rights treaty by a single violation, it would defeat the continuing protective purpose of such instruments.

Another distinctive feature of human rights treaties, as opposed to other treaties in international law, are provisions which permit denunciation. Here states may withdraw unilaterally from their obligations under a treaty, as long as procedure; established by the treaty is complied with. While most human rights treaties provide for the possibility of denunciation, they also provide that state parties will be responsible for any violations of the treaty committed prior to denunciation. In so doing, the treaties ensure that states are not able to avoid their legal responsibilities simply by choosing to opt out of the instrument when its obligations become burdensome.

Finally, some mention should be made here of the methods by which treaties may be interpreted. The traditional rule is the literal rule, which is expressed in Article 31 of the Vienna Convention. This provides that 'a treaty shall be interpreted in good faith in accordance with the ordinary meaning to be given to the terms of the treaty in their context and in the light of its object and purpose'. Where, however, a literal interpretation of the instrument leaves the meaning ambiguous or obscure or leads to a result which is manifestly absurd or unreasonable, resource may be had to supplementary material such as the preparatory works or the drafting history of the instrument. Institutions which are charged with interpreting human rights instruments seldom adopt such a straightforward approach and frequently apply other techniques of interpretation either separately or in conjunction with those enumerated above. Here, the process combines with a number of others factors. Of particular importance is the role of the institution, the context within which it functions, the legal, political and social traditions from which the members of the institution are drawn and their perceptions of their own and their institutions' functions. Thus, for example, the European Court of Human Rights has a predominantly teleological or end-orientated approach to interpretation of the Convention. This does not mean that the Court does not apply the standard techniques when occasion demands, simply that they have a conception of their role as that of maximizing the protective function of the Convention. Critics of the teleological approach including some past judges of the Court, have argued that it leads to judicial legislation. This is undoubtedly true, since the court has, on occasion, read rights into the Convention which are not automatically evident at first sight. However, since judges, as a category of decision makers enjoy a broadly legislative function anyway the only objection to the teleological approach might be the extent of their creativity.

Having pointed out some of the distinctive features of human rights treaties, it might legitimately be questioned whether or not they are qualitatively different to other kinds of treaties. Certainly there is a school of thought which argues that they are, and this school of thought is supported by statements of both the European and Inter-American Courts of Human Rights. The former, for example, declared in Austria v Italy that the obligations undertaken by the parties of the Convention were 'essentially of an objective character being designed rather to protect the fundamental rights of individual human beings from infringements of any of the .... Parties than to create subjective and reciprocal rights for the... Parties themselves'. The Court went on in the same case to say that the purpose of the parties to the Convention 'was not to concede to each other reciprocal rights and obligations in pursuance of their individual national interests but ....to establish a common public order of the free democracies of Europe with the object of safeguarding their common heritage of political traditions, ideals, freedoms and the rule of law'. In similar vein, the Inter-American Court of Human Rights declared in Effect of Reservations that 'the object and purpose of the (American Convention on Human Rights) is not the exchange of reciprocal rights between a limited number of States, but the protection of the human rights of all individual human beings within the Americas, irrespective of their nationality'. Thus, as far as the regional systems are concerned, the competent institutions appear to be claiming that their constituent instruments provide the basis for supra-national legal systems or systems of law superior to national law which can be invoked by individuals within those states.

Tradition and Custom

Although the majority of international transactions are now conducted through the medium of treaties, custom still remains an important source of law. Indeed, some authors would argue that custom is qualitatively more important than treaties, since it is custom which forms the bed-rock of the international legal system. Even treaties derive their binding force from a prior customary rule which states that treaties are binding must be observed in good faith. Furthermore, while states must signify their consent before they can legally bound by treaties, this is not a necessary prerequisite to a state becoming bound by a customary rule of international law.

What then is custom? The description in Article 38(1)(b) gives a hint of its nature. There it is described as a general practice accepted as law, which indicates that it is created by patterns of interaction between states accompanied by an underlying sense of legal obligation. Thus, custom is traditionally said to consist of two elements: a material element and a 'psychological' element. The material element is evidenced by what is called state practice or the conduct of states. Such conduct may be evidenced by a variety of factors which impact on a state's international relations. These might include statements by the competent organs of state in a variety of domestic and international fora such as the UN, domestic legislation, the decision of local courts, and so on. Conduct alone, however, is not sufficient for the creation of a binding rule of customary international law; it must also be accompanied by a sense on the part of the relevant state organ that the conduct is underpinned by a sense of legal obligation. This is usually known by its Latin name, *opinio iuris sive* necessitates or, more commonly, simply *opinio iuris*. There has been much debate about whether *opinio iuris* needs to be proved in any given case or whether it can be inferred from a consistent pattern of conduct. The ICJ, however, still insists that it needs to be proved.

There are a multitude of theoretical difficulties associated with proving the existence of customary international law. Many of these arise because customary law is more frequently associated with the development of law within small, tight integrated human communities, usually known by German sociologist Tonnies' term *gemeinschaft*, rather than the development of law between complex corporate entities such as the modern state. Rather than talking of custom in international law, perhaps it would be more appropriate to coin a new term representing the realities of the situation. Nevertheless, 'custom' remains a potent source of contemporary international law. A state which seeks to rely on custom must prove the rule by demonstrating the existence of state practice which is definite, extensive, which has been extant for an appropriate period of time, and which is supported by the necessary *opinio iuris*.

Two matters which are associated with custom should be mentioned here: the legal status of UN General Assembly resolutions and the concept of *ius cogens*.

UN Resolutions

The legal status of resolutions passed by the General Assembly, the plenary organ of the UN, is frequently misunderstood. 'Housekeeping' resolutions dealing with General Assembly internal organization are legally binding on Assembly members, but resolutions covering other matters are not legally binding per se. Nonetheless, the latter may have certain legal effects depending on their subject matter and manner of drafting. Here a distinction should be made between resolutions dealing with issues of a general nature, such as those urging member states to promote research into environmental degradation, and those of a 'legal' nature which seek to set down the member states' understanding of the appropriate rules of law in a particular area. The precise legal effect of such latter resolutions is controversial and open to a number of characterizations. Some states such as the USA deny that General Assembly resolutions have any normative effect, and assert that they are simply statements of political aspiration. Others argue that resolutions may, in appropriate circumstances, be authoritative interpretations of the UN Charter by the General Assembly. Thus, for example, the Universal Declaration might be regarded as an authoritative interpretation of the meaning of 'human rights' in a number of Charter provisions. Still further, some states and commentators argue that resolutions, where they deal with broadly 'legal' issues, are a clear statement of state practice and can therefore be regarded as material element in the formation of customary international law. This indeed has been the position adopted by the ICJ in Nicaragua v United States, where a majority of the Court held that the Declaration of Principles Resolution and Resolution 3314(XXIX) 1974, the Consensus Definition of Aggression Resolution, both evidenced the international community's understanding of the appropriate customary rules in both areas. Thus, while General Assembly resolutions in no way amount to a form of international legislation, they are nevertheless capable of providing the constituent elements for the formation of customary international law.

If one examines Article 38 of the ICJ statute closely, it is apparent that the sources of law appear to be hierarchical, that is, they tend to move from the more specific to less specific. The hierarchy is not, however, immutable. Although under normal circumstances a treaty setting down precise rules of law would override customary international law, there are occasions when the customary rule is of such fundamental importance to the structure of the international system that it cannot be overridden by any contrary agreement. An example of this would be a treaty between two states to commit an act of genocide, a treaty which international law could not possibly sanction. In many ways, this is analogous to a contract for illegal or immoral purposes under domestic contract law which domestic courts would not enforce on the grounds that it would be contrary to public policy to do so. Indeed, *ius cogens* is occasionally called the international doctrine of public policy or, to use the more precise French term, *orre public*. Article 53 of the Vienna Convention on the Law of Treaties provides a definition of ius cogens and indicates the effects of a treaty which is concluded in violation of such a norm. It states:

> A treaty is void if, at the time of its conclusion, its conflicts with a peremptory norm of general international law [ins cogens]... [A] peremptory norm of general international law is norm accepted and recognized by the international community of States as a whole from which no derogation is permitted and which can be modified only by a subsequent norm of international law having the same character.

When this particular provision was drafted by the International Law Commission, the latter gave as examples of ins cogens norms, the rule prohibiting the use of force in international law, and criminal acts under international law such as the commission of acts of slavery, genocide and piracy. Certain members of the Commission also voiced their opinion that the conclusion of treaties which envisaged human rights violations might also be contrary to *ius cogens*. The view that the human rights have a ius cogens character also finds some support from the ICJ in Genocide Conventions Case and the Barcelona Traction Case and from the Inter-American Court of Human Rights in a number of cases. On a general scale, however, it seems clear that treaties which violate rules having a general humanitarian character run the risk of being classified as a breach of ins cogens, with the corresponding sanction that such treaties may be declared void by a competent tribunal.

General Principles

The third potential source of international law is 'the general principles of international law recognized by civilized nations'. This was included in the ICJ's statute in order to deal with the circumstances where the Court might not be able to decide a dispute because of absence of any treaty or customary law dealing with the issue before it. This situation is generally known as *non-liquet,* a situation which is more likely to arise in the decentralized international legal system than it is in hierarchically integrated domestic legal systems. As with the other sources of international law, there is some dispute over exactly what the phrase means. Some writers take the view that it simply means procedural rules of national or municipal law which have been incorporated into international law, whereas others, such as Waldock, claim that the phrase means that the ICJ is competent to draw from a well of immutable principles of law which are common to all major legal systems. Certainly, the latter view would render this particular source of law more dynamic and better suited to the judicial decision-making process than would the former. It also means that when faced with a *non-liquet,* both the ICJ and other bodies charged with interpreting and applying international law would be able to apply a form of juridical calculus by which they might determine whether or not certain principles possess the necessary qualifications for application at the international level.

Subsidiary Sources

It is from the phraseology employed in Article 38 that judicial decisions and the opinions of writers are little more than subsidiary means for the determination of law. None the less, these can be particularly useful, particularly in determining the existence of customary international law. An example of this 'source' of law in action is a Californian court decision in the case of Filartiga v Pena Irala, in which the judge, after reviewing the appropriate international instruments, declared that the commission of acts of torture was contrary to the customary international law, and as such could be applied by the court in pursuance of the US Alien Tort Claims Statute.

Domestic Application of International Human Rights Norms

The creation of international human rights law, is as we have seen, primarily a function of the international legal system, and the supervision of human rights is largely undertaken by international institutions created for this purpose. It should be noted, however, that domestic tribunals may also have a substantial role to play in the application of international human rights law. Much depends here upon the nature of the domestic constitution under which the local courts function. Some constitutions permit their domestic courts to apply norms of international law origin directly, whereas others require international law to be transformed into domestic law by legislation before the domestic courts can apply them. Since national and international law are regarded as a single integrated system, whereas constitutions in which transformation of international legal obligations into domestic law is required are called dualist constitutions, since domestic and international law are perceived as two separate and distinct systems. The main feature of monist constitutions is that there is usually some form of direct democratic or legislative control over the transaction of international relations by the executive branch of government, while there is an absence of such direct control in dualist constitutions.

Of course, the monist-dualist dichotomy is seldom as simple in actuality as the definition would suggest. Even in dualist constitutions, a distinction is often drawn between international rules of customary law origin and those of treaty-based provenance. Moreover, states with dualist constitutions will often differ in their approach to the question of whether international rules of direct application or municipal laws take precedence in the event of conflict between them. Some constitutions, such as that of Germany, give clear precedence to both customary and treaty rules over domestic federal law, whereas others, such as that of the USA, will only give precedence to particular categories of treaty. The main point to note from this discussion, however, is that some states' constitutions facilitate the direct application by the municipal courts of international human rights law, whereas others do not. In each and every case, the constitution of the state in question must be considered, as indeed must the approach of the municipal courts of the interpretation of the constitution.

Examples of two constitutions might serve to demonstrate the points made above. First, the British constitution, which is often regarded as the archetypal monist constitution. This is perhaps something of a misnomer, since the English courts have always applied rules of customary international law origin where there is no legislative provision to the contrary. However, the appellation 'monist' clearly indicates that, in general, rules emanating from the competent institutions of the European Community excepted, Parliamentary legislation takes precedence over rules of international origin. Thus, as far as treaty-based obligations are concerned, they will have no domestic application in UK unless they have been transformed into domestic law by legislation. In the absence of statutory transformation, rules contained in an international treaty have no legal force in the UK. The English courts have adopted certain cannons of interpretation to deal with the relationship between statute and treaty, such as, where possible a statute will be construed to give effect to the UK's international legal obligations, but in all cases rules emanating from a treaty will give way to a contrary intention expressed by Parliament in its legislation. In the human rights field, the English courts have consistently refused to allow provisions of the European Convention on Human Rights to take precedence over domestic law, even when the latter has clearly been contrary to the Convention.

This position has recently been reaffirmed by the House of Lords in Brind and Others v Secretary of State for the Home Department. This case concerned certain directives issued by the Home Secretary prohibiting the direct broadcasting of statements made by representatives of proscribed organizations in Northern Ireland. The measures adopted by the Home Secretary were in the form of delegated legislation which the appellants complained violated Article 10 of the European Convention (freedom of expression). The appellants further contended that the Home Secretary did not take the convention into account when he made the directives and that he had been wrong in law in not doing so. This argument was rejected by the House of Lords, which held that although the UK courts would interpret domestic legislation in a manner which conformed to the Convention where this was possible, there was no corresponding presumption of domestic law that the courts would review the exercise of an administrative discretion on the basis that such a discretion had to be exercised in conformity with the Convention. In responding to a submission that Article 10 of the Convention was a relevant factor to which the Home Secretary ought to have had regard when exercising his discretion in making the directives, Lord Ackner said: 'If the Secretary of State was obliged to have proper regard to the Convention, i.e. to conform with article 10, this inevitably would result in incorporating the Convention into English domestic law by the back door. It is apparent, therefore, that the UK constitution, as a form of dualist constitution, is not particularly well suited to giving effect to treaty-based international human rights obligations.

An appropriate example of how a broadly monist constitution gives effect to human rights of international law provenance is the constitution of the USA. Article 11(2) of the US Constitution provides that the President has the power to make treaties 'by and with the advice; and consent of the Senate .... provided two thirds of the Senators present concur'. Article 4 of the constitution further provides that treaties made in such a way 'shall be the supreme law of the land; and the judges in every state shall be bound thereby'. The treaty can therefore be an important legislative device in the USA, but unlike; the UK, the treaty-making power of the executive, in the person of the US President, is subject to clear and direct democratic control. Moreover, treaties which are adopted in conformity with the constitution may produce rules which are directly enforceable by individuals before the municipal courts. These are known as self-executing treaties. However, in order for a treaty to be self-executing, it must have a precise quality which is capable of giving rise to individual rights. As the Supreme Courts of California pointed out in Sei Fujii v California, the human rights provisions contained in the UN Charter lacked 'the mandatory quality and definiteness which would indicate upon ratification'. If such qualities are in existence in a particular treaty, then the potential for individual protection in the USA would be considerable. Unfortunately, the USA has steadfastly refused to participate in any international human rights instruments, claiming that its domestic System for human rights protection is more than adequate.

SEVEN

United Nations' Role

Although the institutions and procedures established under the auspices of the UN are sometimes referred to as the universal system for promoting respect for and observance of human rights, the term is somewhat misleading, for although there are a number of supervisory systems established under the umbrella of the UN, none of them enjoy participation by all the states of the world. None the less, the term is convenient for distinguishing those instruments and systems of potentially global application from those which are simply regional in their operation.

There is a bewildering number of institutions and supervisory systems established within the framework of the UN. Some of the institutions and systems are discrete as they have been created by treaties which, while adopted within a UN context, nevertheless apply to specific fields and possess autonomous implementation machinery. An example of this is the ICCPR, which stands as a separate treaty, has an autonomous supervisory body in the Human Rights Committee, but which was drafted and adopted within the UN Organization. Other institutions and supervisory mechanisms have been developed under the Charter either because their creation was mandated by that instrument or because they have evolved under the Charter on an ad hoc basis.

UN Charter

The UN Charter, which is a multilateral treaty and therefore creates legally binding obligations for all UN member states, contains a number of provisions concerning human rights. The Preamble states the determination of the peoples of the UN 'to reaffirm faith in fundamental human rights, in the dignity and worth of the human person, in the equal rights of men and women and of nations large and small', and Article 1(3) includes as one of the purposes of the UN 'promoting and encouraging respect for human rights and for fundamental freedoms for all without distinction as to race sex, language, or religion'. Moreover, under Chapter XI of the Charter, which is entitled 'International Economic and Social Cooperation', Article 55 provides that the UN 'shall promote... universal respect for, and observance of, human rights and fundamental freedoms for all without distinction as to race, sex, language, or religion'. This is further buttressed by Article 56 by which all members 'pledge themselves to take joint and separate action... for the achievement of the purposes set forth in Article 56'.

As might be expected, there is diversity of views on the nature of the human rights obligations imposed on members under the Charter. Some jurists argue that the requirement to 'promote' respect for and observance of human rights is simply hortatory and incapable of being defined with the precision necessary to impose legal obligations on members. They further argue that the obligations to promote human rights in Article 55 does not necessarily infer an obligation to protect human rights. In addition to the imprecision of the Charter obligations, they draw attention to the fact that there is no indication of which human rights are protectable nor any mechanisms for their actual protection.

Other commentators adopt sharply divergent views to those expressed above. They argue that Article 56 imposes a clear obligation on all members to take positive action to achieve respect for and observance of human rights. Thus a state which denies human rights cannot be said to be taking action to respect or observe human rights. The criticism that there is no index of protectable rights is also not insuperable. If one takes a natural law standpoint similar to that of Judge

Tanaka in the South West Africa Cases, the reaffirmation of faith in human rights in the Preamble would seem to assume that such rights enjoyed an existence both prior, and superior, to the positive law of the Charter. Such an argument, however, raises the difficulties associated with the natural law school in general; namely, which rights should be included in any potential list? Happily, this particular problem can be overcome by the pragmatic expedient of examining the Universal Declaration, which might be said at the very least to contain an index of what is meant by the term 'human rights' in the Charter. This is a view which will be addressed in further detail below.

These theoretical arguments have in many ways been overtaken by the actual practice of the UN. Within debates of the various organs of the organizations it is now generally agreed that the human rights provisions of the Charter create legally binding obligations on members to protect human rights. It is also apparent that early objections by some to the competence of the UN and other members to comment on human rights violations on Article 2(7), the non-intervention provision of the Charter discussed above, are now seldom raised.

Universal Declaration

It will be recalled that the Universal Declaration was adopted to remedy the failure of the UN members to agree on the incorporation of a catalogue of protectable human rights within the body of the Charter itself. The Declaration was adopted as a simple resolution of the General Assembly and therefore it was not legally binding in a technical sense. Furthermore, although there were no votes against the Declaration, Byelorussia, Czechoslovakia, Poland, Saudi Arabia, South Africa, Ukraine, the Soviet Union and Yugoslavia abstained. While the abstentions were primarily based on conflicting ideologies to those expressed in the individualistic categories of rights contained in the Declaration, both South

Africa and Saudi Arabia also expressed anxiety that the Declaration might eventually be used to interpret the Charter. This was particularly a prescient assumption.

What, however, is the legal status of the Declaration today? There are a number of potential answers to this question, each of ascending normative importance. First, it is possible that the Declaration has simply retained its status as a non-binding resolution. However, because of subsequent developments in both UN and state practice, which will be addressed below, this minimalist position is unlikely to be correct. Second, it is arguable that the Declaration is an authoritative interpretation of the Charter by one of its competent organs: the General Assembly. This is a highly plausible argument since the Preamble to the Declaration makes it clear by its language that its was adopted to give effect to the obligations contained in Articles 55 and 56 of the charter. Third, it may be posited that the Declaration is now part of the general principles of law recognized by civilized nations. This proposition would be difficult to gainsay, since nearly every written constitution in the modern world contains a commitment to the protection of human rights and a list of the rights to be protected. Fourth, and this is an argument that a significant number of authors find prersuasive, it may be said that after forty years, the Declaration has become part of customary international law. A great deal of evidence is available to support this view. There is a large amount of state practice which indicates that the Declaration is the benchmark against which human rights standards within states is measured. This state practice includes resolutions of international organizations and institutions, ministerial statements, participation in a variety of human rights treaties, domestic legislation, and so on. It is also apparent that the necessary *opinio iuris* is available, since the bulk of state practice is supported by a belief that human rights obligations, as enunciated in the Declaration, are legally binding. Perhaps the most telling point, however, is that the UN Commission on

Human Rights (a body whose functions will be discussed later) is empowered to employ the Declaration in determining whether there have been widespread and gross violations of human rights in states under whose human rights record is being scrutinized by it. A small number of commentators would also advance beyond the basic proposition that the Declaration represents customary international law and state that it now possesses the characteristics of *ius cogens*, that is peremptory norms from which no derogation is permitted. As Lillich points out while certain of the rights contained in the Declaration, such as the prohibition of slavery, do possess a *ius cogens* character, this is not true of all the provisions, especially those which permit derogations under specified conditions.

If the argument that the Declaration represents customary international law were to be accepted, this would mean that all states are legally bound to afford to individuals within their jurisdiction position to adopt, it does pose a number of practical problems. First, the rights in the Declaration include a mixture of first, second and third generation rights. All of these rights are formulated as precise and immediate commands to state. Article 3, for example, simply states: 'Everyone has the right to life, liberty and security of person.' As a general statement of a fundamental right, this formulation is unobjectionable. What, however, is the content of such a right? Does it preclude abortion, euthanasia or the death penalty following conviction and sentencing by competent courts? Is it absolute? Can exceptions to the right be invoked in times of emergency? None of these questions are answered by the Declaration.

The second problem is intimately linked to the first. There is no obvious institution which is specifically empowered to interpret or apply the Declaration. Notwithstanding these objections, it seems that both a number of UN organs, international bodies and domestic courts have been sufficiently convinced that some of the rights stated in the Declaration, as exiguous as those statements might be, are endowed with sufficient precision for application in a general sense. Nor should the political and moral potency of the Declaration be neglected. It has not only formed the basis for the drafting of two international covenants and there regional human rights treaties, but it has also been the paradigm for the drafting of the human rights provisions of over 25 domestic constitutions. The Declaration is also very often perceived by states, international institutions, NGOs and individuals alike as the touchstone of human rights; indeed, John Humphrey has referred to the Declaration as the 'Magna Carta of Mankind'.

UN Organs

There are a plethora of UN organs and institutions which have a greater or lesser degree of responsibility within the general field of human rights. This section will simply attempt to point a broad picture of the organs and their various competencies.

General Assembly: The General Assembly is the plenary organ of the UN and has broad competence under the Charter to consider questions concerning human rights. These questions may be dealt with the General Assembly of its own motion or they may be referred to it by one of its seven main committees. Under Article 13(1)(b), the major obligations of the General Assembly with respect to human rights are to initiate studies and to make recommendations for the purpose of assisting in the realization of fundamental rights and freedoms for all. A number of studies have been commissioned by the General Assembly, and it has made a large number of recommendations of human rights issues. Such recommendations are not legally binding on numbers, but when taken in conjunction with the obligations contained in Articles 55 and 56 of the Charter, they assume considerable legal significance, and may even be said to create legal obligations where they are stated with sufficient precision. Perhaps the most important contribution of the General Assembly to human rights has been the significant number of international instruments adopted by it in the field following reference from the Commission on Human Rights and ECOSOC. These have included the Universal Declaration, the two International Covenants and a number of UN conventions in specialized human rights fields, the most important of which are considered below. It should also be noted that under these UN-sponsored human rights conventions, the General Assembly is the ultimate destination of all reports made on questions of implementation and on any special procedures to be followed.

The General Assembly has also established, in accordance with its powers under Article 22, a number of subsidiary organs to deal with human rights issues. Some of these have enjoyed substantial longevity, whereas others have simply been of a short-term ad hoc nature. Among the more notable of these organs have been the UN International Children's Emergency Fund (UNICEF), the Office of the High Commissioner for Refugees, the Decolonization Committee and Special Committee on Apartheid. Each of these has had a significant impact upon the matters within its purview.

Economic and Social Council: The Economic and Social Council is a political organ of the UN consisting of 54 members. In the field of human rights, it is charged with making recommendations for the purpose of promoting respect for and observance of human rights and fundamental freedoms and, as we have seen above, submitting draft conventions to the General Assembly. ECOSOC is also the organ which is responsible for receiving reports from, coordinating activities with and concluding agreements with UN specialized agencies having certain human rights competencies such as ILO, UNESCO and WHO. ECOSOC is also responsible for coordinating activities with NGOs.

Much of ECOSOC'S work is undertaken by commissions which it is required to establish under Article 68. The most important of these commissions, as far as human rights are concerned, are the Commission on Human Rights, the Sub-

Commission on Prevention of Discrimination and Protection of Minorities and the Commission on the Status of Women.

Commission on Human Rights: The establishment of a CHR was recommended in 1945 by the Preparatory Commission of the UN in order to deal with the outstanding human rights issues which could not be resolved during the original drafting of the Charter. At its first session in 1946, ECOSOC established the CHR. The Commission, which has grown in size over the years, now consists of 43 persons chosen from the UN members who serve the CHR in their capacity as governmental representatives. In this sense, the CHR may be regarded as a political body, and it is therefore not surprising that the debates within the Commission frequently take on an overtly political dimension. The CHR's terms of references were established by ECOSOC in 1946. There were that the Commission should submit proposals, recommendations and reports to ECOSOC regarding:

(a) An international bill of rights;
(b) International declarations or conventions on civil liberties, the status of women, freedom of informations and similar matters;
(c) The protections of minorities;
(d) The preventions of discriminations on grounds of race, sex, language or religion;
(e) Any other matter concerning human rights not covered by items (a), (b), (c) and (d).

In 1979, ECOSOC added the following term to the above: 'The Commission shall assist [ECOSOC] in the coordination of activities concerning human rights in the [UN] system. This addition clearly reflected the transition by the UN to an integrated and holistic approach to human rights matters as reflected in a 1977 General Assembly resolution on the subject.

Despite the fact that the Commission is clearly a political organ of the UN, it has in fact undertaken much useful work in developing the human rights agenda within the organization.

In pursuit of its mandate, the CHR has not only drafted the Universal Declaration and the two Covenants, but also a large number of standard setting declarations and a large number of conventions concerned with human rights.

Sub-Commission: The Sub-Commission, which was established by ECOSOC in 1947, works closely with the CHR. It consists of 26 members who are independent and who serve in their own individual capacities. The terms of reference under which the Sub-Commission functions are:

(a) to undertake studies particularly in the light of the Universal Declaration... and to make recommendation to the [CHR] concerning the prevention of discrimination of any kind relating to human rights and fundamental freedoms and the protection of racial, national, religious and linguistic minorities; and

(b) to perform any other functions which may be entrusted to it by [ECOSOC] or the [CHR].

While the Sub-Commission has performed much valuable work on the question of the protection of minorities, it has drafted a number of instruments relevant to human rights standards and has encouraged bodies such as UNESCO and ILO to undertake studies appropriate to their spheres of competence, it is, perhaps, the protective function of the Sub-Commission in conjuction with the CHR and ECOSOC which deserves particular mention.

When the CHR was established, it received a large number of complaints from individuals alleging human rights violations. The Commission, however, decided that it had no power to take any action in respect of individual human rights violations notified to it. This position was confirmed by ECOSOC Resolution 75(5) in 1947 and reconfirmed in 1959 by Resolution 728(XXVIII). This latter resolution, however, provided for the production of a confidential list of petitions which; although providing useful information, could not be used as a basis for action by the CHR. In 1967, however,

ECOSOC changed its position. Under Resolution 1235(XLII), ECOSOC authorized the CHR to:

> ...examine information relevant to gross violations of human rights and fundamental freedoms as exemplified by the policy of apartheid as practised in the Republic of South Africa ...and to racial discrimination ...contained in the communications listed ...pursuant to ....Resolution 728F(XXVIII)... [emphasis added].

Pursuant to this, the CHR was empowered to make thorough study of situations which revealed a ' consistent pattern of violation of human rights, as exemplified by the policy of apartheid... and racial discrimination... and report with recommendations thereon to [ECOSOC]'. While it is clear that Resolution 1235 appeared to have as its main concern discriminatory policies, the prime examples of which was apartheid, it is also apparent that, by implication, the CHR was to examine other gross abuses to human rights. The expansion of the CHR's mandate to examine all gross violations became clear in Resolution 1503(XLVIII).

Resolution 1503 empowers the Sub-Commission to establish a five member working group whose task is to screen all incoming communications. Communications which 'appear to reveal a consistent pattern of gross and reliably attested violations of human rights and fundamental freedoms' are considered by the Sub-Commission together with any replies from the relevant governments. A confidential report is then sent to the CHR. On the basis of this report, the CHR may decide whether to act, and if so, whether it should undertake a 'thorough study' in accordance with Resolution 1235 or whether to make the matter a subject of study by an ad hoc committee. If it decides on the latter course of action, not only must the consent of the relevant government be obtained, but it must also ensure that individuals involved in making the complaints have 'direct and reliable knowledge of the violations', have exhausted all local remedies and that the communication is not being considered under another form of international procedure, such as a communication to the Human Rights Committee under the ICCPR First Optional Protocol or any of the regional systems. A number of ad hoc committees have been brought into being and have functioned with varying degrees of success. The more important cases in which such committees have operated have been Equatorial Guinea, Chile, Namibia and the Israeli occupied West Bank.

Two points should be noted about the Resolution 1503 procedure. First, it is engaged solely by the accretion of individual communications which reveal 'a consistent pattern of gross and reliably attested violations'. The procedure is not one which results in individual remedies, but simply draws the attention of the UN to states in which the human rights situation is already drier. Second, the procedure is entirely confidential until the CHR decides to make recommendations to ECOSOC. All the CHR's meetings are held in private, and no documents are released until ECOSOC is informed of the CHR's recommendations. None the less, once ECOSOC has received a thorough study under the procedure, it-and the General Assembly to whom it is responsible-may discuss the reports and adopt resolutions calling upon states to comply with their human rights obligations under; the Charter.

The 1503 procedure has a number of obvious defects. First, confidentiality ensures that states are not put 'in the dock'. While this might facilitate state cooperation in proceedings, it denies the UN institutions the power and leverage which accompany adverse publicity. Second, the accumulation of evidence through which gross violations are identified means that the institutions are always working 'in arrears' and may be unable to exercise their influence until it is too late. Third the procedure is open to abuse by states who may be able to place political pressure on the various institutions involved. To some extent, these criticisms have been circumvented by the CHR by relying on a new thematic rather than a country-oriented approach to violations. Under Resolution 2325, the CHR has undertaken studies on enforced disappearances, summary executions, mass expulsions and torture. The Resolution 2325 procedure can be engaged more quickly than the 1503 procedure, since it does not depend on an accumulation of events. Furthermore, it does not suffer the defects of excessive confidentially, since investigations and discussions take place in public. This helps focus public attention directly and immediately upon some of the worst violations and reduces the opportunity for political interference.

Commission on the Status of Women: This institution was established contemporaneously with the CHR. It consists of 32 members whose function is two-fold: first, to prepare recommendations and reports to ECOSOC on promoting women's rights in political, economic, civil, social and educational fields and, second, to make recommendations to ECOSOC on urgent problems requiring immediate attention in the field of women's rights the object of implementing the principle that men and women shall have equal rights and to develop proposals to give effect to such recommendations. The Commission has enjoyed most of its success in the area of setting international standards and has played a major role in the drafting of the Declaration on the Status of Women 1967, the Convention on the Elimination of All Forms of Discrimination Against Women 1979, and the Convention on the Political Rights of Women 1953. Unlike the CHR, the Commission on the Status of Women declared itself competent to receive communications from women alleging violation of their rights from an early stage. Much of this procedure has, however, been overtaken by other, more specific procedures. Nevertheless, it is the organs which are charged with receiving reports from the Committee on the Elimination of Discrimination Against Women under the 1979 Convention.

UNESCO: UNESCO is a specialized agency of UN which has its headquarters in Paris. Under Article 1 of its constitution purpose is:

> ...to contribute to peace and security and promoting collaboration among the nations through education,

science and culture in order to further universal respect for justice, for; the rule of law and for the human rights and fundamental freedoms which are affirmed for the peoples of the world, without distinction of race, sex, language or religion.

As Saba observes, UNESCO has always seen education, the natural and social science and the defence of the human rights as 'indissolubly linked to the safeguarding of peace'. In pursuing these objectives, UNESCO sets standards for the guidance of governments in matters within its competence (and there has been a great deal of dispute as to exactly what lies within UNESCO's competence in recent years) and the drafting of relevant treaties. The organization's Convention and Recommendation against Discrimination in Education is perhaps the clearest examples of its competence in the human rights and educational fields.

Initially, UNESCO took the view that, like the CHR, it had no competence to receive communications from individuals alleging violations of human rights. However, in 1978, it adopted a procedure for considering communications. Like all international procedures, it is predicated upon the exhaustion of local remedies and must disclose violations of human rights which lie within the fields of UNESCO's competence. Communications; alleging human rights violations are considered by he Committee on Conventions and Recommendations, whose primary function is to secure a friendly solution 'designed to advance the promotion of human rights falling within UNESCO's fields of competence'. The procedure is both flexible and confidential. Such confidentiality extends to the Committee's reports which is made to UNESCO's Executive Board at the end of each session. The Committee's report not only identifies individual and specific cases of human rights violation, but also questions the 'massive, systematic or flagrant violations'. Such questions may be discussed by UNESCO's plenary body the General Conference.

International Labour Organization: The ILO which was

we saw earlier, was founded in 1919 by the Treaty of Versailles, was transformed into a specialized agency of the UN under an agreement with ECOSOC. The objectives of the ILO were restated in the Declaration of Philadelphia 1944, which became part of the Organization's constitution. Its major concerns are those of social justice and social welfare through the promotion of social welfare rights. The ILO has sponsored over 150 international instruments which provide the basis for labour and social welfare law in significant number of states.

Supervision under the ILO Constitution takes a number of forms. First, under Article 22, member states are bound to submit periodic reports on the measures which they have taken to give effect to the ILO conventions to which they are party. These are examined by a Committee of Experts consisting of 18 independent persons. The Committee may address requests to members for further information and include its observations on the reports and other information gathered through its requests to the annual session of the International Labour Conference, where they are considered by a Conference Committee on the Application of Conventions and Recommendations.

Second, under Article 24, if a representation is made to the International Labour Office by an association of industrial employers or workers that a member has failed to observe the standards set down in any ILO convention to which it is a party, the Conserving Body of ILO may communicate this to the affected state, which may respond to the allegation. The Governing Body then delegates the hearing of the case to a committee which reports back with recommendations and, if a breach is found to have occurred, can publish the original representation.

Third, there exists an inter-state complaints procedure under Article 25 whereby one member state may complain that another has not been observing an ILO convention to; which both states are party. The Governing Body may refer such a complaint to a Commission of Inquiry, which investigates the complaint and then reports to the Director-General of the ILO who communicates the report of both parties and to the Governing Body which is obliged to publish the report. Each of the members states must within three months inform the Director-General whether it accepts the report of the Commission and indicate whether, as it is entitled to do, it proposes to refer the complaint to the ICJ for adjudication. The first complaint made under this procedure was a complaint by Ghana against Portugal alleging a violation of the Convention or the Abolition of Forced Labour 1957 in Portugal's colonies.

Fourth, there is a special procedure concerning complaints about the violation of the right to freedom of association. In 1951, a Committee on Freedom of Association consisting of nine members was established to examine complaints in this area. After examining such complaints, the Committee submits detailed report to the Governing Body with proposed conclusions and recommendations to be made to the state concerned. In order to deal with serious and politically sensitive cases, a Fact Finding and Conciliation Commission may undertake investigations. The Commission has, however, not been used often, simply because the area in which it operates is too politically sensitive for most of the states concerned.

Other Organs: The picture of competent bodies in the field of human rights under the UN Charter would be incomplete without mention of the Security Council and the ICJ. While the Security Council has no specific responsibility for human rights, it has, on a number of occasions, made pronouncements on such matters acting under Chapter VI (disputes and situations likely to endanger maintenance of international peace and security) and Chapter VII (enforcement action) of the Charter. In particular, the Council has considered, inter alia, the question of apartheid in South Africa and the treatment of Palestinians in the Israeli occupied territories.

The ICJ, which is the principal judicial organ of the UN, clearly has competence to determine questions concerning or involving human rights under its contentious and advisory jurisdictions. This it has done in a number of cases. In the Corfu Channel Case, for example, the Court ruled that Albania ought to have had regard to 'elementary considerations of humanity' in warning British warships of the presence of mines in the Corfu Channel which was under its jurisdiction. Questions of political asylum were raised in the Asylum Case, issues of apartheid were discussed in a series of cases concerning Namibia or South West Africa, and in the Genocide Convention Case the question of genocide as *ius cogens* was touched upon obliquely.

International Covenants

At the time the Universal Declaration was drafted, it was recognized that it would not create legally binding obligations but would simply 'set a standard of achievement for all peoples and all nations'. It was therefore agreed that CHR should undertake the drafting of a legally binding human rights instrument modelled on the Declaration. Although the proposed treaty was to include both economic, social and cultural rights, and civil and political rights within it, problems arose concerning the appropriate methods of implementation for the different categories of rights. It was therefore proposed that two instruments be adopted, one dealing with economic, social and cultural rights and the other dealing with civil and political rights. Two covenants were therefore presented to, and adopted by, the General Assembly in 1966. They did not, however, enter into force until 1976, when the required number of 35 states had ratified them.

Unlike the Universal Declaration, the Covenants create legally binding obligations for the more than 80 states which are now party to them. Thus it is no longer possible, if it ever were, for these states to argue that protection of human rights is simply a matter within their domestic jurisdiction. Furthermore, while the obligations in respect of the protected rights are contained in treaties which normally give rise to reciprocal rights and duties between the parties, these human rights treaties are more in the nature of unilateral legally binding commitments by the states parties to be supervised by international institutions.

Only two provisions are common to both Covenants. The first of these provisions is Article 1, which provides for the self-determination of peoples, that is the right of a cognate group to determine their own political destiny. The common Article 1 also provides for the right of peoples to dispose of their own natural resources and wealth, and not to be deprived of their own means of subsistence. These are clearly third-generation rights, and the rationale for their inclusion in a separate part which lies at the head of both Covenants would seem to be that if people are subject to allien domination and subjugation and are thus denied the right of self-determination, all other rights become meaningless. The second common provision is the rule prohibiting discrimination on grounds of race, colour, sex, language, religion, political or other opinion, national or social origin, property, birth of other status. This broad prohibition of discrimination, which is a constituent central element of the rule of law, is clearly a necessary prerequisite to the proper enjoyment of all other substantive rights.

ICCPR: Whereas the Universal Declaration was drafted in the form of peremptory commands to states to protect certain rights, the ICCPR was drafted to meet the practical problems of protecting human rights. Thus, the Covenant elaborates the protectable rights more specifically and indicates with a reasonable degree of clarity the limitations which may be imposed upon the exercise of certain of the rights in given situations. Furthermore, the rights contained in the ICCPR do not correspond exactly with those in the Universal Declaration. Included in the Covenant is the obligation on states to allow individuals who are members of an ethnic, religious or linguistic minority 'to enjoy their own culture, to profess and practice their own religion or to use their own language' in community with other members of the group (Article 27). Also included is the right to be free from imprisonment for failure to fulfil a contractual obligation (Article 11); the right of all prisoners to be treated with humanity and respect for the inherent dignity of the human person (Article 10(1); and the right of special protection for children (Article 24). Excluded from the Covenant is the right to asylum, the right to a nationality and, largely as a result of ideological differences between the East and West blocs the right to own property.

Although a number of rights protected by the Covenant may not be derogated from under any circumstances. Article 4 provides that the remaining rights may be derogated from 'in time of public emergency that threatens the life of the nations' as long as such derogations are proportionate to the threat to be met and non-discriminatory. Derogations must also be communicated immediately to the other states parties through the intermediary of the UN Secretary-General, together with the reason for which they were taken. Certain rights are also subject to what Professor Rosalyn Higgins calls 'claw-back' provisions, which permit limitations to be imposed on rights for the protection of public safety, order, health or morals or the fundamental rights and freedoms of others. While this gives a margin of discretion to states, a discretion which possesses the potential for abuse, it is nevertheless counterbalanced by Article 5(1) which introduces an element of proportionality. This provides that the rights in questions should not be limited to 'a greater extent than is provided for in the present Covenant'.

Under Article 2(1) of the Covenant, states parties are obligated to 'respect and to ensure to all individuals within a territory and subject to its jurisdiction the rights recognised in the present Covenant' without discrimination of any kind. Where such rights are not already respected and ensured within a state's jurisdiction, it is required by Article 2(2) to introduce the necessary legislative or other measures in order to give them effect. It should be noted that these obligations are absolute and immediate. It should also be noted that the rights are to be accorded to all individuals, whatever their nationality, who find themselves under the jurisdiction of the state. This not only includes the state's territorial jurisdiction, but also the state's personal jurisdiction over its own nationals who might be located overseas.

Human Rights Committee

The body which is charged with supervising the states parties' obligations under the ICCPR is the Human Rights Committee (HRC), which sits either at the UN Headquarters in New York or at Geneva, which is the location of the Human Rights Division of the UN Secretariat. The HRC is a creature of the Covenant and is composed of 18 members who must be national of the parties to the Covenant and 'persons of high moral character and recognized competence in the field of human rights'. Although members need not necessarily be lawyers, Article 28(2) provides that 'consideration should be given to the usefulness of the participation of some persons having legal experience'. In fact, the Committee has, since its inception, been staffed entirely by lawyers, usually of some distinction. Committee members are elected for a four-year period, by secret ballot from nominations by the states parties. No two persons elected may be from the same state, and each serves in their individual capacity, not as state nominees. The personal nature of the duties performed by Committee members is reinforced by the requirement that each must, on appointment, make a solemn declaration that they will perform their functions impartially and conscientiously. Committee members, therefore, owe their allegiance not to their nominating state but to the Committee alone. Committee member are also paid by the UN thus eradicating one particular major source of potential government interference. In order to ensure the widest; representation of legal cultures, Article 31(2) requires that in the election of the Committee, consideration, must be given to equitable geographical distribution and to the representation of different forms of civilization and of legal systems. Given the diverse origins of the Committee members, it might be thought that political and ideological differences would have come to the fore in its proceedings and discussions. As Nowak has indicated, however, the Committee works on the basis of consensus, and although the inevitable disputes over legal doctrine and methodology have occurred, there has been little political confrontation.

Supervisory Mechanisms: The ICCPR in its First Optional Protocol provides one mandatory and two optional mechanisms to enable the HRC to supervise the states parties' obligations. The mandatory means of supervision is a system of periodic reports under Article 40(1), under which states parties undertake 'to submit reports on the measures they have adopted which give effect to the rights recognized [in the ICCPR] and on the progress made in the enjoyment of those rights'. The Committee has now received a large number of state reports, and has developed guidelines both in their representation and for its follow-up procedure. Briefly, the practice is as follows:

Within a year of becoming party to the ICCPR and at periods specified thereafter by the Committee, states parties are required to submit their reports to the Committee via the UN Secretary-General. The Committee then studies the reports and draws up a list of questions requesting the state to clarify to elaborate various parts of the reports. A representative of the state is then required by the Committee's Rules of Procedure to make a final presentation to the HRC in person in order to deal with the general and specific issues raised by it. The HRC then forwards its comments to the state party which is entitled to submit observations on those comments. The main advantage of this procedure is that it enables the Committee to engage in a 'constructive dialogue' with the state party, but it also allows it to investigate the state parties' submissions by probing weaknesses, resolving ambiguities and illuminating obfuscation in reports. Copies of reports and comments are forwarded to ECOSOC for consideration, and the HRC itself is also required to submit an annual report to the General Assembly on its activities. This enables the Committee to isolate particular problems and difficulties identified in any of the country reports studied. It also makes public any matters of concern, and opens the way for possible debate in the General Assembly in respect of certain states.

The second, optional, method of supervision is an inter-state complaint procedure under Articles 41 and 42. This procedure requires acceptance by individual state parties, and it can be utilized only against other states which have also agreed to submit themselves to the procedure. Assuming the condition of reciprocity applies, the procedure operates as follows: A state which considers that another state is violating the Covenant brings that fact to the attention of the state party concerned. That state party must respond to the allegation within a period of three months. If, within six months, the remedies have been exhausted before considering the case in closed session. It may then offer its good offices with a view to achieving a friendly settlement between the states. If friendly settlement is reached, the HRC must make a report on its terms, but if no friendly settlement is forthcoming, the Committee may appoint ad hoc Conciliation Commission consisting of five members which has the power to make recommendations after hearing the submissions of the parties, but these recommendations are not binding on the parties. In all cases, however, the matter will be referred to the General Assembly via ECOSOC by the Committee in its annual report.

The inter-state complaint procedure is most unsatisfactory. Like inter-state procedures in the regional conventions, it is subject to potential abuse since it may be used for overtly political purposes. The emphasis on friendly settlement of the dispute also renders the procedure unsuitable for protecting individuals, the violation of whose rights may have prompted the original complaint. Since there is no adjudicative power either in the Committee or the ad hoc Conciliation Commission, objective determination of the issues is not possible. Finally, the absence of binding decisions does not ensure the rectification of breaches. It is perhaps not surprising that this procedure has never been invoked.

The third, optional, method of supervision and enforcement of rights contained in the Covenant is the individual communication procedure contained in the First Optional Protocol. This has undoubtedly been the most significant development in the universal system of human rights protection, since it allows individuals direct access to an impartial international body, the Human Rights Committee, which has the power to determine whether or not a state has violated the rights protected under the Covenant. Given the significance of the communication system under the Protocol, it is appropriate to consider it in some detail.

The Individual Application System

The conditions for admissibility of communication and the procedures to be followed in dealing with it are contained in the Protocol, the Committee's Rules of Procedure and the jurisprudence of the Committee. Under Article 1, a state party to Protocol must recognize the competence of the Committee to receive communication from individuals subject to jurisdiction who claim to be victims of a violation of any of the rights protected by the Covenant. In order to declare a communication admissible, a number of conditions must be met:

1 The communication must be an individual who claims to be a victim (Articles 1 and 2(1) Protocol).
2 The communication must not be under consideration under any other procedure of international investigation or settlement (Article 5(1)(a) Protocol).
3 The victim must show that he or she has exhausted all local remedies (Articles 2 and 5(2)(b) Protocol).
4 The communication must not be anonymous, abusive of the right of submission or incompatible

with the provisions of the Covenant (Article 3 Protocol).

5 The communication must not be manifestly ill-founded. This requirement is derived from the jurisprudence of the HRC.

There are no definitions of the admissibility criteria contained in the Protocol, but the Committee has developed these through its own jurisprudence. Similarly, there is no time limit for making a communication, but this does not appear to have concerned the Committee to date. Although the Covenant is silent on its temporal scope, the Committee has decided that it cannot take account of violations which took place before the entry into force of the Covenant for the state in question, unless those violations have a continuing character or have produced continuing effects.

The Procedure: Unless a case is rejected by the HRC, all communications must be brought to the attention of the affected state party. Rule 91(2) of the HRC's Rules of Procedure further provides that non communication may be ruled admissible until the state party concerned has been given opportunity to comment upon it. Once a communication is declared admissible, however, the state party must within six months furnish the Committee with written explanations or statements clarifying the matter and any remedial action which it has taken.

The major characteristics of the Committee's procedure both at the admissibility and merits stages is that it is written and confidential with all HRC meetings being held in camera. Once the Committee has examined the written evidence before it, it makes its views known to the state and the individual concerned in accordance with Article 5(4) of the Protocol. Although Article 6 envisages that the Committee should simply include a summary of its activities under the Protocol in its annual report to ECOSOC and General Assembly of the UN, it has, in fact, published complete versions of its procedures and views in the case of every communication.

1. Communications from 'Individuals' who are 'Victims'

This requirement raises a number of issues of interpretation:

(a) Must the author of the communication always be the victim of alleged violation?

If this requirement were taken too literally, it could lead to denial of the right of communication in certain circumstances. A person arbitrarily arrested of the held incommunicado, for example, would not, on a strict reading of the Protocol, be able to avail him or herself of the right to communication. To permit the right of third-party communication on their behalf would not only accord with the overall object and purpose of the Protocol, it would also ensure that states were not able to evade their obligations under the Covenant by 'disappearing' victims.

This view is supported by Rule 90 of the HRC's Rules of Procedure which states that a communication should 'normally be submitted by the individual himself or by his representative' and that it may be submitted on behalf of an alleged victim 'when it appears that he is unable to submit [it] himself. The Committee has had no difficulty in accepting third-party communications in a number of cases. In Massera v Uruguay, for example, the Committee accepted a communication from a woman alleging the arbitrary detention and torture of her husband, mother and stepfather in Uruguay saying: 'The author of the communication was justified by reason of close family connection in acting on behalf of the ... alleged victims' (para. 5.a).

This formula, which has been reiterated in subsequent cases, does not mean that the third-party representative of all alleged victim need necessarily be a family member, but it is clear that the author will need to prove an interest in the proceedings. It will be easy to show an interest where the representative has the express consent of the alleged victim, as in the case of a lawyer representing him or her, but rather more difficult where consent is to be implied. A friend would probably have legal standing, but a member or representative of an organization of which the alleged victim was also a member would probably not.

It is certainly clear that there is no possibility of a class action, or *actio popularis* as it is known, under the Protocol. In the Mauritian Women Case, a number of women complained about the discriminatory effect of a 1977 immigration law which affected the residence rights of the foreign husbands of Mauritian women, but not the foreign wives of Mauritian men. Many of the women complainants refused to be named in the communication, and it was brought on their behalf by some women who were willing to identify themselves. The Committee declared:

> A persons can only claim to be a victim if he or she is actually affected. It is a matter of degree how concretely this requirement should be taken. However, no individual can in the abstract, by way of an *actio popularis,* challenge a law or practice that has not already been correctly applied to the detriment of that individual, it must in any event be applicable in such a way that the victim's risk of being affected is more than a theoretical possibility.

The Committee decided in this case that there were a number of women who were not affected by the law, whereas others were affected even though the law had not been applied to their husband. The Committee's reasoning here was that the mere existence of the law created uncertainty as regards the residence status for the foreign husbands of these women.

(b) Must the victim be an individual? The majority of rights contained in the Covenant are of an individual nature, but Article 1 includes third-generation or group rights which guarantee the right to self-determination. The question, therefore, that arises in this connection is whether a group may submit a communication complaining of a denial of this right. It is clear that the HRC has set its face against this, ruling in a number of cases that, on the wording of the Protocol, communications may only be accepted from individuals and not from groups. It would seem therefore, that the right of self-determination is an unenforceable right under the individual complaints procedure of the Protocol.

(c) Must the author be within the territorial jurisdiction of the state against which the complaints is made either (i) at the time the violation occurred or (ii) at the time of submitting the communication? Before considering these questions, it should be noted under Article 2 of the Covenant and Article 1 of the Protocol that individuals may complain of a violation of their rights by a state though they are not citizens of that state, as long as they are subject to its territorial jurisdiction.

(i) There have been a number of communications from individuals who have been victims of violations by the states of which they are citizens, although they have been resident in the territory of another state at the time. Examples of this have ranged from kidnap of victims by the agents of their own state acting in violation of the sovereignty of the state of residence at the more serious end of the spectrum, to refusal to renew a passport at the less serious end. In an early communication involving the latter, Uruguay refused to renew the passport of one of its citizens who was resident in Mexico. Uruguay claimed that the HRC lacked competence to consider the communication lodged by the complainant, since he was not within its territorial jurisdiction. The Committee, however, took a wider view, indicating that the issue of a passport was a matter which was entirely subject to the jurisdiction of the state, since it alone was competent to determine whether or not it should be issued.

This personal nature of the jurisdiction referred to in Article 1 of the Protocol Article 2 of the Covenant was stated unequivocally by the HRC in Celiberti v Uruguay. Here a Uruguayan citizen had been abducted by agents and returned to Uruguay where he was arbitrarily imprisoned and tortured. Uruguay, contesting the admissibility of the communication, complained that the act had not taken place within Uruguay's territorial jurisdiction. The Committee rejected this contention, stating that the reference in Article 1 of the Protocol was 'not to the place where the violation occurred, but rather to the relationship between the individual and the State in relation to the rights set forth in Covenants wherever they occurred'.

(ii) A glance at the origin of many communications indicates that they have been made by refugees or the relatives of victims who are themselves refugees. A number of early communications involving Uruguayan citizens were authored in Mexico, to which they had fled from Uruguay's right-wing military regime. The HRC has accepted such communications without questions since the Protocol demands on residential requirement.

2. *Overlapping Systems of International Investigation*

Under Article 5(2)(a) of the Protocol, a communication may not be considered by the HRC if it contains the same matter as that which is being examined under another procedure of international investigation. This is to prevent proliferation of proceedings among the various human rights institutions now in existence. In most cases, the Committee will have no difficulty in determining whether or not this requirement has been fulfilled. In a number of cases, applications have been submitted to the American Commission on Human Rights or the European Commission on Human Rights and this has led to inadmissibility before the HRC. In some circumstances, however, the Committee has shown a willingness to be flexible. In Milan Seguira v Uruguay, for example, a two-line reference to the author of a complaint in a list of over one hundred named persons who had been arbitrarily detained by Uruguayan authorities which had been submitted by a third party, was not held to breach the non-duplication requirement. Further, in Celiberti, the Committee held that it was not precluded from examining a communication by reason of the subsequent opening of a case before the American Commission by a third party who was unrelated to the alleged victim. The HRC showed itself to be even more creative in Grille Motta, where it found that a communication which was before the American Commission could not contain the same matters as that currently before it, since the communication before the American Commission concerned events which had taken prior to the entry into force of the Covenant for the state in question.

Difficulties of another kind have arisen for the Committee in cases where the subject matter is the same as that which has been considered previously by either the Inter-American or European Commissions and rejected. Here the questions has been whether the HRC is competent to reconsider such a case? In the communications which have come before it, the Committee has decided that it possesses the competence to consider cases anew, but has declined to do so because of particular reservations to the Protocol made by the state parties in question. These reservations precluded it from considering cases which had already been considered by the European Commission. The HRC's views in these cases have, however, turned very much on the precise language used by the reserving states. On a different but related issue, it should be noted that the Committee itself will not generally review its own admissibility decisions, but if new information comes to light which might have affected its decision, Rule 93(4) of its Rules of Procedure give it the power to do so.

3. Exhaustion of local remedies

All human rights instruments require complainants to exhaust local remedies before international proceedings may be initiated. The Protocol is no exception to this requirement, and although Article 5(2)(b) does not expressly state a complainant must exhaust local remedies 'in accordance with the accepted rules of international law', the HRC has implied this condition. Thus, remedies which are unduly tardy or which do not provide redress for violations, will not be a bar to admissibility on this ground.

Since the HRC's procedure is written, problems arise in determining whether a complainant has exhausted all possible local remedies. It would seem that a state which wished to contest admissibility need only allege that a complainant has not taken the necessary steps to secure redress in domestic institutions. The Committee has not, however, been prepared to accept such general statements as conclusive and has placed the burden of demonstrating that domestic remedies have not been exhausted upon the state. It is not enough for the state to respond simply by referring to general categories of remedies; it must indicate in detail the specific remedies available to the complaint in his or her particular case. This was made clear in Lanza v Uruguay, where the HRC said:

> Specific responses and pertinent evidence (including copies of the relevant decisions of the courts and findings of any investigations which have taken place into the validity of the complaints made) in reply to the contentions of the author.

This device had been remarkably effective in securing fuller cooperation with the Committee by states.

4. Further conditions for admissibility

Article 3 provides that the Committee shall consider inadmissible any communication which is anonymous or which it considers to be abusive of the right of submission of communications or to be incompatible with the provisions of the Covenant. There have been few communications which have been declared inadmissible on the grounds of abuse of process or incompatibility, but one such is Taylor v Canada. Here Taylor complained of an infringement of his right to hold opinions freely and freedom of expression under Article 19 of the covenant in that had been prohibited from transmitting recorded messages over his telephone warning of the dangers of international Jury. The Committee found that this communications was clearly incompatible with the provisions of the Covenant, since states parties were under an obligations by virtue of Article 20(2) to prohibit any advocacy of national, religious or racial hatred.

It is apparent that the HRC has also extended its competence to declare inadmissible communications which are not well-founded. This has been developed by the Committee's jurisprudence, for there is no such explicit admissibility requirement in the Protocol. In adopting this course of action, the Committee has of necessity been obliged to examine the merits of a case as a preliminary to determining its admissibility. While this again does not specifically provide for in the Protocol, it is necessary consequence of its decision to extend its competence and mirrors closely the practice of other human rights bodies. There are a number of examples of the Committee's approach in recent communications. In J.D.B. v The Netherlands, a communication by an unemployed television repair man that Dutch law discriminated against him by punishing him for failing to take employment not related to his trade was held inadmissible on the grounds that no fact had been stated which substantiated the applicant's claim that he had suffered a violation of any of the rights guaranteed by the Covenant. Perhaps a clearer case of rejection on the grounds that a communication was manifestly ill-founded was that of L.T.K. v Finland, in which the author of the communication alleged that the failure of the Finnish authorities to recognize him as a conscientious objector, thus leading to his criminal prosecution and imprisonment, violated Articles 18 and 19 of the Covenant. In finding the claim inadmissible, the Committee simply declared that 'the Covenant does not recognize the right to conscientious objection'.

The Evidence: Under Article 5(1), the Committee is required to consider communications 'in the light of all written information made available to it by the individual and by the state party concerned'. It is apparent, however, that the written procedure has a number of defects. One major problem is the lack of appropriate mechanisms to enforce state party compliance with the obligation to provide information under Article 4(2) of the Protocol. The effective operation of the procedure depends entirely on the cooperation of states and the provision of detailed information by them. Unfortunately, a number of states have been less than cooperative with the HRC, and in its early days, Uruguay, in the words of Tomuschat, 'demonstrated a deplorable lack of cooperation'. This included the failure to respond to the Committee's requests for information, tardiness in the provision of information and the supply of very general information. In order to deal with this lack of cooperation, the HRC developed a number of practices. In the case of non-provision of requested information, the HRC in the first communication with which it dealt, Massera v Uruguay, simply compiled its final views by accepting all the evidence that had been supplied by the complainant. The HRC took the view that by non-compliance Uruguay had not contradicted the evidence which the Committee had in its possession.

Where there has been a lack of information on information of a general nature has been supplied by the state, the HRC has proceeded rather more cautiously. It has pointed out that Article 4(2) implies that states are under an obligation to provide the most detailed information possible within the given time limit of six months. It has further been argued that it is only natural to place the burden of disproving the alleged victim', allegations upon the state, since it is the state which generally has access to the appropriate information. Thus, in Santullo, the Committee decided to accept as proved, '...facts which have either been essentially confirmed by the State Party or are unrepudiated or uncontested except for denials of a general character offering no particular information or explanation'. The Committee therefore phrased its final views in a negative way and indicated that it 'could not find that there has not been any violation [of the Covenant]'.

The HRC has also decided that where specific allegations are made against particular government agents by the author of a communication, those allegations should be fully investigated by the state concerned. This was made clear in Grille Motta v Uruguay, where the complainant alleged that he had been subjected to electric shocks, submarino (immersion of a victim's head in foul water until the victim is close to drowning), insertion of bottles and the barrels of automatic weapons into his anus, standing hooded and handcuffed with a piece of wood thrust into his mouth for several days and nights by identifiable individuals. Uruguay dismissed these allegations as 'a figment of the imagination of the author'.. The HRC found, however, that since the allegations had not been duly investigated by Uruguay, they remained unrefuted. The state should have demonstrated that it had investigated the allegations in accordance with its domestic law and brought those found to be responsible to justice.

Given the limitations inherent in the written procedure, it is arguable that the Committee has been remarkably successful in overcoming the difficulties involved. Its placing the burden of proof on the state to disprove the allegations made by the author of a communication once again finds justification in law policy. Under the Protocol, which is an optional instrument to which states have freely acceded, states parties are required to comply with certain obligations. The requirements that they provide written explanations or statements clarifying alleged violations of the Covenant to the HRC under Article 4(2) requires co-operations in the utmost good faith. Failure to do so would deprive the Protocol of its efficacy if states were able to avoid their obligations by recalcitrance or tardiness.

While it may be argued that the Committee's procedure

favours a complainant, it has none the less maintained that its procedures conform to the standards of natural justice as far as allegedly delinquent states are concerned. In Quinteros v Uruguay, it said:

> In accordance with its mandate under Article 5(1) of the ...Protocol, the Committee has considered the communication in the light of the information made available to it by the author of the communication and by the State party concerned. In this connection the Committee has adhered strictly to the principle audiatur et altera pars and has given the State party every opportunity to furnish information to refuse the evidence presented by the author.

Final Views

The HRC concludes this process of considering a communication by presenting its 'views' usually referred to as 'final views', on the allegations made. This has been criticized as the weakest part of the procedure, since it is argued that; the views are not legally binding. Tomuschat has argued that even so, the views have immense authority which 'proceeds from their inner qualities of impartially, objectiveness and soberness'. While it may be open to a state to challenge the Committee's final views and to refuse to implement them, this would expose it to criticism that it had disregarded the authoritative pronouncement of an independent tribunal to whose jurisdiction it had freely submitted. Further, there can be no doubt that the HRC's views are authoritative. It alone is given exclusive competence to rule on compliance or breach of the Covenant under the Protocol, and although its views may not be binding in a strict legal sense, a finding of breach is to all intent and purposes a potent declaration of international delinquency.

As the views of the HRC are not legally binding, and in the absence of any provision for remedies in either the Covenant or the Protocol; it would not appear to be open to the

Committee to decide that a state must grant compensation to the victim of a violation of any of the rights contained in the ICCPR. However, in line with its practice of declaring breaches, the HRC has also declared that delinquent states are required to grant remedies to victims in order to comply with their obligations under the Covenant. In general, the HRC uses the following formula:

> The Committee... is of the view that the State Party is under an obligation to provide the victim with effective remedies, including compensation, for the violations which he has suffered and to take steps to ensure that similar violations do not occur in the future.

While a state is not under a legal duty to comply with the views of the Committee, it is under an obligation to comply with the obligations established by the Covenant. Again, it would be difficult to argue that the ruling of the Committee here is not authoritative.

The practice of the Human Rights Committee under the ICCPR First Optional Protocol is one of the most important developments in international human rights law in the twentieth century. For the first time, it gives individuals direct access to an impartial international tribunal which is competent to rule on the question of violations of a large number of civil and political rights. The way in which the Committee has gone about its task of forging an effective mechanism of near universal application is also to be commended and bears witness to the calibre of the people who serve on it. As some states, particularly Uruguay and Zaire, have discovered to their cost, the HRC is both creative and tenacious and it is certainly not content to be relegated to diplomatic backwaters. If there is a criticism of the procedure, it is the length of time taken to present final views on communications. At present, this takes approximately three years, but this is no fault of the Committee, which must sit as a single body and cannot sit in 'chambers' of lesser numbers. It might also be commented that there are no procedures for the HRC to act in cases of urgency; this, it would appear, must be left to the regional human rights institutions.

ICESCR: Like its analogue ICCPR, ICESCR both elaborates upon and expands the list of rights contained in the Universal Declaration. Unlike ICCPR, however, it does not require states to give immediate effect to rights recognized, but simply initiates and exhortatory and programmatic approach to their implementation. This approach has led some jurists to argue that economic, social and cultural rights are not real rights, since they do not possess an absolute quality, but are dependent upon economic factors for their implementation. This view is based on Article 2(1) of ICESCR, which provides that each state party 'undertake to take steps to the maximum of its available resources, with a view to achieving progressively the full realisation of the rights recognized in the present Covenant by all appropriate means.

There is only one method of supervision under ICESCR and that is the submission of periodic reports to ECOSOC on the measures which the states parties have adopted and the progress made in achieving the observance of the rights recognized. There is no provision for individual communication, but this is currently under consideration by ECOSOC. Although ECOSOC is the formal supervising body, it has effectively delegated its function under the Covenants to a Committee on Economic, Social and Cultural Rights, which was created in 1985 by Resolution 17. This body mirrors the Human Rights Committee as it consists of 18 experts elected by the states parties who serve in their individual capacities. It considers the periodic reports made by the states parties and forwards its observations to ECOSOC, the UN Commission on Human Rights and to other specialized agencies of the UN concerned with economic, social and cultural right.

Clearly, the implementation procedures and means of supervision under the Covenant are relatively weak and can do little more than highlight the shortcomings of states in the social welfare rights field. None the less, the Committee on

Economic, Social and Cultural Rights had demonstrated in its early sessions a willingness to engage in the same kind of constructive dialogue which has characterized the activities of the Human Rights Committee. A realistic approach to economic, social, and cultural rights, however, suggests that difficulties of implementation are only to be expected, since progress depends not only upon the political will of states, but also upon the availability of resources to fulfil the stated obligations. But as Trubek argues, the minimum position tenable for states parties to ICCPR is that it creates a presumption in favour of social welfare rights which they are clearly legally bound to advance.

Action in Specific Areas

In addition to action in the broad fields of civil, political, economic, social and cultural rights, the UN has also undertaken a variety of activities relating to narrower, more specific areas of human rights promotion and protection. Only the more important conventions adopted under; the auspices of the UN will be examined here.

Genocide: The Convention on the Prevention and Punishment of the Crime of Genocide was adopted by the General Assembly in 1948 and entered into force in 1951. Its drafting and adoption, like the inclusion of the human rights provisions in the Charter, was motivated by the experience of the Nazi extermination of millions of Jews, Gypsies, Slaves and other groups both prior to and during the Second World War. Genocide, which has been described by Whittaker as the 'ultimate crime', is defined by Article of II of the Convention as:

> .... any of the following acts committed with intent to destroy, in whole or in part, a national, ethnical, racial or religious group, as such:
>
> (a) Killing members of the group;
>
> (b) Causing serious bodily or mental harm to members of the group;

(c) Deliberately inflicting on the group conditions of life calculated to bring about its physical destruction in whole or in part;

(d) Imposing measures intended to prevent births within the group;

(e) Forcibly transferring children of the group to another group.

Under Article I of the Convention, the parties 'confirm that genocide .... is a crime under international law which they undertake to prevent and punish'. Not only is the list of acts which constitute genocide punishable, but so too are conspiracy, incitement, attempt to commit and complicity in genocide. Under Article IV, all individuals, whatever their status, are personally responsible for committing genocide, which implies that the position taken in the judgement of the Nuremburg Tribunal that superior orders emanating from high-ranking state of officials is no defence applies within the context of the Convention.

Although Article VI of the Convention recognizes that an international tribunal with jurisdiction to try individuals who have committed genocide may be brought into existence by the parties at some future date, it none the less requires the competent tribunals of the contracting states to adopt jurisdiction over the offence in the meantime if the crime is committed within their territories. Subsequent events have also made it clear that genocide is a crime over which the courts of all states are competent to exercise their jurisdiction wherever and by whomsoever the crime was committed. Thus, genocide is said to be a crime under international law which attracts universal jurisdiction, and a norm of *ius cogens*. Support for this view can be found in the Reservations to the Genocide Convention Case, the Barcelona Traction Case, statements of the International Law Commission and in the practice of a considerable number of states which have given legislative effect to the Convention.

Racial Discrimination: The elimination of all forms of discrimination has been one of the major objectives of the UN since its inception. The Charter, the institutions created under the Charter and the International Bill of Rights all have as a predominant theme the equality of treatment of all human beings., It is therefore not surprising that various institutions of the UN have devoted considerable energy to drafting instruments designed to combat the most pervasive of all kinds of discrimination- racial and sexual discrimination.

The first treaty to deal specifically with racial discrimination was the International Convention on the Elimination of All Forms of Racial Discrimination, which was adopted by the General Assembly in 1965 and entered into force in 1969. The Convention both condemns and prohibits racial discrimination, which is defined by Article 1(1) as:

> ... any distinction, restriction or preference based on race, colour, descent or national or ethnic origin which has the purpose or effect of nullifying or impairing the recognition, enjoyment or exercise, on an, equal footing, of human rights and fundamental freedoms in the political, economic, social, cultural or any other field of public life.

In its advisory opinion in the 1971 Namibia Case, the ICJ held that this definition was authoritative for the purposes of interpreting the non-discrimination provisions of the UN Charter. It might be argued that in view of its widespread acceptance, the definition also forms part of *ius cogens*. It should be noted that under Article 2(2), affirmative action programmes are not prohibited by the Convention, although they are clearly limited in time until the objectives for which they were introduced have been achieved.

States parties are under obligation by Article 2(1) to take 'all appropriate means' to eliminate racial discrimination within their territory and to ensure that all civil, political, economic and social rights are accorded without discrimination. In order to supervise the Convention, a Committee on the Elimination of Racial Discrimination (CERD) consisting of 18 independent experts elected by the states parties is created by Article 8. The main method of supervision is a system of periodic reporting by the states parties similar to that under the International Covenants, but the Convention also provides for a right of individual communication where states have recognized the competence of CERD to receive such communications. As under the ICCPR First Optional Protocol, complainants must have exhausted all local remedies before their commendation may be considered. Once admitted, CERD considers the complaint and may make recommendations to the state party and individual concerned. Although the Convention provide in Article 22 for the compulsory jurisdiction of the ICJ in case of unresolved disputes between state parties, the majority of states have entered reservations to this, effectively rendering nugatory this important provision.

One of the most important challenges to international human rights law in recent years has been South Africa's institutionalized policy of racial discrimination and segregation known as 'apartheid'. While this policy has been subject to constant condemnation by a number of UN organs concerned with human rights, it was not until 1973 that the UN General Assembly adopted the International Convention on the Suppression and Punishment of the Crime of Apartheid. The Convention entered into force in 1976.

Apartheid, which is declared by Article 1 of the Convention to be a crime against humanity, thus placing it on an equal footing with genocide, is defined by reference to 'similar policies and practices of racial segregation and discrimination as practised in southern [sic] Africa. Like the Genocide Convention, the Apartheid Convention then provides a broad definition supplemented by a list of particular practices. Thus, the crime of apartheid applies to acts which are 'committed for the purpose of establishing and maintaining domination by one racial group of persons over any other racial group'. These acts include murder infliction of serious mental and physical harm, arbitrary arrest and illegal imprisonment and the deliberate imposition of living conditions calculated to cause the physical destruction of racial groups in whole or in part. The crime of apartheid is also committed by those who incite, conspire, aid, abet or encourage its commission. In the absence of any international penal tribunal, states parties are to take jurisdiction over the prosecution and punishment of the crime.

Supervision of the Convention is undertaken by the submission of periodic reports by the states parties on the progress achieved to a group of three members of the CHR nominated by the Chairman of the Commission. This group of three must also be representatives of the states parties to the Convention as well as members of the CHR. The Convention also empowers the Commission to prepare studies and reports on apartheid and to prepare lists of individuals, organizations, institutions and representatives of states that are alleged to be guilty of crime. These reports and lists have been made available to the General Assembly via ECOSOC.

Sexual Discrimination: As indicated above, the UN and its organ have undertaken a substantial amount of work in standard setting and taking measures to prohibit discrimination based on sex. The Convention on the Elimination of All Forms of Discrimination Against Women, which was adopted by the General Assembly in 1979 and which entered into force in 1981, comprise together with the International Covenants one of the major instruments in field. Article 1 of the Convention defines 'discrimination against women' as 'any distinction, exclusion or restriction made on the basis of sex which has the effect or purpose of impairing or nullifying the recognition, enjoyment or exercise of women... of human rights and fundamental freedoms in the political, economic, social, cultural, civil or any other field'. State parties are not only required to eliminate such discrimination, but under Article 2 are also required to initiate measures to promote equality of women with men in their social, public, and political life.

Article 5(a) in particular requires state parties to take 'all appropriate measures to modify the social and cultural patterns of conduct of men and women, with a view to achieving the elimination of prejudices and customary and all other practice which are based on the idea of the inferiority or the superiority of either of the sex or on stereotyped roles for men and women'. Despite the large number of states which are party to this Convention, this particular obligation remains more honoured in its breach than in its observance.

As with other UN-sponsored conventions, this Convention is supervised by requiring states parties to submit periodic reports on the measures adopted to give effect to the Convention's provisions. The reports are studied by a 28-member Committee on the Elimination of Discrimination Against Women elected by the parties, but who serve in an independent capacity. Observations on the reports studied by the Committee are sent to the Commission on the Status of Women, which then forwards its observations to the General Assembly via ECOSOC. Under Article 29(a), there is provisions for the resolutions of disputes between the parties by the ICJ, but with other UN conventions in which a similar provision exists, no recourse has yet been had to this procedure.

Torture: A glimpse at either Amnesty International's annual reports or the US Senate's country reports on human rights practices will confirm that torture remains endemic in modern world. It is used by governments not only to obtain information from suspected political opponents, but also to oppress their populations. Although both the Universal Declaration and the ICCPR contain prohibitions on torture, inhuman and degrading treatment, these concepts are nowhere defined within those instruments. The UN Convention Against Torture and Order Cruel, Inhuman or Degrading Treatment, which was adopted by the General Assembly in 1984 and which entered into force in 1987, not only seeks to remedy to this omission, but also provides a supervision mechanism.

There are undoubtedly problems in defining what

constitutes torture. It can be approached from a subjective point of view, which is inherently difficult to measure, or it can be defined objectively. The Torture Convention takes the latter approach. Article 1(1) of the Convention defined torture as:

> ...any act by which severe pain or suffering, whether physical or mental, is intentionally inflicted on a person for such purposes as obtaining from him or a third person information or a confession, punishing him for act he or a third person has committed or is suspected of having committed, or intimidating or coercing him or a third person, or for any reason based on discrimination of any kind, when such pain or suffering is inflicted by or at the instigation of or with the consent or acquiescence of a public official.

Torture does not, however, include pain or suffering 'arising only from, inherent in or incidental to lawful sanction'. This definition is replete with difficulties, not least of which is what is severe pain or suffering? None the less, Article 2 of the Convention makes it clear that there are no exceptional circumstances which will ever justify torture, nor may a torturer ever plead superior orders as a defence to the commission of such an act. If a person is alleged to have committed torture in any state, the state party within whose jurisdiction that person is found is under an obligation either to try or extradite him or her to a requesting state. States parties are also obliged to keep their interrogation rules instructions and methods under review as a means of preventing torture.

Supervision of the Torture Convention is by a ten-person Committee Torture which is elected by the state parties but whose members serve in their individual capacities. The methods of supervision under the Convention are a periodic reporting system (Article 19), an optional interstate complaint procedure (Article 21) and a right of individual petition which is also optional and depends upon state acceptance (Article 22). These by now familiar supervisory mechanisms are supplemented in the Torture Convention by an innovation which allows the Committee to investigate a state party on its own initiative when it receives reliable information that suggests that Torture is being systematically practised in the territory of that state party. Such an inquiry is to be confidential and Article 20 requires the Committee to seek the cooperation of the state party under investigation. If such cooperation is not forthcoming, it would seem that the Committee may nevertheless proceed with its inquiry. What is clear, however, is if the Committee wishes to conduct an investigation within the territory of a state party, it must be granted permission, otherwise the state party's sovereignty would be violated. As with the Committee's other supervisory functions, reference is made to the proceeding in its annual report which is submitted both to the state parties and the General Assembly. A state party which does not with itself desire to be bound by the inquiry procedure must make a declaration to this effect at the time of becoming party to the Convention. This is also unusual, since treaties generally require state to 'opt in' to rather than to 'opt out' of international supervisory systems. Disputes between states parties may also be referred under Article 30 to the ICJ for adjudication, but states may avoid this obligation by entering a timely reservation.

Children: While it might have been thought that the rights of the child were adequately protected by existing human rights instruments, particularly the ICCPR, it was nevertheless agreed in 1979, the Year of the Child, that a working group of the CHR should draft a convention which would give effect to certain child-orientated rights. The UN Convention on the Rights of the Child was adopted by the General Assembly in 1989 and entered into force in 1990. In addition to the protection of a number of traditional civil, political, economic and social rights, the Convention includes certain rights which apply to the child alone, a child being defined by Article 2 for these purposes as 'every human being below the age of 18 years unless, under the law applicable to the child, majority is attained earlier'. Among the 'new' right protected are the right to a name, the right to know and be cared for by his or her parents, the preservation of the child's identity, freedom from sexual abuse and exploitation, narcotic drugs and traffic in. A number of provisions also place obligations on states parties to ensure, by the adoption of appropriate measures, that children will be allowed to develop to their maximum potential.

Supervision under the Convention is by a ten-member Committee on the Rights of the Child. The member of the Committee are to be drawn from the state parties and they serve in their individual capacities. As with other UN treaties, supervision is by a system of periodic reports submitted by the state parties which are studied by the Committee. Under Article 45 of the Convention, the Committee is obliged to forward a biannual report of its activities to the General Assembly via ECOSOC. It is also interesting to note that UNICEF and other competent UN organs are entitled to participate in considering the implementation of the obligations under the Convention. As yet, it is too early to speculate on the likely effectiveness of this particular instrument, but it clearly has the effect of strengthening UN institutional cooperation and supervision in this particular area.

EIGHT

Scene in Americas

Of all the regions in the world, it is perhaps the Americas, sometimes known as the Western Hemisphere, which manifests the greatest divergence in political, economic and social development. It includes not only the wealthy countries of the north, but also the predominantly impoverished state of the Caribbean and Central and Latin America. The northern states, the USA and Canada, are characterized by the longevity and stability of their democratic political state structure and their fundamentally sound domestic system of human rights protection, while certain states lying to the south have been wrecked by frequent violent changes in totalitarian forms of government, the fragility of their economic and social system and their abject failure in protecting human rights. Indeed, the names of certain of these states have become bywords for some of the worst human rights abuses in recent years. Chile, Argentina, Uruguay, Guatemala and El Salvador are countries in which some of the worst excesses of the last decade have been perpetrated by government against their own civilian populations using military units and private; death squads. Disappearances, torture, arbitrary detention and extra judicial executions have been the hallmarks of certain American regimes. It is also ironic to note that, in most of these states, apart from periodic declarations of states of emergency, siege or exception, to use the various terminology, sophisticated constitutional mechanisms for human rights protection were in the place and technically capable of all utilization by individuals. Yet the remedies of *habeas corpus* and *amparo* (a remedy guaranteeing protection of constitutional rights) proved to be entirely illusory, demonstrating the truism that human rights instruments and legal remedies are of little immediate utility in the absence of appropriate political and social conditions for securing their observance. None the less, as a period of democracy emerges in a number—but by no means all—Central and Latin American states, the debt owed to human rights ideology and activism becomes apparent. The strengthening of democratic institutions based on respect for human rights and the rule of law has become a priority of newly elected regimes as a means of reinforcing their democratic base. It is the purpose of this chapter to examine the structure and processes of the inter-American human rights system in order to assess how it helps to underpin this process.

Inter-American System

The inter-American system for the protection of human rights has evolved within the framework of the Organization of American States (OAS). This is an inter-governmental organization that was founded in 1948 and which is defined as a 'regional agency' within the meaning of Article 52 of the UN Charter. In most respects, the objectives and the institutional structure of the OAS mirror those of the global UN organization. Thus, the OAS Charter is concerned with establishing systems for the peaceful settlement of disputes among its members and undertaking regional enforcement action where this is necessary. It is also concerned with the promotion of social and economic development and the promotion and protection of human rights. The work of the OAS is carried out through a number of institutions which, again, mirror those of the UN. The General Assembly is the plenary organ having general competence to oversee the totality of the organization's activities, while the Permanent Council is the analogue to the UN Security Council and serves as the executive organ of the OAS in permanent session having competence to deal with matters of peace and security. There is also an Inter-American Commission on Human Rights, which, as we shall see, has a dual status and general competence in the field of human rights under both the Charter and the American Convention on Human Rights (ACHR).

The inter-American human rights system is distinctive as it has its origins in two separate but substantially interrelated legal instruments. First, part of the system has developed within the context of the Charter itself. All member states have assumed human rights obligations under the Charter simply by becoming members of the Organization. Second, some states have also voluntarily assumed human rights obligations under the ACHR and its Additional Protocol by becoming parties to those instruments. The two parts of the system, however, share a common institution in the Inter-American Commission on Human Rights, although it operates under different procedures depending upon whether it is acting as a Charter or ACHR institution. The Inter-American Court of Human Rights, which was created by the Convention, also has certain advisory competence relating to the human rights provision of the Charter. Furthermore, the normative standards developed under the Charter system and those of the ACHR are capable of overlapping with, and influencing the developments of , each other. Clearly, this does not make the process of explication easy, and perhaps the best way of analysing the system is by examining the two strands of human rights protection separately and noting, where appropriate, their points of convergence and interaction..

Charter System: The regime for the protection of human rights under the OAS Charter has undergone a number of important changes since its entry into force in 1951. The historical evolution of these changes will be considered in this section.

Under the original Charter Article 3(j), now Article 5 (j) the member states proclaimed 'the fundamental rights of the individual without distinction as to race, nationality, creed or sex'. Article 13, now Article 16, further provided that each state in exercising its right to develop its cultural, political and economic life was obliged to 'respect the rights of the individual and the principles of universal morality'. Nowhere, however did the Charter define or elaborate what was partially remedied at the same Bogota Conference at which the Charter was adopted by the passing of a resolution entitled the American Declaration of the Rights and Duties of Man. The Declaration contains a list of civil and political, and economic and social, rights. It also contains a number of duties setting out an individual's obligations to the society in which he or she lives. Like its UN counterpart, which it pre-dated and to which it is similar in many respects, the American Declaration was a simple conference resolution of the organization and was not intended to be legally binding per se nor by incorporation into the Charter system. This, however, is no longer the case. The American Declaration has acquired the status of an authoritative interpretation of the references to human rights within the Charter. How it has assumed this status can only be understood by reference to the institutional development of the Inter-American Commission on Human Rights under the Charter.

Inter American Commission: At the Fifth Meeting of Consultation of Ministers of Foreign Affairs of the OAS in Santiago, Chile in 1959, a resolution was adopted by which the Permanent Council was required to establish in Inter-American Commission on Human Rights charged with the mandate of promoting respect for human rights. The Statute of the seven-person Commission, which was adopted by the Permanent Council in 1960, described it as an 'autonomous entity' of the OAS. This appeared to mean that, being a creature of a resolution, the Commission had no precise legal status as an institution under the Charter. In fulfilling its obligations to promote human rights, Article 2 of the Commission's Statute declared: 'For the purposes of the present Statute, human rights are understood to be the rights set forth in the American Declaration of the Rights and Duties of Man.'

Although under Article 9 of its Statute the Commission

was limited to advisory and recommendatory functions, nevertheless it decided, through a process of auto-interpretation of its constituent instrument, that it had power to make specific recommendations on human rights violations to member states and to undertake studies and make reports on human rights situations in states where large-scale violations were alleged to have taken place. Despite the receipt of a large number of individual communications from persons alleging violations of human rights, the Commission decided that it had no competence to take cognisance of, nor act upon such information. This lack of competence was, however, remedied at a Second Special Inter-American Conference at Rio de Janeiro in Brazil in 1965, when a resolution added Article 9 (bis) to the Commission's Statute. This new provision empowered it to receive communications from individuals alleging, violation of certain specified rights, to seek information on the individual communications and to make recommendations to state in respect of them. The rights of which the Commission was mandated to take particular note in receiving such communications were Articles I (right to life, liberty and security of the person), II (right to equality before the law), III (right to religious freedom and worship), IV (right to freedom of investigation, opinion, expression and dissemination of opinions), XVIII (right to a fair trial), XXV (right to protection from arbitrary arrest) and XXVI (right to due process of law).

Despite its weak constitutional foundations, the Commission was able to fashion a remarkably effective system of protection on the basis of its Statute. As well as dealing with a large number of individual communications and making recommendations to concerned member states thereon, it performed a large number of country studies to investigate allegations of widespread human rights abuses. In making its country studies the Commission established the practice of requesting permission from the state involved to conduct on-site investigations, to review documentation, to visit government institutions such as prisons and to interview authors of communications and government personnel. This was often facilitated by conducting meetings of the full Commission in the territories of the states where widespread violations had been alleged.

In 1970, following an amendment to the Charter by the Protocol of Buenos Aires, the Commission was transformed by Article 51 (e) into an organ of the OAS. A new Article 112 clearly stated the Commission's functions under the Charter. These were 'to promote the observance and protection of human rights and to serve as a consultative organ of the Organization in these matters'. Article 112 also provided, however, that the structure, competence and procedure of the Commission would be determined by, as at that time, a nonexistent American convention on human rights. Until such a convention entered into force, Article 150 provided that the 'present Inter-American Commission on Human Rights shall keep vigilance over the observance of human rights'. This led some commentators to speculate that there might be two Commissions when the ACHR came into being – a Commission for the Charter and a Commission for the Convention. The Commission's new Statute, which was adopted in 1979 when the ACHR entered into force, made it clear, however, that there would be a single Commission with separate procedure under the Charter and the Convention. Article 1(2) of the Commission's Statute therefore provided that:

For the purposes of the present Statute, human rights are understood to be:

(a) The rights set forth in the American Convention on Human Rights in relation to the State Parties thereto;

(b) The rights set forth in the American Declaration of the rights and Duties of Man.

Thus, all member states of the OAS who were not parties to the ACHR continued to be bound by the human rights standards established by the Charter. Furthermore, the mechanisms established by the Commission as a charter institution were specifically preserved. The overall effects of the amendments to the Charter in 1970 were to institutionalize not only the Commission's procedures under Article 9 and 9(bis) but also to confer through the process of incorporations a normative status upon the hitherto non-binding Declaration. What, however, is the status of the Declaration under the Charter? This question has been addressed on two occasions: first, by the Commission itself and, second by the Inter-American Court in an advisory opinion.

The Commission in the 'Baby Boy' case was called upon by a United States NGO, Catholics for Christian Political Action (CCPA), to rule that the abortion of a male foetus by a doctor in Massachusetts violated the right to life of the 'baby boy' which was protected by Article I of the Declaration. The abortion had taken place following liberalizing decisions of the American Supreme Court in Roe v Wade and Doe v Bolton and was not therefore an offence in the USA. Before the Commission could consider the merits of the application, it had to determine whether the case was admissible. This in turn depended upon whether or not the USA was bound by any human rights obligations under the Charter. The Commission held that the USA was so bound. Its reasoning was that as a consequence of Article 3(j) and 16, which obligate member states to respect human rights, and the incorporation of the Commission and its Statute into a Charter system, the American Declaration had acquired 'binding force'. This seems to suggest that the Declaration had taken on a treaty-like quality and provided legally binding obligations for all OAS member states to adhere to the standards established by the Declaration. This view, however, was not espoused by the Court in a request by Colombia by an advisory opinion upon whether the Declaration was a 'treaty concerning the protection of human rights in the American States' within the meaning of Article 64(1) of the American Convention. Here, the Court ruled that while the Declaration was not a treaty within the meaning of Article 2(1)(a) of the Vienna Convention on the Law of Treaties, none the less it constituted an authoritative interpretation of the human rights provisions of the Charter. The Court said:

> ... it may be said that the means of an authoritative interpretation, the members state of the Organization have signalled their agreement that the Declaration contains and defines the fundamental human rights referred to in the Charter. Thus the Charter of the Organization cannot be interpreted and applied as far as human rights are organs of the OAS, to the corresponding provisions of the Declaration.

The Court further observed that Article 1(2)(b) and 20 (which replaced Article 9 and 9(bis) of the Commission's Statute made it clear that the Declaration was a 'source of international obligation related to the Charter of the Organization'. While this language is not particularly clear, it would nevertheless seem to indicate that the Declaration, as an authoritative interpretation of the Charter, creates a legally binding standard for all member states of the OAS. Article 29(d) of the ACHR also supports the view that the Declaration is intended to have legal effects since this provides:

> No provision of this Convention shall be interpreted as
>
> (e) excluding or limiting the effect that the American Declaration... and other international acts of the same nature may have.

It would therefore seem that the American Declaration has since its adoption in 1948 acquired a potent status within the Charter system. It is now without doubt that nearly every state in the Western Hemisphere is legally bound to adhere to the human rights standards established by the Declaration. In its submissions to the Court in the Interpretation of the American Declaration Case, the USA argued that it was undesirable to translate the Declaration into a legally binding obligation since this not only jeopardized a fundamental aspect of treaty law, namely that states can only be bound by their consent, but also because it would be impossible to determine the precise content of the exiguously stated rights in the

Declaration. This objection is not, however, insuperable simply because both the Commission and the Court, exercising its advisory jurisdiction with respect to the Charter, are competent to interpret the extent to the rights in question. This point should not be lost on the USA, whose own Bill of Rights is composed of bare declarations of rights which must be interpreted by its own competent institution, the Supreme Court.

Commission under the Charter: As we saw above, the Commission fulfils a number of functions under the Charter. These might be classified as promotional, advisory, consultative and protective. The Commission serves as the organ of consultation in the field of human rights for the General Assembly of the OAS, it has drafted a number of human rights instruments, including the American Convention and its Protocol of San Salvador, and it has been employed by the OAS to mediate in a number of situations, perhaps the most notorious being when armed conflict broke out between Honduras and El Salvador following a highly charged international soccer match. It is, however, in the performance of its protective function that the Commission might be observed operating most effectively under the Charter. Here, a distinction may be made between the Commission's country studies and on-site investigation procedures, on the one hand and its individual petition system, on the other. These will be examined in turn.

On-site Investigations: Like the UN Commission on Human Rights, the Inter-American Commission, when it was first established by resolution in 1960, received a large number of individual communications claiming human rights violations by OAS member states. Also, like the UN Commission, the Inter-American Commission had no legal competence to act on these individual applications, but could not only deal with them in accordance with its general mandate under Article 9 of its Statute. It therefore utilized the individual communications as evidence in attempting to determine the state of human rights in the member state against which they were addressed. Where a large number of communications were received, the Commission would decide to initiate a country study in order to investigate fully the position in the state in question. Where possible, the Commission undertook the investigation in the territory of the state concerned. This it was empowered to do by its Statute, but since the sovereignty of the state under investigation was at issue, the Commission could only convene in the territory of the state with its consent.

The Commission's first country studies dealing with Cuba, Haiti and the Dominican Republic were prepared in the early 1960s. While Cuba and Haiti were not prepared to allow the Commission to enter their territory, the Dominican Republic granted it permission to carry out its work on-site. These first three studies enabled the Commission to established its modus operandi. It heard witnesses, interviewed government officials and, in the case of the Dominican Republic, visited official institutions and interviewed opposition and community leaders. The practices employed in the Dominican Republic on-site investigation have been followed in subsequent country studies in Argentina, Nicaragua, Guatemala, El Salvador and Surinam.

Once a state has agreed to allow the Commission to conduct an on-site investigation, its obligations are set out in detail in Articles 55-59 of the Commission's Regulations. It is required to place all the facilities necessary for the execution of the Commission's task at its disposal. The members of the Commission are to be allowed to travel freely throughout the state's territory, and the state must ensure the safety of Commission members during their stay and their travels in the country. The state is also obliged to allow the Commission to interview any person requested, and must undertake not to retaliate against individuals who supply information to it. Such on-site investigations are undertaken by a Special Commission convened in accordance with Article 56 of the Commission's Regulations, which precludes nationals or residents of the state under investigation from serving with the Commission in order to prevent a conflict of interests.

On-site investigations have been a particularly useful device. They not only allow the Commission to obtain fuller information about the state of affairs in the country being studied, but they also allow it to corroborate by direct observation allegations made by individuals. Two of the most graphic accounts to the latter are to be found in the El Salvador and Argentina reports. In the former report, the Commission was able to verify the existence of torture chambers used by the armed forces, and in the latter the Special Commission actually discovered the existence of a number of desaparedos in a jail in the northern Argentinian city of Cordoba. Furthermore, as Buergenthal points out, the very presence of the Commission in a state may ameliorate the human rights situation there. Here, he cites the example of the Dominican Republic's civil war in 1965 when the Commission was able to save hundreds of lives and secured the release from prison of large numbers of political detainees.

In preparing country reports, the Commission adopts a three-stage procedure. First, it produces a draft report based on all the evidence it has assembled. Second, the draft report is then submitted to the government of the state concerned for its comments. If the government's comments are considered well-founded by the Commission, it will amend the report to take account of them. Third, the Commission must take a decision whether or not to publish the report. Article 62 of the Commission's Regulations requires it to publish the report if a state has not responded to the request for observations on the draft, but more recently the Commission has decided to publish reports together with the government's observations in full. The Commission may also transmit the report to the OAS General Assembly for consideration. Originally, the General Assembly simply noted receipt of the country reports, but in 1975 it charged its practice by debating fully the report of the Commission on the situation of human rights in Pinochet's Chile and adopting a resolution on the issue calling on Chile to comply with its obligations. Since then, the General Assembly has debated to a greater or lesser degree a number of country reports and the Commission's annual reports. The publicity which attends the Commission's publication of its reports and the debates upon them in the General Assembly is one of the more potent 'sanctions' available within the inter-American system. Governments, for the most part, dislike being castigated as delinquents and, furthermore, an adverse human rights record may affect other aspects of international relations such as defence, trade or foreign aid. The US Senate, for example, is obliged by law to withhold military and economic aid from a state which attracts an adverse report on human rights from the State Department. Of course, when one reaches the realms of political sanctions, such as a condemnatory resolution of the OAS General Assembly, the weightiness of the response is likely to depend on the political complexion of the body itself. During Latin America's 'totalitarian phase' of the 1970s, condemnation of certain events was difficult to achieve. It is easier to attract such condemnation in that region's current 'democratic phase'.

Individual Petitions: As we saw above, the Commission, following amendment of its Statute at Rio de Janeiro in 1965, was entitled to receive and act upon individual communications under Article 9(bis). When, however, the ACHR entered into force in 1979, control of this function was transferred to Article 20 of the Commission's new Statute. Although Article 20 reiterates the list of Declaration rights to which the Commission is obliged to pay particular attention, its Regulations none the less make it clear that it is able to deal with the violation of any rights contained in the instrument, including the economic and social rights.

The procedure of the Commission concerning the admissibility of communications under the Charter is the same as that for admissibility under the Convention. The difference in treatment of the two types of communications lies at the post-admissibility stage, and this will be the main focus here. The requirements for admissibility will be dealt with in detail in the section on the procedures under the ACHR. Suffice it to say at this point that applicants must have exhausted all local remedies and their applications must be timely and well-founded. Once admitted, the Commission investigates the communication by utilizing all information at its disposal, including the observations of the state which is invited to comment on the allegations. Having completed the investigatory stage of its proceedings, the Commission then compiles a final decision which comprises a statement of facts, the Commission's findings or conclusions and, where appropriate, recommendations to the state concerned. Again the 'sanction' on a state which fails to implement the Commission's recommendation is that of publicity, since the Commission is at liberty to publish the final decision in its annual report to the OAS General Assembly. Unlike the case of country reports, however, the General Assembly has generally not shown itself to be particularly concerned with the question of individual communications. Cynics might argue that this is because there is little political mileage to be made out of isolated cases of human rights abuse.

Clearly, while', the possibility of individual communication under the Charter represents an important step forward in terms of international and regional human rights protection, the system is none the less defective in a number of ways. First, there is no possibility—as there is under the Convention—of the Commission securing a friendly settlement between the state and the aggrieved individual. Second, the 'final decisions' of the Commission are not legally binding, although of course the 'sanction' of publicity may have some deterrent force or corrective utility where serious human rights violations are concerned. Third, the Court has no role to play within the individual application procedure under the Charter system, and therefore there is no possibility of legally binding judicial determination of the issues. Finally, there is no provision for the award of monetary compensation for individual victims.

American Convention

The American Convention on Human Rights, also known as the Pact of San Jose, and its Protocol of San Salvador on Economic, Social and Cultural Rights comprise the second part of the inter-American human rights system. The ACHR was adopted at a special inter-governmental conference at San Jose, Costa Rica in 1969 and entered into force in July 1978. The more recent Protocol was approved by the states parties to the ACHR on 14 November 1988 and was subsequently confirmed by the General Assembly of the OAS as its eighteenth regular session in San Salvador, El Salvador.

The format of the ACHR and its institutional structure is similar to that of the European Convention on Human Rights and Fundamental Freedoms of 1950, but it is apparent that the drafters of the American Convention drew on the accumulated experience under the European Convention and thereby managed to avoid some of its defects. The European Convention was not, however, the only source of inspiration for the drafters of the American Convention, who also drew on the ICCPR and, more particularly, the American Declaration. Similarly, the Protocol to the ACHR draws upon both the American Declaration and the IECSCR, but has novel elements both in the rights protected and in the mechanisms for enforcement of those rights.

Both the ACHR and its Protocol contain the traditional range of civil and political, and economic and social, rights, although it is clear that a number of the rights in both the Convention and Protocol are drafted in much broader terms than those in analogous instruments. As in other international human rights treaties, the dichotomy between the two broad groups of rights is identifiable. The civil and political rights are expressed in absolute and immediate terms, whereas the economic and social rights are framed in exhortatory terms and are to be implemented progressively. Article 1(1) of the ACHR requires state parties to 'respect the rights and freedoms recognized' and to 'ensure to all persons subject to their jurisdiction the free and full exercise of those rights and freedoms...', while Article I of the Protocol simply demands that states parties take appropriate measures 'for the purpose of achieving progressively... the full observance of the rights recognized in the Protocol'.

Article 27(1) of the Convention permits states to take measures derogating from their obligations 'in time of war, public danger, or other emergency that threatens the independence or security of a state party ...to the extent and period of time strictly required by the exigencies of the situation...'. Such measures must not, however, be discriminatory, and certain rights are classified as non-derogable in any circumstances. The ACHR further states that the judicial remedies essential for the protection of the non-derogable rights may not be suspended. The Court in an advisory opinion given; at the request of the Commission, declared that this meant that the remedies of *habeas corpus* and *amparo* could never be suspended where they related to such non-derogable rights. Under Article 27(3), all derogations, the reasons for which they were taken and the period for which they are adopted, must be communicated to the other member states of the OAS by informing the Secretary-General.

The institutional structure of the American Convention: Like the ECHR, the American Convention establishes two organs to supervise the implementation and enforcement of the rights contained within it: the Commission and the Court.

The Commission: Under Article 34 of the ACHR, as under the Charter, the Commission is composed of seven members who are required to be nationals of an OAS member state and persons of 'high moral character; and competence in the field of human rights'. The Commission members serve for a period of four years in an independent capacity. As a Convention institution, the Commission's many roles are defined by Article 41. Briefly stated they are educational, investigative, advisory, administrative and supervisory. These tasks are complementary and mutually supporting, and permit the

Commission to oversee the totality of human rights activities in the states parties to the ACHR.

The Court: The Court is also composed of seven members who are required to be nationals of OAS member state. They are elected in an individual capacity for a period of six years from among 'jurists of the highest moral authority and of recognized competence in the field of human rights, who possess the qualifications required for the exercise of the highest judicial functions...'. The Court has two forms of jurisdiction: contentious and advisory. Under Article 62, states must accept the Court's contentious jurisdiction either unconditionally, conditionally, or in specific cases. The Court's advisory jurisdiction, as we shall see below, may be used by any member state of the OAS without prior acceptance.

The Complaint Machinery

There are two categories of complaints which may be made under the Convention. The first is complaints by persons denouncing violations of the Convention by a state party under Article 44 of the ACHR. The second is complaints by state parties that another state party has violated the human rights protected by the Convention under Article 45. In analysing Article 44, two important points should be noted. First, all states which become party to the ACHR automatically should recognize the competence of the Commission to receive complaints from persons alleging violation of their rights. This differs from Article 25 of the ECHR, which as we have already seen, requires a declaration by a state party that it recognizes the competence of the Europe and Commission to receive communications. Indeed, the Court itself in Viviana Gallarclo described the American Convention as 'unique' human rights instruments in making the right of private petition applicable against states parties as soon as they ratify the Convention. Second, while under Article 25 of ECHR only 'victims' may author communications, under Article 44 of the ACHR:

> Any person or group of persons, or any non-governmental entity legally recognized in one or more member states of the Organization, may lodge petitions with the Commission containing denunciations or complaints of violation of this Convention by a State Party.

This is clearly drafted in wide terms and avoids the problem encountered by the European Commission in determining whether petitions may be received from persons who are themselves not victims, but who are petitioning on behalf of alleged victims. Thus, it is clear that unlike the European Convention which does not permit an *actio popularis,* the American Convention does.

In considering the second, inter-state system of complaints, it is clear that while Article 24 of the ECHR makes inter-state complaints mandatory for state parties, the ACHR requires states wishing to allow such complaints to make a declaration to that effect under Article 45. Even then, complaints may only be instituted on a reciprocal basis. The reason for making inter-state complaints subject to an optional declaration under the ACHR probably derives from the political sensitivity which would inevitably accompany such action in a hemisphere with widely differing political systems. An inter-state petition system can, as the ECHR system demonstrates, be abused by states within to make political capital out of disputes over alleged human rights violations.

The procedure for the admissibility of an individual communication under Article 44 of an inter-state communication under Article 45 is contained in Articles 46 and 47 of the ACHR. Article 46 establishes four conditions which must be met for admissibility. These are:

1 It must be demonstrated that all remedies under domestic law have been exhausted in accordance with the generally recognized principles of international law (Article 46(1)(a)).
2 The petition or communication has been lodged within six months from the date on which the party

alleging violation of the rights was notified of the final judgment (Article 46(1)(b)).

3 The subject of the petition or communication must not be pending before another international proceeding for settlement. In the case of individual petitions, this effectively means the subject of the petition must not be under consideration by the HRC under the Optional protocol of the ICCPR (Article 46(1)(c)).

4 In the case of individual petitions, the petition must not be anonymous and must contain details of the nationality, profession, domicile and signature of the person or the legal representative of the person lodging the petition (Article 46(1)(d)).

It should be noted, however, that the first two conditions are not applicable if the domestic legislation of the state complained or does not afford due process for the protection of the allegedly violated rights or if the party alleging violation of the rights has been denied access to the remedies under domestic law or has been prevented from exhausting them. In the latter context, the Court has held that where an individual has been unable to secure legal representation because of a generalized fear in the legal community that representing certain clients will lead to state retribution, it is unnecessary to exhaust local remedies. This is a very real issue in a number of Central and Latin American states where lawyers may be unwilling or afraid to take on criminal defence cases because they are tainted with a 'political' element and may result in threats, maiming or death to them and their families. The court also held in the same case that where indigence may prevent an individual from securing legal representation in circumstances where an absence of representation might affect the right to a fair trial, the individual is not under an obligation to exhaust local remedies. Furthermore, under Article 46(2), if remedies are shown to be either inadequate or ineffective, individuals are not required to exhaust them. In addition, unwarranted tardiness by a local court in giving final judgment in cases where effective local remedies are available will also obviate the need to exhaust domestic remedies. If a state alleges that a complainant has not exhausted local remedies, the burden of proof is upon the state to demonstrate this.

When the Commission is satisfied that the conditions in Article 46 have been fulfilled, it then proceeds to consider whether any of the factors which are contained in Article 47 exist and thereby render a petition or communication inadmissible. Once again, Article 47 contains four grounds occasioning inadmissibility:

1 That any of the requirements in Article 46 have not, in fact, been met (Article 47(1)(a)).
2 That the petition or communication does not state facts which tend to establish a violation of the rights guaranteed by the Convention (Article 47(1)(b)).
3 That the statements of the petitioner or of the state indicate that the petition or communication is manifestly groundless or obviously out of order (Article 47(1)(c)).
4 That the petition or communication is substantially the same as one previously 'studied' by the Commission or other international organization (Article 47(I)(d)).

Once a petition or communication has been declared prima facie -admissible, the Commission then proceeds to its second stage. Here the Commission performs a number of parallel tasks under Article 48 of the ACHR. Its primary function is to obtain all the necessary evidence from the parties both in writing and during the course of oral proceedings. When it considers it 'necessary and advisable', the Commission may carry out an onsite investigation so as to verify the facts disclosed in the communication. Such an investigation depends, of course, on the consent of the state party in question. If, during the course of its proceedings in the second stage, the Commission becomes aware of facts which indicate that the petition or communication ought not to have been admitted in the first place, it may still declare them inadmissible. The procedure contained in Article 48 may, however, be expedited in serious and urgent cases. Here, only the formal requirements of admissibility, that is those contained in Articles 46 and 47, are required before the Commission is empowered to conduct an on-site investigation with the prior consent of the state in whose territory the alleged violation has been committed.

During the investigative process contained in Article 48, the Commission is also required to perform a conciliatory function. Article 48(1)(f) provides:

> The Commission shall place itself at the disposal of the parties concerned with the view to reaching a friendly settlement of the matter on the basis of respect for human rights recognized in this Convention.

If a friendly settlement is reached in accordance with this procedure, the Commission must draw up and transmit a report containing a brief statement of the facts and the solution reached to the Secretary-General of the OAS for publication. Where a friendly settlement is not achieved, the Commission must draw up a report under Article 50 stating the facts and its conclusions and transmit it to the state party concerned within 180 days. The Commission may make any proposal or recommendation which it sees fit to the state party, which is not at liberty to publish the report.

After transmission of the report to the concerned, a period of three months begins to run during which time the case may either be settled by the parties or submitted to the Court either by the Commission or the concerned state. If neither of those occur within the time limit, the Commission may set forth its opinion and conclusions on the issue, together with recommendations concerning the remedial measures which the state must take and time limit within which they must effected. After this time limit has expired, the Commission must decide by a majority of its members whether the delinquent state has taken adequate measures to remedy the breach, and also whether or not to publish its report.

From the foregoing it can be seen that the Commission has a broad discretion to decide whether or not to deal with an issue itself or to transmit it to the Court if, of course, the state concerned has accepted the Court's jurisdiction. There is no guidance in the ACHR or the Commission's Statute, Regulations or Rules of Procedure about when a contentious case should be disposed of by remitting it to the Court rather than by the other methods envisaged by Article 51 in its advisory opinion in Compulsory Membership, the Court's contentious jurisdiction. Here, the Court was requested by Costa Rica to give an advisory opinion on whether a Costa Rican law requiring those who wished to practise the profession of journalism to be members of an organization prescribed by law, conflicted with Articles 13 and 29 of the ACHR. Although submitted as a request for an advisory opinion, the case had its origins in an individual petition presented to the Commission by a US citizen, Stephen Schmidt, who had practised journalism without being a member of the specified organization and who had consequently been convicted and sentenced to three months imprisonment under Costa Rican law. Costa Rica won the case before the Commission, but neither the Commission nor Costa Rica decided at that stage to submit the case to the Court's contentious jurisdiction. The Court nevertheless considered that the Commission should have done so because the case raised controversial legal issues on which neither the domestic courts nor the Commission had been able to agree. Furthermore, the issue was of considerable importance to other states of the hemisphere since it had not been considered by the Court in the past.

While this decision is specific to the Compulsory Membership case, it seems that bearing these characteristics should be referred to the Court as a matter of course. It is also interesting to note that the state which is the object of a communication may also send the case to the Court within the three-month period. This is clearly a safeguard for any state that may wish to contest the validity of a decision reached by the Commission in its case. Like the European Convention, which as yet remains unamended by Protocol No. 9, individuals have no competence to seise the Court of a case.

Although proceedings before the Commission appear to be cumbersome and lengthy, it should be noted that the main objective of the procedure, like that of the European Commission, is the friendly settlement of the dispute between the complainant and the respondent state. There are two opportunities for this: first, during the Commission's investigatory procedure under Article 48 where it exercises its conciliatory function and, second, at the stage of its first report under Article 51 where the state party may simply comply with the recommendations made by the Commission.

Proceedings: As indicated above, under Article 62 contentious proceedings can only be initiated before the Court if the state party or states parties concerned have accepted its jurisdiction in such matters. Furthermore, proceedings cannot be initiated either by the Commission or a state party unless the procedures before the Commission have been fully completed. A state may not waive the Commission's procedures and take the matter directly to the Court. In Viviana Gallardo, Gallardo, suspected terrorist, was murdered in her prison cell by a member of the Costa Rican National Guard who had been instructed to guard her. Costa Rica attempted to bypass the Commission's procedures by waiving them and taking the substantive issues directly to the Court for determination. The Court held, however, that it lacked jurisdiction to hear the case in such circumstances, because first, on a literal interpretation of the relevant Convention provisions, it was clear that completion of the Commission's procedures were mandatory and not optional and, second as a matter of policy, the Commission's procedures had not been created solely for the benefit of states, but in order to allow victims to protect their rights. The main concern of the Court here was that if a state were permitted to take a case directly to the Court, this would circumvent the Commission's important conciliatory function and would thus distort the integrity of the Conventions' structure. None the less, the Court left open the question of whether certain categories of proceedings, particularly inter-state applications might not be taken directly to the Court. Here, the issue of individual rights protection might not be so acute and might not therefore affect the integrity of the Convention's structure.

Once a case has been properly referred to the Court, it has the competence to review the Commission's findings of fact and *law de novo*. Thus, the Court can determine whether or not an individual has properly complied with the procedural requirements, particularly the exhaustion of domestic remedies, before the Commission. In reviewing questions of fact, the Court may also have regard to whether or not the burden of proof has been adequately discharged. This issue has been dealt with by the Court in three cases against Honduras involving the enforced disappearance of a number of individuals. While the Court adopts the general principle of 'equality of arms' in international judicial proceedings, that is both parties stand on an equal footing, and that it is the responsibility of the party adducing a particular fact to prove that fact, it has also made a number of modifications in order to take account of the specific human rights context. In particular, it has noted that the standards of proof in such proceedings are far less formalistic and rigid than in domestic proceedings, and that in cases where states are uncooperative or have actively participated in the suppression of evidence about certain parties, substantial recourse may be had to circumstantial evidence and matters of inference. The Court has also made it abundantly clear that it does not see human rights proceedings as the international analogue of domestic criminal proceedings, since the main objective of such proceedings is to secure state compliance with its obligations and redress for any violations which may have occurred; it is not to punish the state.

In determining questions of evidence and proof, the Court may not only have regard to documentary evidence, but may also hear witnesses in person. States are under an obligation to facilitate the Court's access to such witnesses and are required not to take measure of reprisal against individuals who testify. While proceedings before the Court are normally held in public, it is possible for the Court to sit in closed session where the evidence of certain witnesses may touch upon matters of national security or be otherwise sensitive to the government in question. In fact, this occurred in Velasquez Rodriguez, where the head of Honduran national security was permitted to give evidence in camera.

A contentious case normally terminates with a judgement by the Court that there has or has not been a violation of one or more of the rights in the ACHR. The Court, however, enjoys a discretion to keep a case open in order to ensure effective supervision and enforcement of its judgment. Although a judgment of the Court is final and cannot be the subject of an appeal, it may, at the request of any of the parties, within ninety days of the communication of the judgment to them, be the subject to a request for interpretation. This has already occurred in Interpretation of Compensatory Damages, where the Court was requested to rule whether an award of damages made by it to the victim's next of kin in the Velasquez Rodriguez case inferred any obligation on the part of Honduras to index link the award to ensure that its value was maintained over a long period of time.

If a breach of the Convention is found, the delinquent state is under an obligation to ensure that the injured party enjoys the rights affected, and where appropriate, the circumstances which gave rise to the breach be remedied and fair compensation paid. States parties to the ACHR undertake to comply with the judgment of the Court in cases to which they are party, and therefore decisions of the Court are binding upon them. While the Court has not yet had an opportunity to rule on the question of positive measures to be taken in the event of a violation, it has been able to rule on the issue of compensatory damages.

In Velasaquez Rodriguez-Compensatory Damages, the Court was required to determine the amount of damages which should be awarded to the next of kin of Velaquez who had been disappeared by agents of the Honduran government. The Court took the view here that the objective of the damages was remedy in full the damage caused by the states delinquency. Honduras was required, as far as was possible, to put Velasquez's next to kin in the position which they would have enjoyed had it not been for the breach of the Convention. Thus, the next of kin were indemnified for Velasquez's loss of earnings throughout the remainder of his life, based on an assessment of his career prospects as a teacher and no actuarial principles. The Court also found in this case, however, that the state should compensate for the emotional and moral harm done to Velasquez's wife and children as a consequence of his disappearance and murder. This approach is different to the European Court, which has been reluctant to accept that emotional and moral damage can be quantified in any meaningful way.

In its judgment, the Court also determined how the damages were to be paid to the next of kin. A quarter of the sum was to be paid directly to Velasquez's wife, and the remainder was to be placed in trust for his children. It was this part of the judgment which prompted the Commission to request an interpretation of the judgment under Article 67 of the ACHR. Here, the Commission was concerned about the possible erosion of the children's damages by inflation unless the Court insisted that the award be index-linked. The Court, however, pointed out in Interpretation of Compensatory Damages that by placing a substantial portion of the damages in a trust fund—which was to be managed 'under the most favourable conditions'—implied that an element of indexing was already inherent to the award.

If the Court awards damages against a state, under Article 68(2) the state may, at its option, give effect to the judgment 'in accordance with the domestic procedure governing the execution of judgments against the state'. Although Costa Rica in its headquarters' agreement with the Court has provided that judgments of the Court will be enforced in that state as if they were judgments of local courts, this approach does not appear to be mandatory. The absence of a mandatory enforcement mechanism would seem to be a major gap in the Convention's protective system.

As far as execution of other parts of the Court's judgments is concerned, there is, similarly, no provision which deals with this matter directly. Article 65, however, provides that the Court, when making its annual report to the regular session of the OAS General Assembly, must specify cases in which a state has not complied with its ruling. The issue of noncompliance, therefore, is to be resolved essentially by political processes. Once again therefore, we see that the primary 'sanction' in this realm is that of political pressure and adverse publicity.

The judgments of the Court in contentious cases are in effect declaratory, since technically they are only binding upon the parties of the case in question. Nevertheless, it is clear that the Court's interpretation of the ACHR and the rights protected by it is authoritative and therefore its judgments have a greater practical significance than their formal status would appear to imply. While states which are not party to proceedings are obviously under obligation to comply with the judgment, a prudent state will recognize the authority of the Court's rulings and seek to bring its own laws into line with them. Furthermore, it is evident from the practice of the Court to date that it will, like the European Court, develop a jurisprudence *constante* or a practice of referring back to its own judgments in which it considers it has made a particularly important ruling on some legal principle arising from the Convention. In the absence of any system or precedent, this lends a degree of continuity and predictability to the Court's judgments.

Provisional Measures

One vitally important power of the Court which requires some comment is its ability to order provisional measures in order to deal with urgent situations. Article 63(2) provides:

> In cases of extreme gravity and urgency, and where necessary to avoid irreparable damage to persons, the Court shall adopt such provisional measures as its deems pertinent in matters it has under consideration. With respect to a case not yet submitted to the Court, it may act at the request of the Commission.

The operation of this provision was vividly demonstrated in the Honduran disappearance cases. Here, a number of witnesses who had either testified or were about to testify before the Court were assassinated. A number of other potential witnesses had also had their lives and property threatened. The Court therefore ordered two sets of provisional measures: one requiring Honduras to take measures to protect the witnesses and the second requiring the state to investigate the assassinations and to bring the perpetrators to justice.

Advisory Opinions

The advisory jurisdiction of the Inter-American Court is broader in space than that of any other international tribunal yet in existence, and compares favourably to the exceptionally narrow and technical advisory competence of the European Court of Human Rights under ECHR Protocol 2. Article 64 of the ACHR provides:

> 1 The member states of the [OAS] may consult the Court regarding the interpretation of the Convention or of any other treaties concerning the protection of human rights in American states. Within their spheres of competence, the organs listed in Chapter X of the Charter of the [OAS], as amended by the Protocol of Buenos Aires, may in the manner consult the Court.
>
> 2 The Court, at the request of a member of the [OAS], may provide that state with opinions regarding the

compatibility of any of its domestic laws with the aforesaid international instruments.

While there are a number of points to note about Article 64, perhaps the most salient is that it is not only the parties to the ACHR which have the power to request an opinion from the Court, but also any member state of the OAS whether they are parties to the Convention or not. Furthermore, these states are not only competent to request an interpretation of the instruments referred to in Article 64, but are entitled to ask the Court whether their domestic laws are compatible with such instruments. This gives the Court a jurisdiction reasonably similar to that of the Court of Justice of the EC under Article 177 of the EEC Treaty, and enhances the integrationist potential in this field. Such a conclusion may be further supported by reference to the fact that the Court may also render advisory opinions at the request of a wide variety of OAS organs. The only requirements which an OAS organ need to show in order to seek an advisory opinion are that the issues falls within its sphere of competence and that it has a 'legitimate institutional interest' in so doing. As the Court pointed out in Effect of Reservations, the Commission will, as a matter of principle, always be able to satisfy these requirements and will therefore always be competent to seek a ruling. By extension, it would seem that the OAS General Assembly will always fall into this category.

Since most of the Court's jurisprudence has been developed through the medium of its advisory jurisdiction, it has had considerable opportunity to interpret Article 64 and to define the limits of its application. Thus, the Court has declared that it has a discretion under Article 64 in deciding whether or not to offer an opinion in any given case. This enables it to deal with circumstances in which a request for an advisory opinion might be seen as an abuse of process. Such a potential abuse might occur, for example, where a request for an advisory opinion is, in reality, a disguised contentious case, since it deals with matters which are the subject of an actual dispute. However, even where a request for an advisory opinion deals with an ongoing dispute between identifiable parties, the Court will not necessarily refuse to exercise its jurisdiction if it considers that the opinion might achieve some useful purpose, such as assisting one of the OAS organs to fulfil its role under the Convention. Furthermore, the Court has interpreted a request to rule on the compatibility of a state's domestic law with its international human rights obligations, as including competence to rule on the compatibility to draft domestic laws. In seeking an advisory opinion on all these matters, the request must come from a competent governmental representative. The Court's view here seems to imply that it must be a member of the state's executive; a request from a state's legislature has been found to be inadequate.

Another question arising in the context of Article 64(1) has been the meaning of 'other treaties concerning the protection of human rights in the American states'. Here, the Court interpreted the phrase broadly to mean any treaty to which an OAS member state was party which affected the protection of human right in that state. The Court made it clear that the phrase was not restricted to human rights treaties concluded within the inter-American system. The Court thus empowered itself to interpret any other human rights treaty, such as the ICCPR, if it affected any OAS member. The objection that this might lead to differing interpretations of the same instrument by different human rights institutions, was discounted by the Court, which observed that the possibility of conflicting interpretation existed in all legal systems that were not hierarchically integrated. None the less, it is apparent that the Court will take into account authoritative interpretations of other instruments by the competent institutions, such as the Human Rights Committee, under those instruments.

Since these opinions of the Court are, by definition, advisory, technically they have no legal binding force. Nevertheless, if one examines the competence of the Court, which is to ensure the fulfilment of the commitments undertaken by the states parties and to interpret and apply the ACHR, it is apparent that the force of the Court's opinion's derive from its inherent authority. Clearly, if a state were to act in manner contrary to one of the Court's advisory opinions, it would be difficult to the conclusion that it had, in effect, breached its obligations, as interpreted by the Court, under the Convention.

Court's Techniques

The Court has begun to develop a significant jurisprudence under both its contentious, to a greater extent, its advisory jurisdiction. This has not only involved the interpretation of a number of substantive rights, but the Court has also made the most of its opportunities to develop certain principles of international human rights law which are applicable to the field in general. Before briefly examining some of the advances made by the Court in this area, it is appropriate to analyse its techniques of interpretation. In nearly all its judgments, the Court has declared that the laws appropriate for treaty interpretation are the rules contained in Articles 31 and 32 of the Vienna Convention on the Law or Treaties. Like its European counterpart, however, the Inter-American Court has not been constrained by narrow rules of textuality, but has, to a limited degree-given the relative paucity of decided cases-employed the principles of effectiveness and teleology. In a general sense, however, the Court has been guided by the proposition that the primary object and purpose of the ACHR is to guarantee and protect the rights of individuals. Its approach, therefore, has been to interpret the rights and guarantees in favour of individuals.

This view has also been reflected in the Court's approach to questions of general international human rights law. In particular, it has taken the view that modern human rights treaties are not simply multilateral treaties of the traditional type concluded to accomplish reciprocal exchanges of rights and obligations between the contracting parties, but that they are more in the nature of unilateral commitments made by states in order to ensure the protection of individual's rights. The practical consequences of such a view are that reservations to the ACHR cannot be interpreted in such a way as to limit the enjoyment of individual rights, nor may they be entered against a non-derogable right. This particular line of arguments has also brought the Court close to, but not actually to the point of, declaring that some of the rights in the ACHR and in the American Declaration are representative of *ius cogens*.

In the Honduran disappearances cases, the Court was required to deal with a phenomenon which was not referred to specifically in the ACHR. None the less, it was able to reduce the practice of disappearances to its central components. Thus, the Court found that disappearances violate the right of life (Article 4), the right to humane treatment (Article 5) and the right to personal liberty (Article 7). It was a feature of the Court's judgment in these cases, however, that it did not attempt to elaborate in detail the precise content of these rights. This was perhaps inevitable, since most of the cases were concerned with procedural issues and the proof of evidence. Once the Court had the evidence before it demonstrating that Honduras was responsible for the practice, it apparently felt that it needed to go no further in order to establish state liability.

In its advisory opinions, the Court has dealt with issues concerning the freedom of thought and expression in a case involving the compulsory licensing of journalists and the guaranteed right of reply to published injurious statements; the rights to nationality; and a number of cases involving derogations from, and limitations to, the rights protected by the Convention. Each of these cases is characterized by extremely careful;, well-elaborated judgments of the highest quality which all bear careful scrutiny. Although the Court is, in institutional terms, only in its infancy, it has already begun to make its mark as a human rights organ of considerable importance.

A final question which needs to be considered, however, is why there has not been greater use of the Court's contentious procedure in the last ten years. There is a stark incongruity between the level of human rights violations in the Eastern Hemisphere and the degree of the Court's utilization in individual cases. There are perhaps a number of reasons for this. The first is that the Court's contentious procedure suffers from the same drawbacks as other human rights institutions and procedures. The primary obstacle here is that of state sovereignty. States are notoriously unwilling to submit to international adjudication of any form, preferring instead to operate through the medium of diplomatic and political fora. Within the inter-American context, there could, until recently, be seen to be a general reluctance on the part of states to accept the compulsory jurisdiction of the Court. State resistance to compulsory jurisdiction in the current democratic phase seems to be lessening.

A second major obstacle to the Court's use is that the socio-economic climate in the Western Hemisphere has not generally been conducive to human rights protection. High levels of poverty and lack of education coupled with widespread fear of challenging the state have made human right petitioning under an individual system neither easy nor an attractive proposition if one valued longevity. An associated major factor, as one of the Court's advisory opinions disclosed, is both the availability of affordable legal services in many American states, and, perhaps more pertinently, the willingness of lawyers to offer their services in cases where the victim appears to be politically 'tainted'.

Finally, the structure of the ACHR itself is a hindrance to its effective operations. Individuals, as we have seen, have no direct access to the Court, but must wait for the Commission's procedures to be completed. These procedures can be extremely lengthy and their focus is not on seeking redress for individuals but upon reaching a friendly accommodation between the allegedly delinquent state and the complaint. In the inter-

American context, the opportunity for state interference with this process is self-evident. As Judge Piza Escalante observed in a separate opinion in Viviana Gallardo, the Commission's procedures are 'a veritable obstacle course that is almost insurmountable'. He further observed that there was nothing that the Commission could do which could not be done as effectively by the Court. In addition to these criticisms is the fact that the Commission enjoys a discretion in determining whether to refer a case to the Court. While the Court has been able to offer some guidance to the Commission on when a case should be referred in Compulsory Membership, it is ironic that the Commission had refused to refer that case to the Court and that it had been left to goodwill of Costa Rica to do so, when it clearly had nothing tangible to gain from the reference.

With increasing democratization in number of Latin American states, it is probable that the contentious jurisdiction of the Court will be put to greater use. Certainly, the prospects are for a less despairing statement from a retiring judge than of Judge Maximo Cisneros who said in Compulsory Membership:

> Now, whereas in signing this Advisory Opinion I am performing last acts as a judge of the Inter-American Court of Human Rights, I wish to say that the "love" that we have put into our work has not been sufficient to avoid the sense of frustration that I feel in leaving the Court before it has had the opportunity to hear a single case of a violation of human rights, in spite of the sad reality of America in this field.

NINE

Scene in Europe

The European system for protecting human rights is primarily composed of two major treaties: the European Convention on Human Rights and Fundamental Freedoms (ECHR) and the European Social Charter (ESC). The ECHR, which is focused upon the protection of civil and political rights, was adopted in 1950 and entered into force in 1953. It is thus the oldest specific human rights instrument in existence, its entry into force pre-dating the ICCPR by more than twenty years. The ESC, which covers the implementation of economic and social 'rights and principles', was adopted in 1961 and entered into force in 1965. Both Conventions were drafted under the auspices of the Council of Europe, an inter-governmental organization of 25 European states, the function of which is to facilitate European cooperation across a broad range of subjects. Upon joining the Council, every member must, under Article 3 of its Statute, 'accept the principles of the rule of law and of the enjoyment by all persons within its jurisdiction of human rights and fundamental freedoms...'. And, as Vasak points out, the themes of democracy, the rule of law and the protection of human rights permeate the Council's founding document. These principles are also echoed in the ECHR's Preamble, which reaffirms their crucial importance to the High Contracting Parties.

European Convention

As indicated above, the motivation for the drafting of the ECHR arose from the wish of the participating states to protect against encroaching communism, to sound the alarm against incipient totalitarianism and to strengthen democracy and the rule of law in the member states. It is also clear that the Council of Europe wished to move more quickly than the UN in the drafting of legally binding human rights obligations. In the Preamble to the ECHR, the Universal Declaration is mentioned on three occasions, parties resolve 'to take the first steps for the collective enforcement of certain of the rights stated in the Universal Declaration.'

Much of the work of the Convention's institutions has been directed towards resolving deficiencies in the domestic law of the states parties, rather than dealing with the gross violations of human rights which its drafters originally appeared to envisage. None the less, the ECHR has on occasion had to deal with the eruption of totalitarianism, as in Denmark, Norway, Sweden and the Netherlands v Greece, which, as previously remarked, highlighted some of the weaknesses of the Convention's protective system. It is arguable that the Convention has functioned rather better as a kind of quasi-constitutional device, providing an instrument of last resort where domestic institutions and laws have been found lacking. It should also be noted that the Convention has self-executing status in a large number of the contracting parties and is pleaded by lawyers directly before their domestic courts. Several calls on various occasions to make the ECHR part of the UK's domestic law have met with non success, although it is now arguable that certain of the rights protected take effect within the UK's legal system, since they have been held by the European Court of Justice to be part of the general principles of EC law.

The ECHR and its ten additional Protocols protect most of the rights contained in the Universal Declaration, although there are some omissions and some differences in the drafting of the rights in order to take account of European conditions. The contracting parties are required by Article 1 to 'secure to everyone within their jurisdiction' the rights and freedoms protected by the Convention, and they are required to do so on a non-discriminatory basis. In the event of a violation of any of the rights and freedoms, Article 13 declared that persons so affected 'shall have an effective remedy before a national authority notwithstanding that the violation has been committed by persons acting in an official capacity'. It is clear that Articles 1 and 13 impliedly require states to take the necessary legislative measures in appropriate cases both to implement the Convention's rights and to provide means for redress in cases of violation.

ECHR'S Institutions: In order to ensure the observance of the obligations undertaken by the parties of the Convention, Article 19 provides for the establishment of a European Commission of Human Rights ('the Commission') and a European Court of Human Rights ('the Court'). It should also be noted that both the Committee of Ministers, which is the governing body of the Council of Europe, and the Secretary-General of the Council, also have functions assigned to them under the Convention. All these institutions have their seat at the Palais de 'Europe in Strasbourg, an imposing building which is periodically shared with the peripatetic Parliament of the European Community.

Commission members must be persons of high moral character and should either possess the qualifications required for appointment to high judicial office or be persons of recognized competence in national or international law. They serve for a period of six years in an individual capacity and may not during their period of office hold a position which is incompatible with their independence and impartiality. The Commission consists of a number of members equal to that of the parties to the Convention. No two members may be from the same state, and there is no requirement that a Commission member should be a national of a contracting party. Whereas, in the past, the Commission was required to sit as a plenary body when considering individual applications submitted to it under Article 25, following an amendment to the Convention by Protocol No. 8 in 1985 in order to expedite its procedures, it may now sit in chambers of seven members. The Commission must still sit in plenary session, however, if it is required to deal with interstate applications under Article 24 or if one of the chambers considers it necessary in view of the case before it.

Under Article 24 of the ECHR the jurisdiction of the Commission under the Convention is automatically accepted by states when they become parties to the ECHR. All proceedings before the Commission take place in camera, legally to facilitate the conciliatory function which is the central duty of the Commission if an application is found to be admissible.

The Court

The Court is composed of a number of judges equal to that of the Members of the Council of Europe. The Court is not normally required to sit as a plenary body, but sits rather in less cumbersome chambers of seven. In cases of importance, however, there is provision for the full Court to sit.

The difference between the numbers of the Commission and the number of judges of the Court should be noted. While the Commission members must be equal in number to the parties to the Convention, the number of judges is determined by reference to the number of Members of the Council of Europe. The reason for the difference is that, as Beddard writes, the drafters of the Convention wanted the Court to represent a kind of 'conscience of Europe'. The divergence between the number of judges and members of the Commission has fluctuated from time to time according to differing memberships of the Council of Europe and the European Convention.

In order to be judicial candidates, Article 39(3) ECHR requires nominees to be of 'high moral character' and possess the qualifications required for appointment to high judicial office or be jurisconsults of recognized competence. Although no two judges may be from the same contracting party, there is no requirement that judges possess the nationality of the nominating state. Indeed, Liechtenstein nominated Canadian law professor R. St. John MacDonanld to sit in the Court rather than one of its own nationals.

Unlike the Commission, the jurisdiction of the Court under the Convention is neither automatic nor compulsory. The parties of the ECHR must declare that they accept the Court's jurisdiction to interpret and apply the Convention. This may be done unconditionally, for a specified period, by special agreement in individual cases or on the basis of reciprocity with other states. The nature of the Court's jurisdiction is two-fold. First, it exercises a contentious jurisdiction, where states have accepted this, to make rulings in interstate and individual cases initiated under Article 24 and 25 ECHR. Secondly, under Protocol II to the Convention, the Court has power to render advisory opinions at the request of the Committee of Ministers. This latter jurisdiction is strictly limited to provisions of the Convention which do not relate to the content or scope of the rights or freedoms guaranteed, and it is therefore of marginal utility. It has never been employed by the Court and compares unfavourably with the exceptionally broad advisory jurisdiction of the Inter-American Court of Human Rights which has been frequently utilized.

ECHR Enforcement Mechanisms

There are two types of enforcement mechanism under the Convention: (1) an inter-state complaint system and (2) a right of individual application.

Inter-State Complaints: Under Article 24 of the ECHR, any party may refer to the Commission via the Secretary-General of the Council of Europe, any alleged breach of the Convention by any other party. By becoming party of the ECHR, all states automatically accept the Commission's competence to receive such complaints. This, as we shall see in Chapter 6, is different from the American Convention on Human Rights where states must declare that they accept the jurisdiction of the Inter-American Commission in such matters. It should be noted that the interstate procedure is not predicated upon the alleged violation of one of the substantive rights protected by the Convention, but can be invoked in relation to any provision of the Convention. Even if an alleged violation does infringe or violate one of the ECHR's substantive rights, it is not necessary for the complaining state to demonstrate that it has a special interest in, or relationship to, the victim. In a technical sense, all that states are concerned with here is ensuring that other parties observe their obligations under the Convention. It has been apparent, however, that in the small number of inter-state cases brought to date, the majority have been motivated by political hostility. In Greece v UK, Greece's complaints concerned the treatment of Greek Cypriot (AOKA) terrorists by the British authorities in Cyprus. The case of Austria v Italy was motivated by the alleged inhuman treatment by Italian authorities of German-speaking youths in the Italian Tyrol. In Ireland v UK, the Irish government objected to the use of certain methods of interrogation known as the 'five techniques' employed against suspected Provisional IRA members by the British Security forces which, it claimed, amounted to torture, inhuman and degrading treatment under Article 3 ECHR. Finally, two cases brought by Cyprus v Turkey arose from the circumstances surrounding Turkey's invasion and partition of Cyprus, and its treatment of the displaced Greek Cypriot population.

Two inter-state applications, however, stand out as being motivated not by political hostility, but by genuine humanitarian concerns. These are the cases brought by Denmark, Norway, Sweden and the Netherlands against Greece in 1970 and by the same states against Turkey in 1982. The first case arose from the aftermath of a coup d'etat by a number of Greek military officers ('the Colonels') in which political opponents to the military regime were imprisoned and tortured. The effect of the case was to lead Greece to denounce the Convention and to withdraw from the Council of Europe a short time before it was due to be expelled. The second case concerned allegations of torture and inhuman treatment of prisoners in Turkey. Unlike the Greek, case, the Turkish Case was subject to a friendly settlement.

The Greek case often helps as an example of the inadequacy of international legal instruments in the face of a totalitarian regime bent on systematically denying human rights to its people. While it is true that a legal instrument by itself can achieve very little without the attendant political will to make it effective, the violation of human rights norms by a state deny its actions legitimacy, damage its international reputation and may lead to diplomatic, political and economic sanctions. Although human rights violations may often appear to be cost-free to states, nevertheless they do damage a state's credibility and make international relations more difficult to sustain, as indeed the Greek 'Colonels' discovered.

Individual Applications: Although the term 'petition' is used in Article 25 of the ECHR, the Commission and the Court now use the term 'application' to denote the procedural right of individual to lodge claims with the Commission that one or more of their rights under the Conventions has been violated. The right of application depends, however, upon a declaration of state acceptance. Such declarations may be unconditional or made for a specified period. The UK, for example, adopts the latter approach, making declarations for periods of only five years, the most recent being its declaration of 14 January 1991. The question of renewal of the UK's declaration under Article 25 has occasionally lead to a difference of opinion between government departments. In 1986, for example, it was reported that the Foreign and Commonwealth Office was eager to renew the UK's declaration, whereas the Home Office was apparently reluctant to have human rights issues adjudicated in Strasbourg.

Under Article 25, applications to the Commission may be lodged with the Secretary-General of the Council of Europe by 'any person, non-governmental organisation or group of individual claiming to be the victim of a violation by one of the parties of the rights set for them in this Convention', provided, of course, that the state in question has accepted the right of individual application. From this it is clear that victim, and hence applicants, may be either natural or legal persons. Indeed, applications, have been lodged by a number of corporate groups such as companies, trades union, churches and other representative organizations. The use of the word 'victim' in Article 25 has been held to mean that an applicant must have been actually affected by the alleged violation, although in Marckx the Court held that in certain circumstances it may be enough for an applicant to show that they would be potentially directly affected by the application of a particular measure. What is clear, however, is that there is no possibility of a class action or *actio popularis* under the ECHR. This was stated by the Court in Klass, although it is arguable that the judgment in Marcksx mitigated the rigour of this position to a certain extent. The Commission has also identified a class of individuals who can submit applications who are known as 'indirect victims'. These are persons not immediately affected by an original violation, but who none the less suffer as a result of such a violation or, in the words of the Commission, individuals who have 'a genuine personal interest in the termination of a violation'. An example of an indirect victim might be a spouse whose partner has been arbitrarily imprisoned. The spouse is clearly not a direct victim of the violation of Article 5, but he or she will be an indirect victim because of the consequences of the violation. It should also be noted that on such circumstances the spouse would also be the direct victim of a violation of Article 8, the right to family life, and therefore competent to lodge an application in his or her own right.

There are a number of conditions set out in Article 26 and 27 which must be fulfilled before the Commission can admit an application and thus proceed to consider the merits of a case.

Exhaustion of Local Remedies

Article 26 provides

The Commission may only deal with the matter after all domestic remedies have been exhausted, according to the generally recognised rules of international law, and within a periods of six months from the date on which the final decision was taken.

Article 27(3) further provides that the Commission must reject any application referred to it which does not comply with the exhaustion of local remedies requirement. Although it would seem necessary for states to ensure the local remedies have been exhausted, since states are bringing the claim not on behalf of an alleged victim, but in their own right, the Commission has nevertheless examined the question where individual rights within the respondent state have been in issue.

The rationale for the existence of the local remedies rule is worth remarking that the both the Commission and the Court have fully accepted the basis of the rule. In Application 343, the Commission stated that the rule is 'founded upon the principle that the Respondent State must first have an opportunity to redress by its own means within the framework of its own domestic legal system the wrong alleged to have been done to the individual', and in De Wilde, Ooms and Versyp (Vagrancy Cases) the court held that the rule 'dispenses states from answering before an international body for their acts before they have had an opportunity to put matters right through their own legal system'.

Both the Commission and the Court in applying the rule have adhered closely to the international law concerning the exhaustion of local remedies. Thus, since the rule is for the benefit of states, it has been held that it is open to them to waive the rule. Such a waiver may be express, but more often that not it will be implied in cases where states have been tardy in raising the issue. In DeJone, Baljet and van den Brink, for example, the Netherlands raised the question of non-exhaustion of local remedies for the first time before the Court, without having pleaded it before the Commission at the admissibility stage. The Court held that the Netherlands was precluded or stopped from raising the objection at this later stage, when it should have done so in contesting admissibility of the application before the Commission.

The jurisprudence of the Commission and the Court has also demonstrated that, in accordance with international law, applicants are not required to exhaust local remedies if they are not genuine and effective or if they are subject to unreasonable delay. As the Court said in Van Oosterwijk, an applicant need only exhaust remedies which 'relate to the breaches alleged and at the same time are available and sufficient'. Thus, where a remedy is shown to have been consistently unsuccessful, it will be deemed not to have been sufficient. This does not mean, however, that if a remedy is uncertain an applicant is absolved from attempting to seek redress through the domestic system of appeals; he or she is required to attempt all reasonable avenues to obtain a remedy.

An important exception to the rule requiring exhaustion of local remedies which has been developed by the Commission and the Court arises in circumstances where there exists an 'administrative practice' within the state in question. An administrative practice has been defined by the Court as 'an accumulation of identical or analogous breaches which are sufficiently numerous and inter-connected to amount not merely to isolated incidents or exceptions but to a pattern or system'. It is unnecessary that such practices be formalized in legislative or quasi-legislative measures; it is enough that there is official toleration of the practice. Such official toleration would, as the Court stated in the Greek case, tend to render judicial remedies ineffective, since it would be practically impossible to obtain evidence through the cooperation of official bodies. Indeed, in the Irish Case, techniques for interrogating Provisional IRA suspects had not been authorized in any official document, but they had been taught to OK security forces at an official training centre. This was enough to signify government toleration of the practices and obviate the need to exhaust local remedies.

The burden of proving that the local remedies have been exhausted lies initially with the applicant. If the Commission is not satisfied that the application discloses an attempt to exhaust all available genuine, effective and timely remedies, it must reject the application. The determination by the Commission at this stage that all local remedies have been exhausted is not conclusive, since it is open to the respondent state to raise the question of non-exhaustion later in the proceedings before the Commission. If a state does raise this issue as a barrier to admissibility, the burden of proof is upon the state to demonstrate non-exhaustion.

Intimately linked to the exhaustion of local remedies rule is the requirement that the application must be lodged within six months of the final decision. What, however, is meant by the term 'final decision'? In Application 214, the Commission ruled that this 'refers exclusively to the final decision concerned in the exhaustion of the domestic remedies according to the generally recognised rules of international law, so that the six months period is operative only in this context'. Thus, it would seem that where an individual applies to a domestic tribunal which clearly has no power to grant a remedy for a violation, it is the date on which the previous decision was given which will count as the final decision. A potential applicant would therefore have to determine carefully whether or not there was any real likelihood of success before attempting to secure redress before a particular domestic tribunal. If, however, there is a violation of the Convention which is of a continuing nature and there is no domestic remedy available, the obligation to submit an application within a six-month period is clearly otiose. This occurred in De Becker, in which a journalist was denied a licence to practise his profession in Belgium. There was no recourse to any tribunal against the decision of the licensing authority, and it was therefore held that the violation of Article 10 (freedom of expression) was of a continuing nature to which the six-month limitation period did not apply.

Article 27 Requirements: Once an applicant has demonstrated that local remedies have been exhausted, he or she must also satisfy three further criteria contained in Article 27 before the application can be ruled admissible by the Commission. Article 27 reads:

(1) The Commission shall not deal with any application submitted under Article 25 which:
   (a) is anonymous, or
   (b) is substantially the same as a matter which has already been examined by the Commission or has already been submitted to another procedure of international investigation or settlement and if it contains no relevant new information.

(2) The Commission shall consider inadmissible any application submitted under Article 251 which it considers incompatible with the provisions of the present Convention, manifestly ill-founded or an abuse of the right of application.

Anonymity: This requirement it not taken too literally by the Commission. As long as the application contains sufficient information to allow the applicant to be identified, it will be admitted.

Substantially the same matter which has already been examined by the Commission: The Commission has applied this provision so strictly that it has developed a doctrine of *res judicata*. None the less, the Commission has indicated that it is prepared to be flexible where there is new information forthcoming. It is clear that where a previous application has been ruled inadmissible because of a failure to exhaust local remedies, the Commission will not subsequently reject the same application if it is re-submitted following the exhaustion of local remedies.

Submitted to another procedure of international investigation: In the first decades of the operation of the Convention, the possibility of duplication of individual application procedures under different international instruments was remote. However, with the entry into force of the First Optional Protocol to the ICCPR, it became apparent that individuals could make applications under both systems. Because of this, the Council of Europe recommended to states which wished to recognize the right of individual application under both systems that they make a reservation when ratifying the Protocol excluding consideration of applications by the Human Rights Committee of matters which had already been considered under the ECHR. As we saw in Chapter 4, reservation by European states to the First Optional Protocol have been pleaded, with mixed results, in an attempt to prevent the HRC from effectively rehearing a case previously rejected as inadmissible by the European Commission. It would seem that the application of such reservations might, if accepted by the HRC without qualification, work to the detriment of individuals whose applications are rejected on the basis that they concern rights not covered by the Convention. It is arguable that applicants should have the opportunity to correct their error before the Committee.

Incompatible with the provisions of the Convention

The Commission may declare applications inadmissible on this ground under a variety of circumstances. There are a number of potential categories of inadmissibility under this heading:

1. Where an application claims a violation of a right not guaranteed by the Convention, otherwise known as *inadmissibility ratione materiae*. This has often involved the claimed violation of rights protected by the Universal Declaration or the European Social Charter but not by the ECHR, such as the right to holiday pay. Sometimes, however, the right claimed is not covered by any instrument such as the right of prisoners to holidays.

2. Where the applicant is not a victim or an indirect victim, otherwise known as *inadmissibility ratione personae*. This has already been covered above in the context of Article 25.
3. Where the alleged victim did not fall within the jurisdiction of the respondent state at the time of the claimed violation. This is known as *inadmissibility ratione loci*.
4. Where the violation took place before the entry into force of the ECHR, unless the breach is of a continuing nature as in De Becker, known as *inadmissibility ratione temporis*.
5. Where the application violates Article 17, which provides:

Nothing in this Convention may be interpreted as implying for any State, group or person any right to engage in any activity or perform any act aimed at the destruction of any of the rights and freedoms set forth herein or at their limitation to a greater extent than is provided for in this Convention.

Manifestly ill founded

This admissibility requirement essentially requires the Commission to determine whether the facts of the application disclose a prima facie breach of the Convention. In order to do this, the Commission must undertake a preliminary investigation of the facts of the case. Sometimes not much more than a cursory investigation is required in order to ascertain whether or not a prima facie breach of the Convention is disclosed. In other occasions, such as in Klass, the Commission has been required to undertake an extensive analysis which has come close to determination of the merits of the case.

Abuse of the Right of Application

A rough equivalent of this term in domestic law might be the rules prohibiting vexatious litigation. It is primarily designed to prevent applicants from making false claims and allegations, but it has also been used in the case of Rafael v

Austria to rule inadmissible an application in which the applicant used abusive and defamatory language about certain members of the respondent state's government. This latter decision has been criticized as being contrary to the spirit of the Convention, since the Commission should be concerned with the question of whether protected rights have been violated and not with whether an applicant has used objectionable phraseology. The Commission's decisions under this heading also make it clear that the motive of an applicant is irrelevant. In Lawless, for example, the Irish government claimed that the applicant's motives were simply political and not primarily concerned with securing a remedy for violated rights. The Commission rightly rejected this contention.

Given the number of hurdles placed in front of a potential applicant, it is not surprising that the majority of applications, approximately 96 per cent, never proceed beyond the admissibility stage. The question may legitimately be asked, therefore, why is it so difficult for an individual to bring a case to the merits stage? The answer to this is probably two-fold. First, the emphasis of the Convention is on respect for national sovereignty and the primary obligation of states to provide the initial avenues of redress by means of their own legal systems. Second, in any international system of protection, it is necessary to sift out applications which clearly have nothing to do with human rights issues either because they claim the protection of rights which do not exist or because they are simply frivolous.

Derogations

As we saw in earlier in this book that, the possibility of derogations exists in most human rights instruments. These allow states to modify or opt out of the protection of certain rights in certain specified circumstances. This does not mean, however, that states have a free hand to do what they like simply by declaring a derogation, since both the circumstances giving rise to the derogation and the operation of the derogation itself will be subject to the supervisory institutions in each instrument. None the less, a derogation may stand in the way of effective human rights protection by precluding or limiting the possibility of redress by an applicant. As in the case of the ICCPR, however, certain rights protected by the ECHR are non-derogable.

Article 15(l) of the ECHR provides:

> In time of war or public emergency threatening the life of the nation any High Contracting Party may take measures derogating from its obligations under this Convention to the extent strictly required by the exigencies of the situation, provided that such measures are not inconsistent with its other obligations under international law.

It is apparent from Article 15(l) that derogations may only be made in circumstances in which the very fabric of the state is under threat, and even then any derogations must be proportionate to the threat. Thus, derogations involve a paradox. They demand the denial of rights or aspects of certain rights in order to protect the totality of rights which can only be guaranteed by the continued existence of the state. Derogations also involve balancing the interest of the state in taking measures which it deems necessary for its survival together with the interests of the Convention's institutions which are charged with supervising its observance.

Both the Commission and the Court have developed important jurisprudence under Article 15(1) to determine whether or not a state is entitled to make derogations in particular circumstances. From this it is clear that there must be an actual or imminent crisis of exceptional proportions, which affects the whole population of the state by threatening the organized life of the community. In determining whether or not such a state of affairs exists, a Party enjoys a degree of discretion which is known as the 'margin of appreciation'. The exercise of this margin of appreciation is, however, subject to the supervision of the Commission and, in the final analysis, the Court. It is they which determine whether or not the conditions permitting the making of derogations exists, in fact and whether or not the state has properly exercised its discretion. It would seem that where derogations are properly made they excuse parties from breach of the Convention, although Judge Sir Gerald Fitzmaurice argued in a separate opinion in Ireland v UK that a derogation properly made actually nullifies a technical breach of the Convention. Parties which avail themselves of the right of derogation must make the derogation public and keep the Secretary-General of the Council of Europe fully informed of the measures which they have taken and the reasons giving rise to them.

The majority derogations under the ECHR have been made by both the UK and Ireland to deal with the terrorist threat in Northern Ireland. In Lawless, the Court held that Ireland had legitimately proscribed membership of the IRA by means of derogation because the extra-constitutional and violent activities of that organization not only affected the fabric of Irish society, but also placed Ireland's relations with the UK at risk. Similarly, in Ireland v UK, the Court found that the terrorist activities of the IRA justified the UK in taking the necessary measures by way of derogation. In contrast, the Commission held in the Greek case that there was not a public emergency in Greece at the time of the military overthrow of the constitutional government by 'the Colonels'. The Commission found that allegations of a communist takeover and a deterioration in the state of public order following a constitutional crisis in 1967 had not been demonstrated.

Post-admissibility Procedure

Once an application has been declared admissible, the Commission must then perform a number of separate tasks. First, it must act as an investigatory body by undertaking a thorough review of the facts alleged in the application. This is not done by the whole Commission, but rather by use of a rapporteur or an individual Commission member who undertakes a review of the facts and reports back to the Commission. If in the course of its investigation of the facts the Commission finds the existence of one of the grounds in Article 27 which would have initially rendered the application inadmissible had it been discovered at the admissibility stage, the Commission may still reject the application. Such a decision must, however, be taken as unanimous of the Commission. This procedure is clearly designed to deal with those applications which ought not to have been admitted, but where this only becomes apparent on close examination.

Second, once the Commission has established the accuracy of the facts alleged in the applications, it must then undertake the role of conciliator. Article 28(b) requires the Commission to 'place itself at the disposal of the parties concerned with a view to securing a friendly settlement of the matter on the basis of respect for Human Rights as defined in this Convention'. All this takes place in camera. In the view of one former President of the Commission, Sir Humphrey Waldock, the drafters of the Convention were right to make friendly settlement the central remedy within the Convention structure. He said:

> Investigation of the shortcomings of a State in regard to human rights is a very delicate form of intervention in its internal affairs. The primary duty of the Commission is to conduct confidential negotiations with the parties and to try and set right unobtrusively any breach of human rights that may have occurred. It was not primarily established for the purpose of putting States in the dock and registering convictions against them.

Clearly, the Commission must steer a via media and must not be seen to favour one party at the expense of another, although it might be felt that the conciliatory function allows states to escape lightly on some occasions. In Amerkrane, for example, an application was filled by Mrs Amerkrane against the UK on her own behalf and on behalf of her husband. Her husband had been an officer in the Moroccan Air Force who had taken part in unsuccessful coup against the King of Morocco. Amekrane escaped to Gibraltar where he sought asylum but was immediately returned to Morocco where he was shot and killed. Mrs Amekrane claimed a number of breaches of the ECHR including Article 3 (inhuman treatment) because of the circumstances of her husband's return to Morocco. Mrs Amekrane, however, reached a friendly settlement with the UK in which she was given an ex gratia payment of £ 37,500 without any admission on the part of the UK that it had violated the Convention. The results of all friendly settlements are recorded in a report by the Commission that is published and which contains a brief statement of the facts and the solution reached between the parties.

Third, if a case cannot be settled by friendly means, the Commission must, under Article 31(1), 'draw up a report on the facts and state its opinion as to whether the facts found disclose a breach by the State concerned of its obligations under the Convention'. This phase of proceedings by the Commission may be regarded as quasi-judicial in nature. The report compiled by the Commission is drafted as if it were the judgment of a court and can contain concurring, separate, and dissenting opinions. The report is not, however, conclusive, since the Commission is not competent to reach decisions binding upon the parties; that competence lies solely within the purview of the Committee of Ministers or the Court.

When the Commission has drawn up its report it must transmit it to the Committee of Ministers with any proposals that it sees fit. The reports is also transmitted to respondent state and, if the case is an individual application under Article 25, to the applicant. None of the parties is at liberty to publish the report. If the respondent state has not accepted the jurisdiction of the Court or has accepted it with reservations which preclude consideration of the instant case, the case must be disposed of by the Committee. If a respondent state has accepted the jurisdiction of the Court but the case has not been referred to the Court within a period of three months, the

Committee of Ministers must similarly dispose it of at the end of that period. The decision on whether a case should be referred to the Court is dealt with by Article 48. This provides that the following may refer a case to the Court:

(a) the Commission
(b) a party whose national is alleged to be a victim;
(c) a party which referred the case to the Commission;
(d) a party against which the complaint has been lodged.

When Protocol No. 9 of 1990 is enforced, a consequential amendment to Article 48 will allow a fifth category of persons to refer a case to the court. This category will include the person, NGO or group of individuals who lodged the complaint with the Commission. The reason for this additional protocol was to broaden access to the Court by individuals and thus make the system more responsive to the individuals which it is meant to serve. The potential amendment to Article 48(2) makes it clear, however, that individuals will not be entitled to refer a case to the Court as of right, since a procedure is established for screening such referrals. Where a case is referred by an individual, it must first be considered by a panel of three judges, one of whom must be a member of the respondent state. If the panel decides by unanimous vote that the case does not raise a serious question affecting the interpretation or application of the Convention and does not warrant consideration by the Court for any other reason, it may decide that the case should not be considered by the Court. If the panel takes such a decision, then the matter falls to be dealt with by the Committee of Ministers in the usual way under Article 32. Britain has already indicated that it has no intention of becoming party to Protocol 9.

To date, the vast majority of cases have been referred to the Court by the Commission. There are no guidelines contained in the Convention as to how the Commission is to exercise its discretion in deciding whether to refer a case to the Court or whether to leave it to be dealt with by the Committee of Ministers. From the Commission's referrals, however, it is apparent that cases in which difficult points of law emerge or where there are sharp divergences of opinion between Commission members will be referred to the Court if the state concerned has accepted its jurisdiction. It has also been suggested that the Commission prefers to refer cases to the committee that has a political complexion, although, of course, there is no satisfactory definition of what might be considered political in this context.

The Committee of Ministers: Where a case is referred to the Committee of Ministers for decision in the circumstances outlined above, the Committee must decide by a majority of two-third whether there has been a violation of the Convention. If it is decided by the requisite majority that a Party is in breach, the Committee of Ministers is required to prescribe the remedial action which the state must take and the time within which it must be taken. Such decisions are legally binding on the states to which they are addressed. The representative of the respondent state party may take part in all these decisions, an approach which runs counter to the principle of *memeo index* in *sua causa* (no-one should be a judge in their own cause).

Although it is clear that the Committee has adjudicative power, it is also clear that it is not required to adopt a judicial approach to the Commission's reports. This is because the Committee, being composed of Council of Europe member state's representatives, is a political institution. Scrutiny of the Committee's decisions under Article 32 appears to indicate, however, that it avoids political conformation and tends to agree with the position taken by the Commission in most cases. There have been exceptions to this, but they are comparatively rare.

Cases before the Court

Article 47 provides that the Court may deal with a case only after the Commission has acknowledged the failure of efforts to secure a friendly settlement and within the period of three months referred to in Article 32. It is also worth reiterating that application of Article 47 is, of course, predicated upon the prior acceptance of the Court's contentious jurisdiction by the respondent state party.

Until protocol 9 enters into force, only the Commission and ECHR parties enjoy the competence to bring a case before the Court. None the less, the gradual amelioration of the position of the individual under the application system has been one of the noteworthy features of the development of the Convention. In Lawless, which was the Court's first case, it became apparent that the applicant was effectively excluded from proceedings before the Court, since only the Commission was given standing to present the case. Thus, although being the applicant who would ultimately be the beneficiary of any decision, he was prevented from making his voice heard directly by appearing before the Court. The Court overcame this particular problem by allowing the applicant to append his own written observations to the Commission's statement, and the Court also reserved the right through its Rules of Procedure to hear at the request of the Commission or state party 'any person whose evidence or statements seem likely to assist it in the carrying out of its task'. Manifestly, this meant that the Court could hear the applicant, if the Commission deemed this appropriate. Since 1983, under Rule 30 of the Court's Rules of Procedure, applicants have been entitled to plead their own case before the Court. This, however, still does not entitle them to become a party to the proceedings.

Once the Court gives its judgement in a case it is final and admits of no appeal. Furthermore, if the respondent state is found to being in violation of the Convention, it must, under Article 53, 'undertake to abide by any decision of the Court'. Such a decision may include the award of monetary compensation, but increasingly the Court has taken the decision that a declaration of breach of the Convention is sufficient remedy for the applicant, especially where only moral damage has been suffered. The Court does not have the power to make punitive awards, nor, would it appear, that it has the competence to make orders for specific performance, that is to direct a state to take positive action in a particular area. However, if a state has been found to be in breach of the Convention through the application of a particular piece of legislation, it is clearly incumbent upon that state to take the appropriate remedial action in accordance with its obligations under Article 1 of the ECHR.

Supervision of the execution of the Court's judgements are undertaken under Article 54 by the Committee of Ministers. Once the Court has made a judgment, it is transmitted to the Committee of Ministers which places it as an item on its agenda. The delinquent state must then inform the Committee of the measures which it has taken to give effect to the judgment. This may include a statement to the effect that the state has paid damages awarded by the Court to the applicant, or that is has taken the appropriate legislative measures to remedy the breach. Given delays in the domestic legislative procedures, however, makes it clear that the Committee needs to keep a watching brief over state activities in this field. It is also arguable that the Committee is not the most effective body for policing this particular aspect of the system, since a determination of whether legislative amendments have indeed remedied the breach and forestalled any potential breaches in the terms of any judgment by the Court, may be a particularly nice question; a question for which the Committee as a political body may not necessarily be adequately equipped to answer. A number of states have been required to modify domestic legislation both in order to remedy and to foreclose upon future breaches of the Covenant. Britain, following the *Sunday Times* Case, for examples, modified its laws concerning contempt of court, and Belgium, in the aftermath to Marckx, amended its legislation concerning children born out of wedlock.

Interpretation of the Rights

It is impossible, given the constraints of space in this book to offer more than cursory attention to the significant and detailed jurisprudence which has been amassed by the ECHR since it heard its first case in 1961. None the less, it is possible to give a flavour of the Court's approach by examining the subject matter of, and the decisions in, some of its more important cases relating to one particular Convention article. At the outset, however, comment should be made about the Court's technique of interpretation. The approach adopted by the Court towards interpreting the substantive rights contained in the Convention is clearly dynamic in nature. The Court has not been constrained by apparent gaps in the protection of certain rights protected by the Convention and has, arguably, engaged in forms of broad judicial legislation in order to achieve results consistent with its overall philosophy. The Convention is seen by the Court as a 'living instrument', the role of which is to deal with the problems of contemporary Europe and not simply the problems which the drafters may have contemplated in the 1950s. In many ways, therefore, the Convention is similar to the Bill of Rights of the American Constitution, not only in the subject matter with which it deals, but also in the way in which the rights protected have been developed through alternating periods of judicial activism and restraint.

In order to give an idea of the way in which the Court decides cases involving alleged breaches of the Convention's substantive provisions, it is intended here to examine, albeit briefly, its interpretation of Article 3. This article, which provides that 'no one shall be subjected to torture or to inhuman or degrading treatment or punishment', has given rise to a series of important cases, the majority of which have involved the UK as respondent. The first of these was an inter-state case, Ireland v United Kingdom, in which the Irish government accused the UK of breach of Article 3 by the use of so-called 'five techniques' by British security forces in

Northern Ireland to extract intelligence from detainees who were suspected of being IRA terrorists. The 'five techniques' involved making detainees stand in a painful posture against a wall, depriving them of light by hooding them, subjecting them to prolonged periods of noise, depriving, them to sleep and placing them on a severely restricted diet. The Commission found unanimously that these procedures amounted to torture, but the Court departed from the Commission's finding and held that the acts complained of were not of the 'particular intensity and cruelty implied by the word torture'. None the less, the Court did find that the use of the 'five techniques' violated Article 3, since it amounted to inhuman and degrading treatment. It is interesting to note here that the Court took a very subjective view of what might amount to breach of Article 3. It was clearly of the opinion that in order to come within the meaning of Article 3, the conduct complained of 'must attain a minimum level of severity', but that this was correlative and depended upon all the circumstances of the case, and, in particular, the personal characteristics of the individual involved. Thus, what might amount to a breach or Article 3 in the case of a person who was sick and old might not be a breach in the case of a person who was young and healthy.

It is apparent that such a subjective approach may raise more problems than its solves, and that determining the perceptions of the individual might cause acute difficulties for states. It is interesting to note that the specialist torture conventions actually work from an objective definition of torture by concentrating on the intention and motivation of the person inflicting the torture rather than from the point of view of the victim.

In Tyrer v United Kingdom, the Court was faced with the question of whether punishment of minors breaching constituted degrading punishment within the meaning of Article 3. Here it held that the infliction of physical violence by one person against another was compounded by its institutionalized nature and the aura of official procedure which was attached to it. This, the Court found, was an attack upon Tyrer's dignity and therefore amounted to degrading treatment. Again, the Court held that the assessment of whether punishment was degrading was relative and depended upon the circumstances of the case and, in particular, 'on the nature and context of punishment itself and the manner of its execution'. It also took the view that physical punishment itself was not necessary for a violation of Article 3, and that apprehension of the physical punishment itself might be sufficient to constitute a breach.

A case involving the UK in which a breach of Article 3 was alleged but not found by the Court was that of Campbell and Cosans. Here, the applicants were the parents of two children who were being educated in the Scottish school system. The use of corporal punishments was till permitted in Scotland and the parents of the children complained that the threat of the use of such punishment, even though it had not been used upon their children, amounted to a violation of Article 3. While the Court found that there had been no breach of Article 3 in this case, it nevertheless held that the threat of torture might itself amount to inhuman treatment.

Of all the cases recently decided by the European Court of Human Rights in this area, perhaps the most farreaching has been that of Soering v United Kingdom. In this case, the applicant, a German citizen, had been arrested in the UK and was serving a prison sentence for fraud, when a request for his extradition was made by US authorities for a murder he and his girlfriend were alleged to have committed in Virginia in 1985. Soering argued that if the UK were to extradite him to US, this would amount to inhuman treatment because, if he were convicted of murder (which was likely since his girlfriend accomplice has already been convicted of the crime), he would be exposed to Virginia's 'death row' phenomenon upon conviction, since that state still maintained the death penalty for such crimes. In this landmark judgment, the Court held that there would be a breach of Article 3 if the decision to extradite an individual were made in circumstances where 'substantial grounds have been shown for believing that the person concerned, if extradited, faces a real risk of being subjected to torture or to inhuman or degrading treatment or punishment in the requesting country'. This, said the Court, would hardly be compatible with the underlying values of the Convention nor with the spirit and intendent of Article 3'. In Soering, the Court also reaffirmed elements of its earlier judgments in Ireland v United Kingdom and Tyrer. It made clear once again that the treatment concerned must reach a minimum level of severity before Article 3 was violated, but that it also depended on 'all the circumstances of the case', including the characteristics of the victim him or herself. Furthermore, the Court observed, in line with Tyrer, that it was not only physical pain with which Article 3 is concerned, but also 'the sentenced person's mental anguish of anticipating the violence he is to have inflicted upon him'. Thus, the Court found that the possible extradition of Soering to the US would amount to inhuman treatment and therefore a breach of Article 3. In the subsequent case of Cruz Varas v Sweden, the Court also held that the principles elaborated in Soering were equally applicable to cases involving the expulsion or deportation of aliens to state where torture or persecution was likely. In Cruz Varas v Sweden, however, the fact found by the Court did not suggest that the applicant was like to face such circumstances when the Swedish government decided to deport him to Chile.

From the cases referred to above, it will be evident that the Court has a clear conception of its role within the general context of the European Convention, and a clear understanding of the limits and potentialities of the Convention itself. Examination of the Court's extensive case law in other areas would tend to confirm this view. The Court's case law in the field of protection of freedom of the person (Article 5) and the right to a fair trial (Article 6) has been both voluminous and important. It has also extended the ambit of the substantive rights in question beyond unexpected limits. In Golder, for example, the Court held that the right to a fair trial in Article 6 also implied the right of access to courts for the determination of an individual's civil rights and obligations or in answer to any criminal charge. As Sinclair has pointed out, if one examines the plain words of Article 6, it is difficult to escape the conclusion that the Court engaged in judicial legislation in this particular case. Similarly, in Marckx, a case concerning the legal disabilities of illegitimate children in Belgium that the right to family life (Article 8) not only prevented the state from intervening in such matters, but also required it to create conditions in which such family life might be enjoyed to its maximum potential. Again, this judicial legislation was criticized by dissenting British Judge, Sir Gerald Fitzmaurice, as being 'a misguided attempt to read-or rather introduce-a whole code of family law into Article 8 of the Convention, thus inflating it in a manner wholly incommensurable with its true and intended proportions'. Despite the criticisms of judicial legislation, however, it is clear that the dynamic teleological approach adopted by the Court is consistent with the overall object and purpose of the Convention, which as the Court has pointed out recently is 'for the protection of individual human beings'. This being so, the Court went on to say that the provisions of the Convention must be 'interpreted and applied so as to make its safeguards practical and effective'.

The European Convention on Human Rights was unarguably one of the successes of post-1945 human rights developments. While it may not have fulfilled its original primary purpose in acting as a warning signal against the emergence of totalitarian regimes, nevertheless it has provided an extremely useful and potent mechanism of last resort for large numbers of individuals whose grievances have not been redressed by the relevant institutions in their own state. Citizens of the UK may, in particular, have good cause to look upon the European Convention as a safeguard against a domestic system which is ill-suited to protecting the rights and freedom of individuals.

European Social Charter

The primary purpose of the European Social Charter (ESC) is, in the words of thee Committee of Ministers, to act as 'the complement to the ECHR'. Thus, whereas the ECHR is designed to protect the civil and political rights of individuals from state interference, the primary aim of the ESC is to secure state participation in realizing the rights involved. As we saw in the context of the ICCPR and the ICESCR, the obligations on states concerning the implementation of the different categories of rights varied. Whereas in the case of the civil and political rights protected by the ICCPR, implementation is to be immediate and absolute, in the cast- of economic, social and cultural rights recognized by the ICESCR, the implementation is to be programmatic. The same divergence is evident in both the ECHR and ESC. The ECHR requires the civil and political rights protected to be secured immediately; the ESC demands a progressive approach.

Part I of the ESC states that the parties 'accept as the aim of their policy, to be pursued by all appropriate means ...in which the following rights and principles may be effectively realised ...'. A list of 19 rights and principles dealing with a wide variety of economic, social and cultural rights then follows. In a sense, therefore, Part I establishes the policy goals to which the parties commit themselves; it does not, however, at this stage create legally binding obligations for the parties. This is done by Part II of the ESC, which defines both the scope and content of the rights and principles set out in Part I in greater detail.

The obligations assumed by the states parties under the ESC are set out in Article 20. This adopts an unusual formulation by first placing an obligation on states to commit themselves to pursuing the policy goals set out in Part I and then giving the parties a choice as to which of the substantive rights it will consider itself bound to. Thus, Article 20(1) provides:

Each of the Contracting Parties undertakes

(a) to consider Part I of this Charter as a declaration of the aims which it will pursue by all appropriate means, as stated in the introductory paragraph of that Part;

(b) to consider itself bound by at least five of the following articles of Part II of this Charter: Article 1 [right to work], 5 [right to organise], 6 [right to bargain collectively], 12 [right to social security], 13 [right to social and medical assistance], 16 [right of the family to social, legal and economic protection] and 19 [right of migrant workers and their families to assistance and protection].

(c) in addition to the articles selected by it in accordance with the preceding sub-paragraphs, to consider itself bound by such a number of articles or numbered paragraphs of Part 11 of the Charter as it may select, provided that the total number of articles or numbered paragraphs by which it is bound is not less that 10 articles or 45 numbered paragraphs.

The apparently curious method of establishing state party obligations has a number of advantages which relate directly to the practical problems inherent in implementing the ESC. As Vasak points out, the object of committing states to the 'inner nucleus' of five out of the seven articles referred to in Article 20(1)(a) is to secure protection for what are seen as essential economic and social rights. The remaining 'outer nucleus' must therefore be considered as the foundation for a complete system of social justice. The obligations of the ESC are clearly flexible in nature, allowing account to be taken of the disparities in the economic conditions between the member state of the Council of Europe. States parties are therefore able to undertake their obligations progressively and programmatically, which is in line with rights implementation in the general field of economic, social and cultural rights.

Supervision: The present method of supervision under the ESC is by now a familiar system of periodic reports. Unlike the international instruments examined so far, however, the ESC requires two types of reports: first.. a biennial report concerning the implementation of the Part 11 rights which the Party in question has accepted and, second, report at intervals prescribed by the Committee of Ministers detailing the status of Part 11 rights not accepted by the Party. These reports are considered by a body known as the Committee of Independent Experts, which consists of seven 'independent experts of the highest integrity and of recognised competence in international and social questions' who are nominated by the parties and elected by the Committee of Ministers. The Committee of Experts is also assisted in its deliberations by a consultant supplied by the ILO. This is an interesting development, since it demonstrates the potential for the cross-fertilization of ideas in the field of economic, social and cultural rights.

The state reports, together with the conclusions of the Committee of Experts, are referred to a sub-Committee of the Governmental Social Committee of the Council of Europe. This is a political body, since it is composed of governmental representatives. It is, however, assisted by four consultants, two of whom are representative of employers' organizations and two of whom are trade union representatives. The Governmental Social Committee, in accordance with Article 27 of the ESC, then forwards its views to the Council of Europe. The state reports and the conclusions of the Committee of independent experts are also sent to the Consultative Assembly of the Council of Europe. This body is composed of delegations of elected members of the legislatures of each of the member states, and thus has a degree of democratic influence on the activities of the Council. Not surprisingly, there has sometimes been a divergence of opinion between the Committee of Ministers, which is composed entirely of government representatives, and the more democratic Consultative Assembly as to the course of action which should be taken on the reports of the Committee of Experts. As might be expected, the Consultative Assembly has, in general, favoured specific action by states where there appear to have been shortcomings in the implementation of their obligations under the ESC, whereas the Committee of Ministers has preferred to proceed more diplomatically and therefore at a general level. None the less, through the process of discourse between the various Council of Europe institutions and from the recommendations for state action which emerge at the end of it, the progressive implementation of certain economic and social rights does take place. An examination of the reports of the Committee of Experts and the recommendations which follow, clearly indicate an incipient jurisprudence in the field. It must be admitted, however, that the mechanisms for the development of rights in this area is imperfect in comparison to the ECHR. Although there have been proposals to incorporate the ESC as a protocol to the ECHR and make it subject to the enforcement mechanisms of that instrument, non concrete progress has been made to date. A protocol to the ESC has been adopted, but this simply extends the range of rights to be protected under the existing system of implementation.

In order to improve the implementation system under the ESC, the Council of Europe adopted a further Protocol to the Charter in Turin in 1991. While the Protocol is not in force at the time of writing, it is perhaps appropriate to examine its silent features since its entry into force is likely to take place in the near future. Under the Protocol, the membership of the Committee of Independent Experts is increased from seven to nine, but of greater importance is the enhanced role given to the Committee. Here, Article 2 of the Protocol (amending Article 24 of the Charter) gives the Committee exclusive competence to interpret the Charter and to write the reports of the Governmental Committee (the present Governmental Social Committee). The Charter's supervisory system will also be simplified by the Protocol and it will enhance the role of trade unions and NGOs in the process.

Since the major criticisms of the Charter have consistently been the indeterminate status of the Committee of Independent Experts' reports and the poverty of the supervisory system, the Council of Europe hoped that when the Charter is eventually amended by the Protocol, these criticisms will be addressed.

European Convention

Although the ECHR contains in Article 3 a clear prohibition on the use of torture, inhuman and degrading treatment was decided by the Committee of Ministers following a proposal from the Council of Europe's Consultative Assembly in 1983 to consider the adoption of a treaty which would introduce a preventative mechanism in this area. The present Convention, which entered into force in 1989, is the fruit of that proposal. It establishes a European Committee for the Prevention of Torture and Inhuman or Degrading Treatment composed of competent persons of high moral character of a number equal to that of the parties which are given authority to visit and investigate any place in which individuals deprived of their liberty are held. Such visits may be periodic or at times considered necessary by the Committee. Parties must allow the Committee access to its territory, the right to travel freely throughout its territory, full information on the places where persons deprived of their liberty are being held and unlimited access and freedom of mobility within such places. Further, the parties must not hinder the Committee's procedures, including the right to communicate within any person deprived of their liberty or any other person the Committee feels may be able to help it. Parties may in exceptional circumstances make representations to the Committee against a visit on grounds of national defence, public safety or serious disorder, but such representations are not conclusive and the Committee may make proposals to the party to institute different arrangements in order to facilitate fulfilment of its task.

Following a visit, the Committee must draw up a report

containing any necessary recommendations which it must then forward to the party concerned. If after consultation with the Committee a party refuses or fails to improve the situation concerning persons deprived of their liberty, then the committee by a two-third majority may decide to make a public statement on the matter. This threat of adverse publicity is clearly one of the most potent tools at the Committee's disposal.

The Convention represents an interesting departure from the traditional type of human rights treaty in two major ways. First, it is concerned primarily with the prevention of human rights abuses by taking pre-emptive action rather than relying on *ex post facto* control as is the case with most of the instruments so far examined. Secondly, it makes on-site investigation in the territory of a party the norm. States, by becoming party to the Convention, automatically concede the right to the Committee to undertake investigatory visits without prior approval. There is no question here of a state being able to plead that there has been an intervention in its internal affairs, since this is subject to explicit prior waiver.

TEN

Scene in Africa

While having dealt with human rights instruments and institutions which have been in place and functioning for some time in this book, it is the purpose of this chapter to examine a system of more recent origin.

Charter on Peoples' Rights

The African Charter, sometimes known as the Banjul Charter after the capital of the Gambia where it was drafted, is the most recent of the regional human rights instruments to come into force. It was adopted at the Eighteenth Assembly of Heads of State and Government of the Organization of African Unity (OAU) in Nairobi, Kenya in June 1981 and entered into force on 21 October 1986. As we shall see, the Charter differs considerably from its other regional counterparts, both in the catalogue of rights protected and in the means of implementation and protection. This is not surprising, since it was drafted to take account of African culture and legal philosophy, and is specifically directed towards African needs. Indeed, the Preamble to the Charter speaks of 'the virtue of the [member states] historical tradition and the values of African civilization which should inspire and characterize their reflection on the concept of human and peoples 'right'.

It might also be argued that of all the regional instruments, the African Charter faces the most acute challenges. Many African states are recently decolonized and are struggling with the legacies of economic underdevelopment, lack of education and inter-communal strife resulting from the colonial imposition of artificial boundaries. Furthermore, many of the political systems in a number of African states are not conducive to the proper functioning of democratic institutions-whether one uses the term democratic in a Western or an African sense—underpinned by the rule of law. None the less, the OAU Charter—which was adopted in 1963—committed the member states 'to promote international cooperation, having due regarded to the Charter of the United Nations and the Universal Declaration of Human Rights'. The African Charter may be seen as the fruit of this commitment.

Protected Rights

This is the first area in which the African Charter differs considerably from its other regional analogues. Not only does the Charter seek to protect individual civil and political rights, it also seeks to promote, within the single instrument, economic and social rights and the controversial category of third-generation rights. It also spells out clearly the duties owed by individuals to family, society and the state. This holistic approach to human rights is prefaced by the Preamble to the Charter, which states:

> ... that it is henceforth essential to pay particular attention to the right to development and that civil and political rights cannot be dissociated from economic, social and cultural rights in their conception as well as universality and the satisfaction of economic, social and cultural rights is a guarantee for the enjoyment of civil and political rights.

The civil and political rights, which are protected by Articles 2-13, comprise the traditional range of rights that are included in the ICCPR and the other regional instruments. One particular freedom that represents a particular African concern is Article 12, which prohibits the mass expulsion of non-nationals and is aimed at national, racial, ethnic or religious groups. There have on occasion been mass expulsions of all Ghanaians from its territory in 1983, and it is this form of action at which Article 12 is directed. All the substantive rights in the Charter are to be accorded to individuals without discrimination on any ground. It is interesting to note that this includes the injunction that there should be no discrimination on the grounds of a person's 'fortune', which implies African recognition that the enforcement of rights may depend upon a person's general circumstances or status in society.

The economic and social rights contained in the Charter also largely reflect the range of such rights in other international instruments. However, there are a number of additions which are worthy of note. The right to education, for example, in Article 17, is supplemented by a duty upon the state whose obligation it is to promote and protect the 'morals and traditional values recognized by the community'. Article 18 reflects similar African concerns and provides:

1 The family shall be the natural unit and basis of society. It shall be protected by the State which shall take care of its physical and moral health.
2 The State shall have the duty to assist the family which is the custodian of morals and traditional values recognized by the community.

Article 18(3) also contains one of the most comprehensive clauses concerning the prohibition of discrimination against women by providing that 'the state shall ensure the elimination of every discrimination against women and also ensure the protection of the rights of the woman and the child as stipulated in international declaration and conventions'. This extremely broad incorporation of other international instruments clearly makes no distinction as to whether or not they are in force for states parties to the Charter: those state will automatically be bound by the standards established by the relevant instruments on becoming party to the Charter.

The African Charter is the only regional human rights instrument to incorporate third-generation rights. In protecting the right to self-determination, the Charter not only traverses the familiar ground of the UN Covenants, but also includes rather more controversial rights such as the right to economic, social and cultural development 'with due regard to their freedom and identity and in equal enjoyment of the common heritage of mankind'. Article 24 of the Charter also includes the right of peoples to peace and security and to a general satisfactory environment favourable to their development'. Clearly, these rights impose obligations on states not only to order their internal affairs in such a way as to preserve or improve environmental factors, but they also require that they pursue particular forms of foreign policy calculated to achieve such an end.

Although the American Declaration deals with the question of duties as well as rights, it is only in the African Charter that duties are imposed on individuals as a matter of international legal obligation. Again, the reason for this is that the African sense of family and community places great emphasis upon the individual's responsibility to both groups. Many of the rights contained in the Charter thus have a correlative duty attached to them. Broad concepts of duty to the family, society and the state are established by Articles 27 and 28 of the Charter, while Article 29 lists the specific duties which are imposed upon the individual. Some of these duties have a particularly nebulous quality, and in many cases it is difficult to see where their limits might lie.

Another area in which the African charter differs from other human rights instruments is the absence of a provision permitting derogation from the rights protected in particular circumstances. While the rights concerning the physical integrity of the person to be absolute, many of the individual rights which deal with matters such as freedom of expression and association are formulated in a manner which implies the possibility of derogations.

Articles 8-13 provide for the enjoyment of rights within certain limitations. Article 8 provides for freedom of conscience and religion and declares that 'no one may, subject to law and order, be submitted to measures restricting the exercise of these freedoms'. Article 9(2) provides that 'every individual shall have the right to express and disseminate his opinions within the law'. Article 10(1) states that 'every individual shall have the right to free association provided that be abides by law'. Articles 11-13 continue in similar vein. It may be argued, however, that far from implying a right of derogation, these formulations simply indicate that the limits of these rights are prescribed by law in accordance with the concept of democratic legitimacy. This conclusion can, however, only be tentative, because unlike the preambles to the European and American Conventions, the African Charter nowhere refers to the fundamental importance of democracy and democratic institutions. None the less, since the Charter is a human rights instrument, it must be assumed that its provisions must be construed in favour of the primacy of rights and against state interference, even if it is justified by normally adopted legal measures. Here again, the notion of constitutional legitimacy may be implied. It is arguable however, that the formulation of the individual civil and political rights in the Charter is weaker and more susceptible to being undercut by 'legal' measures than those in its European and American counterparts.

Supervision

Article 1 of the Charter requires states to recognize the rights, duties and freedoms enshrined in it and to undertake to adopt legislative or other measures to give effect to them. The Charter also imposes two further classes of obligations upon states parties. First, under Article 25, they are 'to promote and ensure through teaching, education and publication the respect of the rights and freedoms contained in the ... Charter and to see to it that these freedoms and rights as well as their corresponding obligations and duties are understood'. Second, by Article, 26, parties are under a duty to guarantee the independence of the courts and 'shall allow the establishment and improvement of appropriate national institutions entrusted with the promotion and protection of the rights and freedoms guaranteed by the present Charter'.

The major perceptible difference between the institutional

structure of the Charter and that of other regional human rights instruments is the absence of any court to settle disputes between states or to rule on individual grievances. The reason for this, according to one African jurist, is that Africans tend to focus on reconciliation and consensus as a means of settling disputes, rather than upon contentious procedures. Article 30 of the Charter simply provides for the establishment of a Commission 'established within the framework of the [OAU] to promote human and peoples' rights and ensure their protection in Africa'. The Commission is composed of eleven members elected by the Assembly of Heads of State and Government of the OAU 'from amongst African personalities of the highest reputation, known for their high morality, integrity, impartiality and competence in matters of human and peoples' rights' for a period of six years. The African Commission, therefore, unlike its other regional analogues, is drawn from all members of its sponsoring regional organization, rather than parties to the Charter. The probable reason for this is that in the absence of any court, the Commission must exercise quasi judicial functions and needs therefore to reflect the wider, African community. The members of the Commission, however, serve in their individual capacities and not as government representatives.

Commission's Mandate

The Commission enjoys a broad and multifaceted role under Article 45 of the Charter. It operates under four main heads: promotional, protective, interpretative and consultative. Its promotional role entails the totality of activities commonly associated with this field. It is required, inter alia, to undertake 'studies and researches [sic]' on African human and peoples' rights problems, to organize seminars, symposia and conferences, and so on. More importantly however, it is also mandated 'should the case arise' to give its views or to make recommendations to governments. This language is reminiscent of the OAS Charter in so far as it relates to the competencies of the Inter-American Commission. We have already seen how creative that institution has been in developing its country studies and on-site investigation procedures, but it will be interesting to see if the African Commission can similarly develop its competencies.

Within the context of the Commission's promotional activities, it is also possible to discern a standard-setting role. Article 45(1)(b) requires the Commission to 'formulate and lay down, principles and rules aimed at solving legal problems relating to human and peoples' rights ... upon which African Governments may abuse their legislation'. This implies a proactive and quasi-legislative role for the Commission which, on the basis of this provision, may undertake drafting programmes of its own motion.

The protective function of the Commission comprises two aspects : an inter-state and an individual communication procedure. As we have already seen, these are common to the other regional human rights instruments, save that in the case of the African system, the procedures begin and end with the Commission since there is no court. These procedures will be examined in detail later.

The Commission's interpretative task once again assumed substantial significance in the absence of a court which is competent to offer authoritative interpretations of the Charter. Under Article 45(3) of the Charter, the Commission is mandated to 'interpret all the provisions of the present Charter at the request of a State party, an institution of the OAU or an African Organization recognized by the OAU'. This gives the Commission a role similar to that of the Inter-American Court of Human Rights under Article 64 of the American Convention. Whether the Commission will utilize the competence as creatively as the Inter-American Court remains to be seen. It should be noted that in addition to this formal quasi-judicial power to the Commission under Article 45, it will also be required to exercise its interpretative competencies under the communications procedures under Chapter III of the Charter.

Before leaving these general matters concerned with the Commission's mandate, some mention should be made of Articles 60 and 61. These are omnibus provisions which have the effect of integrating regional African human rights standards and practices with those of the universal and other regional system. Article 60 provides that the Commission 'shall draw inspiration from international law on human and peoples' rights'. It then lists, by way of example, a large number of universal instruments, both actual and potential, including the UN Charter, the Universal Declaration and all the human rights instruments made or to be made under the auspices of the UN. The effect of this provision is to create a deep reservoir of principles and rules from which the African Commission can draw. The depth of the reservoir is further increased by Article 61, which provides that the Commission `shall also take into consideration, as subsidiary measures to determine the principles of law' other international instruments, which would seem to mean in this context the other regional human rights instruments, and `African practices consistent with international norms on human and peoples' rights, customs generally accepted as law, general principles of law recognized by African states as well as legal precedents and doctrine'. The net effect of Articles 60 and 61 is to provide the Commission with the means by which to ensure the adequate integration of the African regional system into the mainstream of human rights law. In this respect, it is more adequately equipped than its American counterpart, which in turn occupies a better position than the European Commission.

Commission's Procedures

Before examining the Commission's inter-state and individual communications procedures it is appropriate to note that the Charter provides an extremely wide competence to that institution in carrying out its functions. Article 46 states : 'The Commission may resort to any appropriate method of investigation; it may hear from The Secretary-General of the [OAU] or any other person capable of enlightening it.'

Inter-state Complaints

There are two forms of inter-state complaint mechanism contained in the Charter. The first, under Article 47, permits a state party which believes another to have violated its obligations under the Convention to address a communication directly to the delinquent state. The communication must also be copied to the Secretary-General of the OAU and to the Chairman of the Commission. Within three months, the state to which the communication is addressed must respond fully, indicating the redress already given or the courses of action available to remedy the violation. If within three months the issue is not settled to the satisfaction of the two states through bilateral negotiations or through other mechanisms of peaceful dispute settlement, then either party may refer the matter to the Commission. This procedure does not differ from other forms of international dispute resolution, save in the fact that the Commission' jurisdiction is mandatory for parties to the Charter if either of the parties should choose to submit the matter of the dispute to the Commission. If neither of the parties wishes to submit the dispute to the Commission, then there is no time limit to the proceedings. Should the dispute be submitted to the Commission, the procedures for dealing with it are exactly the same as those where a dispute is brought before the Commission under Article 49.

The alternative procedure is initiated under Article 49 by a state complaining directly to the Commission that another state party has violated the provisions of the Charter. Before the Commission can deal with a complaint under Articles 47 or 49, however, it must satisfy itself that 'all local remedies, if they exist, have been exhausted'. There is no need to exhaust local remedies where the procedure for obtaining them is unreasonably prolonged. The inclusion of this particular provision in an inter-state procedure seems to be superfluous. If there is a breach of the Charter by a state, whether it relates to a substantive right or some other matter, under the general principles of international law, that will automatically give rise to a direct international wrong. Here, there is no requirement-indeed, there is no possibility-for another state to exhaust local remedies, since a state is unlikely to have the necessary legal standing before an appropriate domestic tribunal. Similarly, if the breach relates to the ill-treatment of an individual who must exhaust the local remedies within the respondent state, before the complaining state can take up the individual's cause. If the individual has not exhausted the available local remedies, there can, by definition, be no breach of the Charter.

Once the Commission has satisfied, itself, however, that local remedies have been exhausted, it then may ask states concerned to present to it all relevant information. There is no indication of who is to determine what is or is not relevant information, but presumably this lies within the province of the Commission. Furthermore, the Commission when considering the matter, may ask the states involved to submit written or oral representations to it. This should also be read in the light of Article 46 which, it will be recalled, allows the Commission to hear 'from any other person capable of enlightening it'. It would seem, therefore, that the Commission has a very wide power to call witnesses, including the alleged victim if there be one. If, after following this procedure, no 'amicable solution based on the respect of Human and Peoples' Rights' has been achieved by the Commission, it must draw up a report which is to be sent to the OAU Heads of State and Government. The report must not only contain the facts and findings of the Commission, but it may also contain such recommendations as the Commission 'deems useful'. Two points may be noted about this procedure. First, the reference to an 'amicable solution' in Article 52 suggests that the primary concern of the Commission is to achieve a friendly settlement. This is nowhere explicitly stated, but such an approach would seem consistent both with African legal philosophy and the techniques of other human rights institutions. Second, the final destination of the Commission' report is clearly the dominant political organ of the OAU. This implies that any final decision on the report is likely to be based on political rather than legal considerations. This conclusion is further reinforced when it is recalled that these are inter-state disputes under the Charter, which are hardly likely to be conducive to good relations between the parties. This may very well translate itself into the political alliances in the meeting of the Heads of State and Government.

Personal Communications

It is perhaps a misnomer to refer to individual communications under the Charter, since the heading of the appropriate part refers to 'other communications'. A quick perusal of the procedure to be applied in such cases also indicates that it is unlike that utilized in the two other regional conventions, but appears to be a fusion of ECOSOC and the regional conventions' procedures.

Article 55 requires the Secretary of the Commission to draw up separate lists of inter-state and other communications under the Charter and to transmit them to the Commission. It would seem that the use of the term 'other communications' together with the admissibility requirements in Article 56 implied that the drafters of the Charter envisaged such communications would be most likely to originate from individuals, but the absence of exclusive language in Article 55 suggests that communications may also be received from NGOs and other bodies. What is clear, however, is that the African Charter does not require, like Article 45 of the American Convention, that the complainant be a victim of a violation. This means that only can a person, group of persons or NGO submit a communication on behalf of another individual or individuals, but the Charter also recognizes Class actions.

The admissibility requirements in Article 56 are similar to those of other human rights instruments. Thus, communications must not be anonymous (although anonymity can be insulting language). Local remedies must also have been exhausted, although there is no stipulation that this must have been done in accordance with the general principles of international law. It must be assumed, however, that the Commission would be willing to imply such a requirement, especially since Article 56(5) states that such remedies must not be unduly tardy. Once local remedies have been exhausted, communications must be submitted 'within a reasonable time'. One admissibility requirement peculiar to the African Charter is that communications must not be 'based exclusively on news disseminated through the mass media'. Perhaps it would have been easier here for the drafters simply to refer to the Commission to dispose of communications relying exclusively on media coverage, and also to allow it to deal with other cognate matters casting doubt upon the legitimacy of a communication's admissibility.

The main feature of the Charter's individual petition system which distinguishes it from the other regional systems and the Optional Protocol to the ICCPR is that it deals not with individual violations of human rights, but only with 'special cases which reveal the existence of series or massive violations of human and peoples' rights'. In this respect, the Charter's individual communication procedure has more in common with the Commission on Human Rights' procedures under ECOSOC Resolutions 1235 and 1503. Thus, if an, individual communication does not reveal a series of serious or massive violations of human rights, the Commission will not take any notice on it. The Commission must therefore wait until an accumulation of individual petitions discloses such a state of affairs. It can hardly be said that it assists the Commission to carry out its preventive function, and indeed, it may be asserted that the mechanism is highly unsatisfactory. However, the right of individual communication was clearly excluded for particular reasons. The recent history of human and peoples' rights in Africa has been one which has involved particularly widespread and brutal violations, largely based on inter-communal disputes. It may be said that these gross violations are of greater concern of African than the more 'peripheral' violations which occur within the European context. It may also be argued that the African concern for community above the individual, makes these matters of greater import within the African context.

If the Commission decides that a complaint or series of complaints discloses the series of serious or massive widespread violations required by Article 51, it must then be referred to the OAU's Assembly of Heads of State and Government. The Assembly must than decide whether or not to request the Commission to undertake 'an in-depth study' of the cases and to make a factual report and recommendations on its findings. In cases of emergency duly notified to the Commission, the Chairman of the Assembly is mandated to take this decision on behalf of the plenary body. Whether the Commission undertakes an 'in-depth study' depends upon the determination of the OAU's political organ. Under Article 10 of the Charter of the OAU, all such decisions must be taken by a two-thirds majority of states present and voting.

Any in-depth study which is authorized by the Assembly remains confidential until such time as it decides that it might be made public. Similarly, the annual report of the Commission's activities may not be published until it has been considered by the Assembly. Both these provisions seem to suggest that, in the absence of the appropriate two-third majority, both the studies and reports may remain confidential. This deprives the system of one of most valuable sanctions available in the human rights field-the sanction of adverse publicity. It is, perhaps, a mark of lack of effectiveness of this system, that after four years in existence, the Assembly has not yet taken any decisions on reports on individual communications.

ELEVEN

Scenario in Asia

The humanitarian principles embodied in the UN Charter and the Universal Declaration of Human Rights marked the beginning of a full-blown global human rights regime. The Declaration, signed fifty years ago, established a standard of civilised conduct, which applies to all governments in the treatment of their citizens. For example, the Declaration requires States to provide subsistence needs and basic welfare provision as well as a panoply of civil and political rights. Although the latter assumed prominence in the subsequent history of the post-1945 regime, it is important to underscore that from the outset, universal human rights encompassed a concern for positive rights (such as collective provision of education and healthcare) as well as negative rights (freedom from repressive government policies).

The framers of these basic documents assumed that there was no necessary conflict between the principles of sovereignty and non-intervention and respect for universal human rights. This represented a historic evolution in the norms of international society, which from the seventeenth century onwards had maintained that the domestic practices of governments were not a subject of international concern. According to the Westphalia conception of legitimacy, a government's claim to be recognised as sovereign was not dependent upon how it behaved towards its own citizens. As a consequence of the experiences of totalitarianism, governments recognised that there was a need to challenge the Westphalia model of unlimited sovereignty. In these emerging human rights norms, there was a clear consensus that States must be made accountable for their behaviour.

Underlying the evolution of human rights principles was the conviction held by the framers of the Charter that there was a clear link between good governance and the maintenance of international peace and security. It was believed that the aggressive foreign policies of the Axis powers were caused by the militaristic nature of their political systems. Diplomats and State leaders in the early post-1945 period endorsed the 'democratic peace thesis, which has been rejuvenated in the theory and practice of international relations since the end of the Cold War.

The manifesto for human rights and international security contained within the Charter and the Declaration, represented, therefore, a radical assault on the existing principle of international legitimacy. Sovereignty remained the constitutive norm of the society of States, but the meaning that was given to sovereignty had been modified. In R.J. Vincent's words, the way a government treats its people exposes the internal regimes of all the members of international society to the legitimate appraisal of their peers.

Since the first wave of standard setting, successive decades have seen the growing codification of human rights into both treaty and customary international law. Alongside this strengthening of the regime, there has emerged a growing moral awareness among world public opinion of human rights issues and concerns, reflected in the existence of NGOs like Amnesty International which act as the conscience of the regime. An informed and active citizenry has a crucial role to play in monitoring State behaviour for the reason that there is a disjunctive between the declaratory commitments of governments to protect and promote human rights and their compliance with these standards. For example, Amnesty International pointed out in its 1997 Report that of the world's 185 sovereign States, 123 routinely practise torture. Even more striking is the feet that the crime of genocide which is outlawed by the 1950 Genocide Convention has not been banished from the practice of world politics, as the appalling tragedy of

Rwanda illustrated in April 1994. In short, governments—many of whom drafted and signed the International Bill of Rights—have massively defaulted on their normative commitments.

One of the principal purposes of Human Rights in Global Politics is to reflect critically upon the stark contradiction between the idea of universal human rights and practices of human wrongs. To this end, we have brought together a distinguished group of scholars and practitioners to engage with the question: why are there all these human rights standards but the bodies keep piling up? The assumption here is that there is a universal standard of human rights but States fail to live up to it. However, a recurring theme in the volume is the questioning of the foundation of this universal standard. Perhaps another reason for this compliance gap is that political communities interpret universal human rights very differently. On this reading, the explanation for the fifty years' crisis in the human rights regime is expressed succinctly by E. H. Carr, "the question is not who are the standard-bearers, but what is the standard?" Two possible responses suggest themselves. First, different societies 'sign up' to the idea of universal human rights but disagree over the meaning and priority to be accorded to these rights. This intersociety critique, when wielded by non-liberal States, becomes an assault on the West's understanding of what counts as human rights. Second, and more subversive from a human rights perspective, is whether there is a shared discourse of human rights *per se*. In this chapter, we provide an overview of the explanations given by our contributors for the existence of the compliance gap and their prescriptions for closing it.

Developments in post-modern social and political theory challenge the very quest for moral certainty, which underpinned the vision of the post-1945 human rights regime. Post-modernists tell us to be incredulous towards metanarratives such as 'humanity': surely, they argue, the presumption of universal human rights is but another example of Enlightenment mythology. An underlying theme of this volume is to reflect upon the implications for the practice of human rights of the contention, made by post-moderns, that the architecture of the human rights regime has no epistemological warrant for the foundations it assumes.

Historically, the idea of rights has embodied two foundational claims. First, that there is an identifiable subject who has entitlements; and secondly, that to possess a right presupposes the existence of a duty bearer against whom the right is claimed.

A right in this sense can be thought of as consisting of five main elements: a right-holder (the subject of a right) has a claim to some substance (the object of a right), which he or she might assert, or demand, or enjoy, or enforce (exercising a right) against some individual or group (the bearer of the correlative duty), citing in support of his or her claim some particular ground (the justification of a right).

It is this last point, that there is 'some particular ground' upon which right-holders can justify their claim to rights, which has framed the dominant discourse on human rights.

The idea of human rights, for a liberal natural rights theorist, is that we all have rights by virtue of our common humanity. Individuals have certain kinds of rights as members of particular communities, but human rights belong to humanity and do not depend for their existence on the legal and moral practices of different communities. Thus, even if individuals are denied rights by the laws of a particular state, they still can make a claim to rights by virtue of their membership of common humanity. What, then, philosophically grounds such a claim to universality?

One attempt to furnish a defence of common morality historically has been made by the natural law tradition. At its core, natural law maintains that there is a unity among all peoples of the world irrespective of cultural difference. For Victoria, writing in the sixteenth century, humankind was governed by natural laws of love and amity. Later, society-of-

States theorists recognised the intrusion of the 'law of nations' into the idea of a cosmic moral law, but nevertheless hold on to the idea that natural law provides an underlying moral foundation. Whilst classical thinking on natural law placed duties at the centre of its moral deliberations, the challenge for contemporary advocates is to show how natural law can support a theory of universal rights.

Epistemology plays a central role in discerning the content of natural rights. Claims to know what is right are founded on "those basic precepts of common morality [which] are accessible to human reason, they can be known by anyone capable of thought and action". Thus, the faculty of reason which is assumed to be transcultural enables individuals to deduce the correct moral code by which to live their lives. This is an appealing idea but the fundamental weakness of 'practical reason' is that it cannot easily explain why moral practices vary within and between cultures.

Recognising that natural law is a problematic justification for human rights, we nevertheless agree with Chris Brown's contention that "some idea of natural law must underlie all genuinely universal approaches to human rights". Contemporary liberal universalisers like R.J. Vincent and Henry Shue find themselves occupying the same epistemological terrain as the natural law tradition (our lower-right cell) but put rights rather than duties at the centre of their moral reasoning. The kernel of this natural rights position is that all individuals have certain basic rights because they share the same essential human nature. Shue's understanding of 'basic rights' develops out of the idea that without the satisfaction of needs such as 'subsistence' and 'security' it is impossible to enjoy all other rights. However, as Vincent argues, some natural rights thinkers identify "a second, and deeper, appeal not to our physical but to our moral nature. It is in this context", Vincent continues, "that human rights are sometimes called inalienable".

Liberal natural rights thinking has underpinned the

development of the international legal regime on human rights. For evidence of the widespread acceptance of the discourse of 'natural rights', we need look no further than the United Nations Charter which seeks 'to reaffirm faith in fundamental human rights'. Similarly, the Preamble to the 1948 Universal Declaration of Human Rights states that the "recognition of the inherent dignity and of the equal and inalienable rights of all members of the human family is the foundation of freedom, justice and peace in the world". The fundamental problem with defending the human rights regime in terms of natural rights thinking is the failure of its advocates to provide a convincing theory of human nature which would ground notions of human dignity.

Ken Booth argues that defending the idea of human rights in terms of a fixed theory of human nature corrupts our thinking about the possibilities for humanity at the end of the millennium. For Booth, the question 'Are human rights universal?' is an unhelpful one because it is too soon in human history to give a definite answer. By locating the subject of human rights at the interface of the disciplines of International Relations and Anthropology, Booth is able to identify three tyrannies that oppress the theory and practice of human rights: 'presentism', 'culturalism' and 'positivism'. 'Presentism' views the social world as natural and immutable, whereas social anthropology tells us that humanity is constantly evolving and that appeals to human nature as the 'clinching argument' are always overturned by changing social relations. This, for Booth, is the starting point for thinking about the question of the universality of human rights.

The second tyranny is 'culturalism'—the belief that cultures can be black-boxed in the same way that realists in International Relations black-box States. Booth rejects the exclusivity of cultures on the grounds that it privileges traditional values at the expense of emancipator ones. The claim of cultural authenticity should not be allowed to stop the conversation on human rights any more than the appeal to a particular view of human nature should close discussion on the possibility of a warless world. In the past, Booth has cautioned against the dangers of ethnocentrism – seeing other cultures through the prism of one's own sense of cultural superiority – but he argues that sensitivity to the cultural values of others should not be allowed to degenerate into the dogma of culturalism.

The idea of emancipation is the only effective escape from regressive human rights thinking but Booth acknowledges that this raises as many questions as it answers. Finally, he tries to answer some of these questions through a critique of the third tyranny of 'objectivity' and a defence of human rights as universal values. The problem with claims to objectivity in the social world is that they naturalise the existing order as given and immutable. As Booth argues, this is threatening to human rights because by leaving power where it is, the daily round of human wrongs is reproduced. Cultural relativists and post-modernists argue for toleration of diversity, but Booth thinks that we should change the focus to asking 'how much diversity should be tolerated?' The people who have to be heard are not governments, journalists or even human rights NGOs; rather, they are the victims of world politics who should be placed at the centre of theory and praxis in world politics. In deciding how much diversity is tolerable in world politics, Booth argues that a good place to start would be to 'ask the victims' whether they want to remain hungry and oppressed. If the answer is no, then he claims that there is no intelligible reason for saying, "this is not my concern."

In response to the question of what are the foundations for human rights, Booth follows Geoffrey Warlock and Mary Midgley in asserting that it is wrong to torture, starve, humiliate and hurt others. Human rights are not a matter of opinion, cultural prejudice or one community's story as opposed to another's; they are a response to these 'universal social facts'. These derive, according to Booth, 'from our animal nature (the need for food and shelter) and from our social character and potentiality'. Human rights, then, are an idea whose time has come, and this is reflected in the almost universal acceptance of the language of universal human rights.

Reading the human rights story as part of the moral evolution of the human race is echoed by Jack Donnelly. Like Booth, Donnelly identifies a critical relationship between the ideas of human rights and human dignity. Historically, societies have secured human dignity through other mechanisms than human rights, but Donnelly shows how the idea of human rights emerged as a specific historical response to the challenges of modernity. Rather than depending upon an historical account of the subject, he advances the claim that human rights arose in the West in the early part of the twentieth century as a way to overcome threats to human dignity posed by repressive political and economic structures.

Donnelly's willingness to side-step the question of how we ground universal human rights reflects his belief, like Booth's, that any attempt to resolve the meta-ethical foundations of human rights is a distraction. What matters for Donnelly is the 'remarkable international normative consensus on the list of rights' found in the Universal Declaration, the 1966 International Covenants on civil/ political, and economic/ social rights and the 1993 Vienna Declaration. He supports this contention by appealing to the cross-cultural consensus on basic rights such as "the rights to life, liberty, security of the person; the guarantee of legal personality; and protections against slavery, arbitrary arrest, detention, or exile and inhuman or degrading treatment". What further strengthens Donnelly's claim that there is a normative consensus underlying the human rights regime is the fact that in the daily round of diplomacy, State leaders justify their human rights policies in terms of these standards.

Whilst arguing that the various legal instruments which constitute the international bill of rights command 'a remarkable international normative consensus', Donnelly recognises that States do not always uphold these standards. Individuals claim human rights against their State because States are the only bearers of correlative duties, but they frequently fail to fulfil these duties. It is this discrepancy between the human rights commitments of States and their actual practices, which Donnelly sees as the central problematic of the contemporary human rights regime. The challenge then is to close the gap between the standard embodied in the regime and States' compliance with it. Liberals like Donnelly are cautiously optimistic that the regime can be mobilised by its supporters as a means to pressurise those States, which transgress its rules and flout its conventions. Through public censure, promises of rewards for good behaviour, threats of economic sanctions, and, ultimately, armed intervention; the society of States has the potential to use human rights as a civilising force against repressive governments.

In stark contrast, Chris Brown argues that the existence of the standard is itself the problem. Rights, in short, are a consequence of the civilised practices of liberal polities and not the cause of these. Therefore, Brown argues forcefully, any attempt by international society to close the compliance gap is a 'near-impossible task'. Brown criticises defenders of the regime from a communitarian perspective, which holds that we have rights by virtue of our community and not some abstract notion of 'common humanity'. This is an argument that has traditionally been mobilised by cultural relativists. The central claim here is that morality is culturally bound and values can only be brooded in tradition. The idea, then, of individuals possessing inalienable rights which they claim against the State if unthinkable in many societies where the individual is embedded in a complex network of communal duties and familial responsibilities. Following Molly Cochran, we interpret cultural relativism as a form of moral discourse which founds and enables the ethical discourse in which social judgements are possible.

Cultural relativists are often accused of being unable to judge between competing values. Brown's chapter shows the difficulties that relativists have in responding to this criticism. He argues that whilst 'some kind of lowest common denominator' might be present in diverse cultures, such a moral standard lacks a 'critical cutting edge' because it is reducible to these cultural practices. He qualifies this by recognising that certain human wrongs like genocide and mass murder will be caught by this moral minimalism. Although this 'general moral standard' provides a means to judge and criticise egregious regimes like Hitler's Germany, Pol Pot's Cambodia and Amin's Uganda, Brown argues that he is unable to deal with more routine human rights abuses.

In showing the difficulties that relativists have in criticising other cultures, Brown does not argue for a universalist position. Instead, he seeks to transcend the debate between relativists and universalists by arguing that the problem with both positions is their dependence upon epistemological foundationalism: the problem with universal critiques of relativism is that they assume that there is some non-relativist position upon which to stand. It is this claim which Brown rejects and he does so by drawing on the arguments of the post-modern philosopher Richard Rorty. For a pragmatist like Rorty, the idea that reason or science can access 'justified true belief (epistemology) is nothing but a myth. Our beliefs are no more than contingent preferences, which help us to cope with the complexity of late modern life. Rights, for Rorty, are nothing more than a story that liberal societies have decided to 'tell' and, as a consequence, it is only liberal societies which provide an epistemological context for human rights justifications.

The rejection by pragmatists of all narratives which posit universal truths would appear, at first sight, to sound the death-knell for defenders of human rights. However, Rorty argues that the jettisoning of epistemological foundationalism does not mean that liberals cannot defend human rights values.

Rather, he argues that it is 'we twentieth century liberals' who have the responsibility to nurture and strengthen the 'human rights culture', which is a fact of the post-Holocaust world. Crucially for Rorty, this culture "seems to owe nothing to increased moral knowledge, and everything to hearing sad and sentimental stories". What human solidarity depends upon is the manipulation of the sentiments such that 'we liberals' come to realise that our differences with others are less important than our shared capacity to experience pain and suffering. As Brown points out, Rorty's position has nothing to say to those societies, which have not undergone a process of 'education of the sentiments'. Thus, Rorty tells us that there is no knockdown argument against those Bosnian Serbs who choose to construct Bosnian Muslims as sub-human. He does not want to call these people inhuman or morally wrong as this implies the existence of universal human nature; instead, he wants to argue that they have been deprived of the conditions in which to develop feelings of human solidarity. Brown recognises Rorty's position 'does not solve all the problems of relativism' and sentimentality is an 'inadequate' response to human wrongs but reluctantly admits that 'it is difficult to see what other moral vocabulary is available to us once we reach the limit of an ethical community'.

The strength of Brown's position—which we label as 'communitarian pragmatism' is his attempt to hold on to human rights whilst jettisoning their philosophical foundations. What the debate between the upper-left side of the figure and the upper-right illustrates is that dispensing with epistemological certainty has not resolved key questions about the nature and limits of an ethical community within which rights claims are situated. Whilst the contours of this new post-pragmatist debate between cosmopolitanism and communitarianism are not as clear-cut as between traditional communitarianism and natural rights theory, the conversation between communitarian and cosmopolitan pragmatism—represented in this volume by Brown on the one hand and

Booth, Parekh and Midgley on the other – contributes to recent philosophical reflections on the possibilities for universal values in the wake of the Enlightenment.

The moral philosopher, Bhikhu Parekh, argues for a conception of universal values which steers a course between the opposites of moral relativism and foundationalist claims of an essential and knowable human nature. Parekh agrees with Booth that the fundamental problem with relativism is 'that we have no means of judging a society's moral beliefs and practices'. At the opposite pole to relativism stands 'moral monism', a position which maintains that 'we cannot only judge other societies but also lay down what way of life is the highest or truly human' (lower-right cell in Figure 1). Parekh finds this equally unsatisfactory because it assumes an essential human nature which can be revealed after the superstructure of cultural embeddedness has been stripped away.

Between these two extremes lies 'minimum universalist' which recognises the fact of moral diversity but believes "that moral life can be lived in several different ways, but insists that they can be judged on the basis of a universally valid body of values". He identifies this position with H.L.A. Hart, Michael Walzer, John Rawls, Stuart Hampshire and Martha Nussbaum. Although this theoretical position has more to commend it than the other two, Parekh argues that it does not overcome the following objections. First, it relies on an account of human nature which brings it perilously close to monism; secondly, contrary to Donnelly, it is questionable whether there is a normative consensus on prohibiting even the most cruel and inhumane practices; and thirdly, universal principles are too abstract or too weak to provide the possibility of judgement across cultures. Parekh is dissatisfied with all three existing approaches, advocating a theory of non-ethnocentric universal values. These, he contends, can only be constructed by means of a dialogue between equals. It is important to pause and reflect on what Parekh means by a dialogue and why we think it represents 'cosmopolitan pragmatism'.

The point of a cross-cultural dialogue is to arrive at a body of values to which all the participants can be expected to agree. Our concern is not to discover values, for they have no objective basis, but to agree on them . . .Values are a matter of collective decision, and like any other decision they are based on reasons. Since moral values cannot be rationally demonstrated, our concern should be to build a consensus around those that can be shown to be rationally most defensible.

In emphasising that universal values can have no 'objective basis', Parekh can be located. Universal values are possible but have to be decided through argumentation. What he is espousing is a very different position to that articulated by Rorty and Brown who reject the idea that reason can arbitrate between rival validity claims. Brown opines that communitarian pragmatists can supply us with an account of how we should live, but their justification is only intelligible within the limits of an ethical community. In contrast, Parekh's cosmopolitan pragmatism believes it is possible to recognise the reality of cultural embeddedness whilst leaving open the possibility for a transcultural consensus which is more than just 'the lowest common denominator of different cultural traditions'.

How, then, does Parekh try to balance the centrifugal tendencies of ethnocentrism and universalism? Towards the end of the chapter, he shifts the focus to the 'Asian values' debate as a way of exploring how non-foundational universal values can be arrived at through cross-cultural dialogue. In contrast to Booth's critique of the language of 'Asian values', Parekh welcomes the fact that Singapore and China, as participants in the human rights dialogue, bring to the 'table' their own ethnocentric biases. Singapore's challenge to Western values rests upon a defence of a different form of life, which privileges communal values over individual rights. Parekh argues that this alternative understanding of human dignity 'is fully consistent with universal values'. By contrast, China's rejection of the fundamental freedoms, which underpin the human rights regime, such as free speech, freedom of association and political participation, 'offends' against universal values. The key question here is why is Singapore's ethnocentrism acceptable and China's not? As we have seen above, Parekh wants to differentiate his position from that of minimum universalism but his criteria for judging between the moral practices of Singapore and China seem to rely on a conception of universal values, which precedes the dialogue. He argues that there are certain 'universal constants' such as human dignity, worth, equality and fundamental interests which 'generate appropriate universal values' (our emphasis). If these constants are already built into the structure of all societies, Parekh's attempt to derive cosmopolitanism without foundations through dialogue is vulnerable to the criticism that he is presupposing the very foundations, which he seeks to deny.

Parekh argues that an outsider's judgement of another society's interpretation of universal values is strengthened if there is internal criticism of the justifications, which its own government puts forward. He cites Chinese human rights activists who argue that torture, arbitrary arrest and imprisonment without proper trial are not compatible with the language of universal human rights which Chinese State leaders proclaim. Whilst internal critique adds legitimacy to the West's moral condemnation of China's human rights practices, it raises the broader issue as to whether the criticisms of outsiders are only valid in those situations where values are internally contested. Ultimately, this is not an acceptable position because it denies the validity of outsiders making moral judgements in the absence of internally disputed values and practices.

A good illustration of this problem is the case of Koranic punishments in Islamic societies. The practice of amputation of the right hand for theft is morally abhorrent in the West, but Muslim societies defend this cultural practice on the grounds that however severe the punishment might seem, 'it is in fact extremely lenient and merciful in comparison to what the offender will suffer in the next life should the religious punishment not be enforced in this life'. The Sudanese human rights scholar An-Na' im argues that whilst the values of the Koran are open to interpretation and contestation in relation to some practices, there is no interpretation of Islam which would prohibit this religious punishment for theft. This essentialist view of Islam is open to the critique mobilised by Booth.

An-Na'im argues that Muslim governments see no incompatibility between this cultural practice and their acceptance of the right (embodied in the Universal Declaration and the International Covenants) that 'no one shall be subjected to torture or to cruel, inhuman or degrading treatment'. But if the amputation of limbs is consistent with universal human rights norms, then where does the concession to cultural diversity stop? If the regime is to have any normative force, it must provide an independent moral standard which is not reducible to cultural particularism.

The case of Koranic punishments challenges the advocates of cross cultural dialogue. Whilst such a dialogue would provide an opportunity for Islamic societies to justify their legal practices as being in accord with internationally agreed human right standards, conversation requires that the participants be open to changing their practices. However, States enduring Islamic law have been reluctant to reflect critically on their religious practices and this has prevented any meaningful cross-cultural dialogue.

A further area of dispute where ethnocentric biases have hitherto proved resistant to genuine dialogue is that between the United States and China. This issue is emerging as a key foreign policy challenge for the United States at the end of the twentieth century, and it presents scholars working in the human rights field with a case which illustrates the ideological and practical constraints acting upon negotiators. How should we characterise the US-China debate on 'rights'? It is often argued that 'rights talk' is alien to Chinese culture and traditions. An example cited in support of this argument is the radically different social relations found in Chinese society. In place of Western ideas of independence, equality and liberty, Chinese culture has developed a very different set of moral and communal relations emphasising hierarchy, deference and interdependence. This picture of the self which underpins Chinese culture is radically at odds with the West's understanding of what it means to be human. From a Chinese perspective, it does not make sense – so the argument runs – to speak of humanity as an attribute of an individual; rather, "an individual can only become a human being in community".

Whilst cultural difference has played some part in shaping China's response to the human rights regime, it is an inadequate explanation. In the first instance, an obvious danger with this line of argument is that it counterposes two distinct and homogeneous 'Chinese' and 'Western' identities. It is not clear that the cultural differences between the USA and China are greater than those which exist between the USA and other non-liberal States which publicly endorse the human rights regime. More to the point, it is up to defenders of difference to show how the incorporation of universal human rights into Chinese traditions would undermine their culture.

The belief that China is different led the Beijing government to criticise the discourse of human rights. Their stance was clearly spelt out in a 'White Paper' entitled, *Human Rights in China* published in 1991. It argued that China was a developing country with limited resources and a huge population. For this reason, social turmoil could threaten the people's most important right, 'the right to subsistence'. Although rejecting the emphasis upon civil and political rights, China is at the same time appealing to a collective right to subsistence, which is more minimalist than the economic and social rights contained in the Covenant. The implication of this position is that the State has a moral responsibility to curtail individual freedoms and political participation in the name of the higher good of the community. Moreover, China rejected any international criticism of its human rights record since this constituted interference in its internal affairs.

What should we make of these arguments put forward by the Chinese government? China's position is open to two possible interpretations. Either China is part of the dialogue over universal values—albeit advancing a very different conception of what it means to be a human being than in traditional rights-based discourse—or China is using the language of human rights as a foreign policy instrument designed to deflect criticism of the regime (whilst promoting economic interests in the bargain). Even if China is sincere in its aim to promote a particular form of life, it is difficult to see why we should value this type of political order if it treats fundamental human rights with contempt.

The Clinton Administration made it clear that China's human rights practices were unacceptable, but fell short of pursuing a policy of diplomatic and economic isolation. In the aftermath of the UN Human Rights Commission's decision not to debate China's human rights record, Secretary of State Madeleine Albright warned in April 1997 that the United States will continue to 'shine the spotlight' on violators. 'China is changing', she added, 'but the Chinese Government's repression of political dissent has not'. Despite these strong words, the Clinton Administration elevated human rights beneath commercial interests on the foreign policy agenda. Al Gore's visit to China typified the Democrat's Janus-faced attitude to China. Following the agreement to buy Boeing aircraft worth 425 million dollars, Gore genuflected to his guests with the words 'we are greatly honoured by this order from our valued customer and old friend'. It would be unreasonable to single out the United States for prioritising commercial diplomacy over human rights. Despite the efforts of progressive small States like Denmark to cajole their fellow European Union members into 'getting tough' with China, few European States supported the Danish proposal to censure

China at the UN Commission. During the same week that the resolution was rejected, the Chinese premier Li Peng gave a timely speech to the International Chamber of Commerce in Shanghai, in which he dangled the carrot of $300 billion of business opportunities in China before 2000.

Western States might respond to this criticism of elevating commercial interests over human rights concerns by arguing that the two are pulling in the same direction. The idea behind the Clinton policy of 'commercial engagement' is that it is better to trade and criticise a recalcitrant State than to isolate it. This was essentially Clinton's justification for the renewal of China's most favoured nation trade privileges. "1 believe if we were to revoke normal trade status it would cut off our contact with the Chinese people and undermine our influence with the Chinese Government." Yet this begs the obvious question why Clinton imposed economic sanctions on Burma, which has an equally appalling human rights record to that of China? The US President repeatedly criticised the Burmese government, calling it a 'gangster state' in his keynote address to the ASEAN Regional Forum meeting in Manila in 1997. Critics of this move, particularly in the Asia region, contrast the tough stand against Burma with the lukewarm relations maintained with the equally repressive, albeit far richer, China.

In addition to the above commercial and geopolitical considerations, one further reason why China escaped moral censure at the 1997 Human Rights Commission in Geneva was its muted indication that it might be about to sign the 1966 Covenants. Such a move would be further evidence of China's progressive enmeshment in the human rights discourse. The key turning point here was its decision to sign the 1993 Vienna Declaration on Human Rights. In signing, China consented to Paragraph 3 which states that "all human rights are universal, indivisible and inter-related". An important implication of this is that under-development cannot be "invoked to justify the abridgement of internationally recognised human rights". By publicly endorsing a position which was at variance with its 1991 White Paper, China has unwittingly left itself open to criticism of its continuing human rights abuses.

China's entanglement in the diplomacy of human rights has had some effects in legitimising human rights practices, but in no way can this interaction be called a dialogue in the sense understood by Parekh. China is playing a tactical game designed to deflect Western threats to its regime, but it shows little sign of fully participating in the post-Cold War conversation on human rights. Evidence in support of this claim can be seen in the statement by the head of the Chinese delegation to the Vienna Conference, Liu Huaqiu, who argued "one should not and cannot think of the human rights standard and model of certain countries as the only proper ones and demand all other countries to comply with them". The problem here is that China has signed up to universal human rights standard at Vienna and at the same time has justified its stance on human rights by claiming there is no standard, and that those who seek to enforce one are playing the game of power politics.

In order to have a dialogue on the content of non-foundationalist universal values, participants must be prepared to reflect critically on whether their human rights practices are 'rationally defensible'. As was seen from the above, neither Chinese nor Western State leaders have been prepared to empathise with the ethnocentrism of the other. Instead, each party has used the diplomacy of human rights to try and convert the other to its position. What is required is for the United States and China to enter into the conversation in the knowledge that they must be open to changing their position.

How, then, should we respond to states which refuse to enter into a dialogue and which continue systematically to abuse basic rights? Mary Midgley argues that the moral vocabulary of human rights provides a compass for finding our way in the world. She argues that public opinion in the West has a responsibility to protest against global human wrongs and that no one can claim to be an innocent bystander.

Although Midgley recognises that there are always limits to the possibilities for ethical conduct, she warns against accepting the 'common sense' of realism with its impoverished conception of the moral imagination. Instead, she argues for an expansion of our moral horizons such that we come to recognise that 'we can often do enormously more than we are inclined to claim'.

At the heart of her critique of realism's moral boundaries is the conviction that we all have moral duties to come to the aid of 'distant humans'. Midgley supports this claim by drawing on her own recollections of what it meant to be a concerned citizen living in Britain in the 1930s. The victims of Nazism were not distant strangers in faraway places; rather, their suffering 'mattered to everybody'. Buttressing her belief that there is always space for moral agency, she argues that 'we in the West' should have put more pressure on the Nazi state. The key question raised by Midgley's discussion of the moral implications of the Nazis is of why we should go to the rescue of 'distant humans'? One answer is that we all share a common humanity, but this only brings us back to the philosophical conundrum of how we ground this ethical position. Rorty's communitarian pragmatism leads him to argue that the rescuers—those who risked their lives inside Nazi Germany and occupied Europe to save Jews—did not do so because of a belief in a shared humanity but because of more particularistic identifications with those whom they rescued. Set against this is the personal testimony of the rescuers that they acted because of a belief that the Jews were their fellow-humans. The philosophical question of why we have duties to 'distant humans' is important, but the salient fact is that these metatheoretical disputes did not prevent people from becoming rescuers in Nazi Germany.

The experience of the Holocaust—which, in Midgley's words, 'altered the colour of the sky for everyone'—led to the emergence of the global human rights regime. The collective determination to never again repeat the terror of the Nazi death camps led to the signing in 1948 of the Genocide Convention. As with the general language of human rights, the importance of the Convention is that it sharpens our moral awareness and makes us conscious of our responsibilities to 'distant humans'. If the assumption was that the existence of the Genocide Convention would safeguard humankind from this terrible crime, Richard Falk argues that the genocidal experiences in Cambodia, Bosnia and Rwanda reveal the hollowness of the cry 'never again'.

The general moral indifference shown by the Western powers to Nazi Germany's treatment of the Jews has been, according to Falk, paradigmatic of the responses of the society of States to the practice of genocide in post-1945 world politics. Despite establishing criminal accountability for political leaders engaging in acts of genocide, international society has not been prepared to pay the price and bear the burden of collective armed intervention to enforce compliance upon those States and political groups breaking the rules of the Convention. Indeed, the terrible tragedy of Rwanda in 1994, where the international community stood by and watched as hundreds of thousands were slaughtered in a matter of weeks, illustrates how far we are away from what Falk has elsewhere called an 'anti-genocide capability and culture'.

The ineffectual response to genocidal politics, argues Falk, is evidence of the 'low priority accorded to moral dimensions of foreign policy by the governments and elites of leading States'. He recognises that armed humanitarian intervention might fail for operational reasons and this could be one of the factors contributing to the reluctance of decision-makers to intervene. However, he rejects this rationale for non-intervention because States have not allowed logistical considerations to prevent them from intervening when important geopolitical interests are at stake.

Falk identifies two key factors, which explain the poverty of the moral imagination exhibited by statist elites. The first is the grip of the realist mindset on policy-makers, which limits armed intervention to instances where strategic interests are paramount. This might have helped the people of Kuwait in the oil-rich Persian Gulf, but it left millions in Cambodia, Burundi, Bosnia and Rwanda to perish.

The second factor contributing to the persistence of genocidal politics is the deleterious effect of the global market on the moral capacities of governments and civil societies. Falk worries that the impact of globalisation is narrowing our moral horizons by reducing 'the overall capacity and will of governments to address human wrongs either within their own society or elsewhere'. If Falk's prognosis is correct, economic globalisation is likely to compel societies to turn inwards thereby depleting the resources that can be devoted to the amelioration of poverty and malnutrition on a global scale. The slow death of millions in the South who are deprived of basic subsistence rights has been named the 'holocaust of neglect' by Henry Shue, and Falk's chapter alerts us to the importance of widening our category of genocidal politics to include these victims of global human wrongs.

In the face of these powerful ideological barriers against the development of an ethical foreign policy, Falk follows Booth and Midgley in arguing that 'moral purpose' must be injected into foreign policy decision-making. Here, he identifies an important role for global civil society in promoting values of human rights, nonviolence and democracy as a counter to the hegemonic ideologies of realism and *laissez faire* economics.

The role of transitional civil society in holding States leaders and political groups accountable for their exercise of power is the theme, which Mary Kaldor addresses. She focuses on the changing role of transitional civil society in the 1980s and 1990s. Her central thesis is that having achieved the liberalisation of authoritarian State structures in Eastern Europe through the process of 'detente from below', the challenge facing transitional civil society in the 1990s is how to cope with the human suffering produced by the collapse of State structures brought about by the triumph of ethnic and exclusives conceptions of identity.

The starting point for 'detente from below' was the 1975

Helsinki Final Act. At the time, the Soviet Union's signing of the human rights provisions of Basket 3 was seen as little more than a rhetorical commitment. However, as Kaldor shows, what the Soviet Union and its Eastern European allies interpreted as 'paper commitments' were pivotal in legitimising the human rights struggle of groups like Charter 77 in Czechoslovakia, KOR in Poland and the Democratic Opposition in Hungary. Furthermore, the emergence of the Peace Movement in Western Europe added a further transitional impetus to this process. The opposition groups in East-Central Europe, and the peace activists in the West, developed a dialogue based on the shared values of dismantling the militarised structures of the Cold War and developing democratic forms of politics. Kaldor argues that it was transitional social movements which made possible the emergence of Gorbachev, which in turn facilitated the revolutions of 1989 and the ending of the Cold War.

In her chapter, Kaldor makes a convincing case for the capacity of transnational social movements to civilise state institutions. Whilst this was decisive in dismantling the Iron Curtain she argues that these agents were ineffective in stopping the descent into barbarism in the former Yugoslavia. She points out that before war broke out in Bosnia in April 1992 there were groups and individuals committed to the defence of civic values across the former Yugoslavia, but these supporters of civil society could not survive without the protection afforded by the rule of law.

Like Midgley, Kaldor believes that the language of human rights is a powerful tool in promoting the rights of distant humans, but she argues that we need to add to human rights the idea of civil society because it makes concrete the idea of 'individual responsibility for respect of human rights through political action'. But if the lesson of the war in Bosnia is that local supporters of civic values can only succeed if they have 'outside support and access to those international organisations that can influence governments', Kaldor leaves unanswered the question of how the voices of the victims of ethnic and political violence are to be heard in the foreign offices of the leading Western States.

This is the central issue, which is investigated by Martin Shaw. His point of departure is a comparison between the zone of contentment in the West, where war has become virtually unthinkable, and the series of humanitarian crises which have afflicted large parts of the developing world as a consequence of State disintegration and civil war. Shaw agrees with Falk that left to their own devices, Western States will not intervene for humanitarian reasons unless there are clear strategic interests at stake. However, Shaw's thesis is that where there is extensive television coverage of human suffering, Western governments will come under pressure to come to the aid of innocent civilians.

In support of this argument, the main body of his chapter focuses on the rationale for the international rescue of the Kurds. The initial position of the United States and British governments was that they were not responsible for the fate of the Kurds after their failed uprising. In the course of the unfolding refugee crisis, Western State leaders were forced to shift their ground. None of this would have been possible, Shaw argues, without the mobilising power of television which 'took up the plight of the Kurds in an unprecedented campaign which successfully forced governments' hands'. Bush and Major tried to act as though they did not have responsibility for what was happening in the mountains of Northern Iraq, but television journalists were determined to hold these leaders accountable for the consequences of their actions during the war and their incitement to the Iraqi people to revolt against Saddam. It was this exposure by television of the contradiction between their words and deeds, which led Major and Bush to move decisively behind the calls for intervention.

In arguing that it was the televisual media and not newspapers of transitional social movements, which constituted the Western intervention in northern Iraq, Shaw recognises that television as a medium for representing victims has important limitations. The most basic is that television depends upon the presence of journalists. Where were the cameras, Shaw asks, when the Iraqi Republican Guard brutally suppressed the Shi'ite rebellion? Or scores of other long-term humanitarian crises which did not receive ιelevisual attention, such as the civil wars in Tadjikistan, Georgia, Angola, Liberia and Sierra Leone? The presence of television journalists is clearly a key factor in mediating responses to human suffering, but extensive coverage of the atrocities in Bosnia did not lead Western governments to intervene militarily. This suggests that televisual coverage is a necessary but not a sufficient condition for governments to intervene. A second limitation is that television rarely allows the victims of global human wrongs to speak for themselves. Rather, as in the case of the Kurds, it is the 'authoritative voices' of foreign journalists who determine whether and how victims are represented. The cries for help on the part of Kurdish refugees, trapped and dying on the Iraqi-Turkish border, were heard because their plight was a direct consequence of Western intervention in Iraq. But as Gil Loescher reminds us, the refugee crisis in northern Iraq in 1991 represents the tip of the iceberg of the global challenge posed by the millions of asylum-seekers and internally displaced peoples.

The new approach of UNHCR is to resolve the internal conflicts and severe human rights abuses, which produce a refugee crisis. However, Loescher is not optimistic about UNHCR succeeding in this crisis prevention role. It lacks the resources, logistics, training and expertise necessary, and requires the support of governments which remain jealous of their sovereign prerogatives. Additionally, Western States are reluctant to invest money in long-term programmes designed to prevent conflict and promote development in war-torn societies. Instead, they seem to prefer to cope with humanitarian emergencies when they occur. But the effect of this is to channel the scarce resources of the international donor community into emergency short-term aid, which addresses the symptoms of violent conflict but does little to tackle its underlying causes.

The way forward, Loescher argues, is for UNHCR to recognise that the problem of refugees cannot be separated from those of human rights, economic development, international security, and migration. In particular, he argues that the existing human rights machinery needs to be strengthened and applied more effectively to deal with refugees, particularly with regard to State compliance with the 1951 Convention. However, the increasing emphasis on short-term emergency aid has ensured that no extra funds have been provided for the UN's human rights regime "despite its potential to strengthen civil society, promote democratic and pluralistic institutions and procedures and, thereby, to prevent human rights abuses and mass displacements".

To compensate for their unwillingness to incur the costs of developing an integrated approach to the global refugee crisis, donor governments increasingly fund NGOs to act as agents of humanitarian relief and development, as well as contribute to early-warning human rights monitoring and conflict prevention. Loescher recognises the value of NGOs as agents of humanitarian assistance, protection, mediation and conflict resolution, but cautions more generally against too much faith being placed in the preventative approach to the global refugee crisis. He is worried that the belief that the problem can be addressed at source will reinforce the growing practice of Western governments to see "asylum-seekers as an unwanted burden and as an unnecessary inconvenience".

This view of asylum-seekers confirms Richard Falk's prognosis that economic globalisation is producing 'compassion fatigue' on the part of Western States and societies. The asylum-seeker is a distant human who has now become the stranger knocking at the door. The repines of the 'culture of contentment' to these victims of global human wrongs shows the limits of Rorty's idea of 'sentimental education' because our moral imagination is failing to realise 'what it is like to be in her situation—to be far from home, among strangers'. It is instructive that Rorty should talk about 'her', because the majority of refugees are women, and the tragic fact is that many of these suffer physical and sexual abuse at border crossings from those charged with responsibility to protect them.

But as Georgina Ashworth shows, it is not only refugee women who are violated and treated as sub-human. Rather, ordinary women are victims of a gender bias in global politics, which produces systematic violations of their rights. In addition to suffering the same kinds of human wrongs that are inflicted upon men, many women are victims of specific crimes such as enforced prostitution, domestic violence, rape (including rape in war) and physical (or emotional) mutilation. Given the widespread practices of physical violence against women, graphically portrayed by Ashworth, it is perhaps not surprising that feminists claim that 'violence against women is perhaps the most pervasive yet least recognised human rights abuse in the world'.

What explanation does Ashworth provide for the screaming silences of the regime in the face of this litany of human rights abuses towards women? As the opening sentence of her chapter suggests, one of the enduring problems has been the assumption that 'human rights are gender neutral' (an assumption which is severely undermined by the list of gender-based human wrongs). Added to the presumption of neutrality in the regime itself is the persistent silencing of women's voices in mainstream academic approaches to politics, sociology, economics and law. In recent years, however, Ashworth recognises that women's human rights issues are beginning to be heard, in part as a consequence of the interdisciplinary dialogue which many feminist academics have pioneered across the social sciences.

In the body of the chapter, Ashworth points to the progressive coalitions which women's human rights groups have forged, and the relative success they have had in articulating the need for a gender-sensitive regime. For feminist human rights activists, the prime objective is to expose the contradictions between the Universal Declaration's claim to universality and the specific practices of human rights abuses against women, thereby bringing these violations within the remit of the human rights regime. What is particularly important about the story Ashworth tells is the immanent possibilities which exist for transitional social movements to cajole the UN regime into bringing the regime into line with its own standards. An example of this is the way in which NGOs like 'Change' pressurised the regime in the Vienna Declaration to recognise the human rights of women and the girl child as an 'inalienable, integral and indivisible part of universal human rights'.

The victories that women's human rights groups achieved in Vienna, and more recently at the World Conference on Women in Beijing, must be tempered with the recognition that there are more battles to be won. NGOs will play a crucial role in monitoring the new gendered dimension of human rights in the daily practices of States and international institutions. The question of State compliance with human rights norms is an issue taken up by Andrew Hurrell. Human rights concerns are often subordinated to other foreign policy goals, but Hurrell argues that governments find it increasingly difficult to ignore their human rights obligations. The human rights regime, he argues, works through the 'mobilisation of shame' on the part of governments, NGOs and domestic groups fighting for human rights. The effect of this, Hurrell argues, is to make States increasingly sensitive to 'reputational concerns'. He points to China's carrot-and-stick strategy, which it employed to avoid censure at the UN Commission on Human Rights.

An important debate at the end of the Cold War concerns the question of whether the society of States should coercively enforce compliance with the human rights standard. A key development here is the way in which the UN Security Council is, in the 1990s, defining human rights abuses and humanitarian concerns as a threat to 'international peace and security' thereby legitimising coercive intervention under Chapter VII of the UN Charter. Whilst UN authority has provided a degree of legitimacy for armed intervention, Hurrell is sensitive to the criticisms of many non-Western States about the risks of double standards and of self-interest being cloaked in humanitarian garb. He argues that recent collective interventions illustrate the trade-off between 'short-term effectiveness' measured in terms of the relief of human suffering and the dangers of 'a long-term erosion of legitimacy'.

Most writers share the underlying belief that the problem of global human wrongs stems from the failure of statistic elites to comply with the global human rights standard. However, Hurrell returns to the central problematic, which is the claim to universality masking the particular interests and values of its exponents, and having it increasingly contested as a consequence of the rise of new power centres in world politics. Hurrell explores this question in terms of the relationship between human rights and power in the debate between the West and Asia.

He argues that the 'Asian values' challenge to the West reflects the growth of the economic and political power of States like China, Malaysia and Singapore, which interpret human rights concerns on the part of the West as a manoeuvre in the competition for relative gains. Even if the discourse of Asian values is 'manipulated and abused by governments' as part of traditional power politics, Hurrell argues that the debate reveals 'real and genuine conflicts over the nature of human rights'. As a consequence he suggests that instead of worrying about the 'foundations' of our human rights claims, we should "build on and develop the human rights culture and community that has evolved in practice—the element of consensus visible in the actual practice of states".

In searching for a human rights culture without foundations, Hurrell is explicitly recognising the impact that post-modernism has had on the contemporary human rights debate. His acceptance of this and the fact of cultural heterogeneity places Hurrell towards the upper-left corner of our matrix. The only values which morally divergent States can agree on are the norms of sovereignty and nonintervention. Like Hedley Bull, Hurrell is dissatisfied with the limits of a pluralist conception of international morality, and looks to the possibility of moving to a more solidarist society of States. A key component of this vision is that State leaders should act as 'guardians of human rights everywhere'. But the question which Hurrell leaves unanswered is how can the society of States deal with 'gangster' States unless it is prepared to condemn those who commit human rights abuses behind the walls of sovereignty.

ASEAN's decision in 1997 to accept Burma into its regional forum despite extensive pressure from the United States and the European Union illustrates the moral limitations of a pluralist society of States. Western States argued that Burma's human rights record should disqualify it from admission, but this was countered by a number of ASEAN member States on the grounds that the primary rule of the organisation was the right of each member State to sovereign jurisdiction. The metaphor often invoked by ASEAN State leaders, when under pressure from Western states, is that all member States agree not to peer into each other's 'backyard'.

A further problem with Hurrell's contention is suggested by Parekh, whose notion of a human rights dialogue assumes that all participants try to empathise with the ethnocentric biases of their partners. In allowing sovereignty and non-intervention to trump substantive values, Hurrell is leaving open the possibility that conversationalists will veto any moves towards a consensus, which offends against their cultural predilections and interests.

Although Hurrell's attempt to build bridges between procedural and substantive conceptions of legitimacy is problematic, he provides a more convincing account than Parekh of why the Asian value debate has become a prominent issue at the end of the Cold War. Drawing on a tradition of thinking about the practices of statecraft, Hurrell alerts us to the constant intrusion of power in shaping the contours of moral discourse in international society. Hurrell cites Singapore's spokesman for foreign affairs, Kishore Mabhubani, who commented in 1995 that 'All human rights covenants were created when the West was in power'. A precondition for a genuine dialogue is equality, according to Parekh, but the Asian value debate illustrates the limits of an ideal conversation in the hierarchy of States.

The theoretical and empirical investigations into the possibility of a diplomatic dialogue on human rights is predicated on the assumption that states have agency. This returns us to Jack Donnelly's central contention that the only duty-bearing agents are States, but this assumes that States which fail to comply with human rights norms can be pressurised into changing their behaviour. What is interesting about the final part of Hurrell's chapter is the suggestion that the traditional approach to viewing the State as violator needs to take on board that the culpability 'of State authorities may be difficult to demonstrate, or may indeed be wholly absent'.

If we cannot rely on States to combat human wrongs, either because they are the problem (the view espoused by Booth and to some extent Falk) or because they may not be able to be the solution (Hurrell), then we are driven back to considering the emancipator potential of transitional civil society (Kaldor, Shaw, Ashworth). What sustains the latter is an active citizenry campaigning for cosmopolitan values. Finally, Ken Booth and Tim Dunne examine the role that education can play in sustaining these values. They open the discussion by pointing to the link between education and promoting the 'good life' which has been an undercurrent in Western philosophy since Plato; virtuous citizens of the cosmopolites had to be educated in philosophy and ethics. With the rise of modernity, pedagogy has increasingly been redefined as a process where technical knowledge is imparted rather than discovered through an intellectual encounter. Booth and Dunne argue that this spirit needs to be revived if generations of students are going to grow up believing in universal human rights values.

From the outset, education has been an important part of the human rights regime. Article 26 of the Universal Declaration proclaimed that education was a universal human right, a commitment, which has been, refined in subsequent human rights documents. The regime goes beyond stipulating a right to an education insofar as it begins to adumbrate the need for an education in human rights. By this, the UN system means the promotion of 'understanding', 'tolerance', 'respect for fundamental freedoms' and 'friendship'. In other words, to conform to the spirit of the regime, States would have to promote human rights values in the curriculum as well as meet the standards for provision embodied in the regime. Booth and Dunne make a persuasive case for thinking about both aspects of the regime instead of the traditional emphasis upon the provision (rate than the content) of education.

Consistent with many of the contributions to this volume, the chapter on education and human rights illustrates the contradiction between the host of principles, declarations, conventions and programs of action, and the stark fact that there are almost one billion people in the world who are illiterate. In addition to the problem of compliance, there is also the question addressed by Booth, Brown, Parekh and Midgley, as to how we promote universal values, must be a view from somewhere. But crucially, Booth and Dunne argue that a key requirement of such an education is to avoid the parochialism and intolerance that a sense of cultural difference can breed. Building on the arguments of contributors to the volume, the authors offer a list of cosmopolitan values, which they believe to be integral to nurturing a global human rights culture.

TWELVE

The Feminine Side

Violence affects the lives of millions of women worldwide, in all socio-economic and educational classes. It cuts across cultural and religious barriers, impeding the right of women to participate fully in society. Violence against women takes a dismaying variety of forms, from domestic abuse and rape to child marriages and female circumcision. All are violations of the most fundamental human rights.

In a statement to the Fourth World Conference on Women in Beijing in September 1995, the then United Nations Secretary-General, Boutros Boutros-Ghali, said that violence against women is a universal problem that must be universally condemned. But he said that the problem continues to grow.

The Secretary-General noted that domestic violence alone is on the increase. Studies in 10 countries, he said, have found that between 17 per cent and 38 per cent of women have suffered physical assaults by a partner.

In the Platform for Action, the core document of the Beijing Conference, Governments declared that "violence against women constitutes a violation of basic human rights and is an obstacle to the achievement of the objectives of equality, development and peace."

Special Rapporteur

The issue of the advancement of women's rights has concerned the United Nations since the Organisation's founding. Yet the alarming global dimensions of female-targeted violence were not explicitly acknowledged by the international community until December 1993, when the United

Nations General Assembly adopted the Declaration on the Elimination of Violence against Women.

Until that point, most governments tended to regard violence against women largely as a private matter between individuals, and not as a pervasive human rights problem requiring State intervention.

In view of the alarming growth in the number of cases of violence against women throughout the world, the Commission on Human Rights adopted resolution 1994/45 of 4 March 1994, in which it decided to appoint the Special Rapporteur on violence against women, including its causes and consequences.

As a result of these steps, the problem of violence against women has been drawing increasing political attention.

The Special Rapporteur has a mandate to collect and analyse comprehensive data and to recommend measures aimed at eliminating violence at the international, national and regional levels. The mandate is threefold :

- To collect information on violence against women and its causes and consequences from sources such as governments, treaty bodies, specialised agencies and inter-governmental and non-governmental organisations, and to respond effectively to such information;
- To recommend measures and ways and means, at the national, regional and international levels, to eliminate violence against women and its causes, and to remedy its consequences;
- To work closely with other special rapporteurs, special representatives, working groups and independent experts of the Commission on Human Rights.

Domestic Violence

Some females fall prey to violence before they are born, when expectant parents abort their unborn daughters, hoping for sons instead. In other societies, girls are subjected to such traditional practices as circumcision, which leave them maimed and traumatised. In others, they are compelled to marry at an early age, before they are physically, mentally or emotionally mature.

Women are victims of incest, rape and domestic violence that often lead to trauma, physical handicap or death.

And rape is still being used as a weapon of war, a strategy used to subjugate and terrify entire communities. Soldiers deliberately impregnate women of different ethnic groups and abandon them when it is too late to get an abortion.

The Platform for Action adopted at the Fourth World Conference on Women declared that rape in armed conflict is a war crime and could, under certain circumstances, be considered genocide.

Secretary-General Boutros-Ghali told the Beijing Conference that more women today were suffering directly from the effects of war and conflict than ever before in history.

"There is a deplorable trend towards the organised humiliation of women, including the crime of mass rape," the Secretary-General said. "We will press for international legal action against those who perpetrate organised violence against women in time of conflict."

A preliminary report in 1994 by the Special Rapporteur, Ms. Radhika Coomaraswamy, focused on three areas of concern where women are particularly vulnerable: in the family (including domestic violence, traditional practices, infanticide); in the community (including rape, sexual assault, commercialised violence such as trafficking in women, labour exploitation, female migrant workers, etc.); and by the State (including violence against women in detention as well as violence against women in situations of armed conflict and against refugee women).

In the Platform for Action adopted at the Beijing Conference, violence against women and the human rights of women are two of the 12 critical areas of concern identified as the main obstacles to the advancement of women.

Official Commitments

Governments agreed to adopt and implement national legislation to end violence against women and to work actively to ratify all international agreements that relate to violence against women. They agreed that there should be shelters, legal aid and other services for girls and women at risk, and counselling and rehabilitation for perpetrators.

Governments also pledged to adopt appropriate measures in the field of education to modify the social and cultural patterns of conduct of men and women. And the Platform called on media professionals to develop self-regulatory guidelines to address violent, degrading and pornographic materials while encouraging non-stereotyped, balanced and diverse images of women.

Ascertaining Gender-based Abuse

The Declaration on the Elimination of Violence against Women is the first international human rights instrument to exclusively and explicitly address the issue of violence against women. It affirms that the phenomenon violates, impairs or nullifies women's human rights and their exercise of fundamental freedoms.

The Declaration provides a definition of gender-based abuse, calling it "any act of gender-based violence that results in, or is likely to result in, physical, sexual or psychological harm or suffering to women, including threats of such acts, coercion or arbitrary deprivation of liberty, whether occurring in public or in private life."

The definition is amplified in Article 2 of the Declaration, which identifies three areas in which violence commonly takes place :

- Physical, sexual and psychological violence that occurs in the family, including battering; sexual abuse of female children in the household; dowry-related violence; marital rape; female genital mutilation and other traditional practices harmful to women; non-spousal violence; and violence related to exploitation;

- Physical, sexual and psychological violence that occurs within the general community, including rape; sexual abuse; sexual harassment and intimidation at work, in educational institutions and elsewhere; trafficking in women; and forced prostitution; and
- Physical, sexual and psychological violence perpetrated or condoned by the State, wherever it occurs.

The importance of the question of violence against women was emphasised over the last decade through the holding of several expert group meetings sponsored by the United Nations to draw attention to the extent and severity of the problem. In September 1992, the United Nations Commission on the Status of Women established a special Working Group and gave it a mandate to draw up a draft declaration on violence against women.

The following year, the United Nations Commission for Human Rights, in resolution 1993/46 of 3 March, condemned all forms of violence and violations of human rights directed specifically against women.

The World Conference on Human Rights, held in Vienna in June 1993, laid extensive groundwork for eliminating violence against women. In the Vienna Declaration and Programme of Action, governments declared that the United Nations system and Member States should work towards the elimination of violence against women in public and private life; of all forms of sexual harassment, exploitation and trafficking in women; of gender bias in the administration of justice; and of any conflicts arising between the rights of women and the harmful effects of certain traditional or customary practices, cultural prejudices and religious extremism.

The document also declared that "violations of the human rights of women in situations of armed conflicts are violations of the fundamental principles of international human rights and humanitarian law," and that all violations of this kind—including murder, systematic rape, sexual slavery and forced pregnancy—require a particularly effective response."

Many Sorts of Violence

Violence against women in the family occurs in developed and developing countries alike. It has long been considered a private matter by bystanders— including neighbours, the community and government. But such private matters have a tendency to become public tragedies.

In the United States, a woman is beaten every 18 minutes. Indeed, domestic violence is the leading cause of injury among women of reproductive age in the United States. Between 22 and 35 per cent of women who visit emergency rooms are there for that reason.

The highly publicised trial of O. J. Simpson, the retired United States football player acquitted of the murder of his former wife and a male friend of hers, helped focus international media attention on the issue of domestic violence and spousal abuse.

In Peru, 70 per cent of all crimes reported to the police involve women beaten by their husbands. In Pakistan, Prime Minister Benazir Bhutto strongly defended a 35-year-old mother of two who was severely burned by her husband; in a domestic dispute.

"There is no excuse for such a behaviour," the Prime Minister declared after visiting the hospitalised victim. "My presence here is to send a message to all those who violate Islamic teachings and defy laws of the land with their inhuman treatment of women. This will not be tolerated."

According to the Human Rights Commission of Pakistan, in the 400 cases of domestic violence reported in 1993 in the province of Punjab, nearly half ended with the death of the wife. According to the Special Rapporteur's report, many governments now recognise the importance of protecting victims of domestic abuse and taking action to punish perpetrators. The establishment of structures allowing officials to deal with cases of domestic violence and its consequences is a significant step towards the elimination of violence against women in the family.

The Special Rapporteur's report highlights the importance of adopting legislation that provides for prosecution of the offender. It also stresses the importance of specialised training for law enforcement authorities as well as medical and legal professionals, and of the establishment of community support services for victims, including access to information and shelters.

In many countries, women fall victim to traditional practices that violate their human rights. The persistence of the problem has much to do with the fact that most of these physically and psychologically harmful customs are deeply rooted in the tradition and culture of society.

According to the World Health Organisation, 85 million to 115 million girls and women in the population have undergone some form of female genital mutilation and suffer from its adverse health effects.

Every year an estimated two million young girls undergo this procedure. Most live in Africa and Asia, but an increasing number can be found among immigrant and refugee families in Western Europe and North America. Indeed, the practice has been outlawed in some European countries.

In France, a Malian was convicted in a criminal court after his baby girl died of a female circumcision-related infection. The procedure had been performed on the infant at home.

In Canada, fear of being forced to undergo circumcision can be grounds for asylum. A Nigerian woman was granted refugee status since she felt that she might be persecuted in her home country because of her refusal to inflict genital mutilation on her baby daughter.

There is a growing consensus that the best way to

eliminate these practices is through educational campaigns that emphasise their dangerous health consequences. Several governments have been actively promoting such campaigns in their countries.

Son preference affects women in many countries, particularly in Asia. Its consequences can be anything from foetal or female infanticide to neglect of the girl-child over her brother in terms of such essential needs as nutrition, basic health care and education.

In China and India, some women choose to terminate their pregnancies when expecting daughters but carry their pregnancies to term when expecting sons.

According to reports from India, genetic testing for sex selection has become a booming business, especially in the country's northern regions. Indian gender-detection clinics drew protests from women's groups after the appearance of advertisements suggesting that it was better to spend $38 now to terminate a female foetus than $3,800 later on her dowry.

A study of amniocentesis procedures conducted in a large Bombay hospital found that 95.5 per cent of foetuses identified as female were aborted, compared with a far smaller percentage of male foetuses. The problem of son preference is present in many other countries as well. Asked how many children he had fathered, the former United States boxing champion Muhammad Ali told an interviewer: "One boy and seven mistakes."

Marriage-related Violence

In some countries, weddings are preceded by the payment of an agreed-upon dowry by the bride's family. Failure to pay the dowry can lead to violence.

In Bangladesh, a bride whose dowry was deemed too small was disfigured after her husband threw acid on her face. In India, an average of five women a day are burned in dowry-related disputes—and many more cases are never reported.

Early marriage, especially without the consent of the girl, is another form of human rights violation. Early marriage followed by multiple pregnancies can affect the health of women for life.

The report of the Special Rapporteur has documented the destructive effects of marriage of female children under 18 and has urged governments to adopt relevant legislation.

Within Community

Rape can occur anywhere, even in the family, where it can take the form of marital rape or incest. It occurs in the community, where a woman can fall prey to any abuser. It also occurs in situations of armed conflict and in refugee camps.

In the United States, national statistics indicate that a women is raped every six minutes. In 1995, the case of a Brazilian jogger raped and murdered in New York City's Central Park drew international attention once again to the problem. The incident occurred only a few years after an earlier sensational jogger-assault case in which the victim—an American assaulted in the same general area of the park — barely survived after her assailants left her for dead.

Relations between residents of the Japanese island of Okinawa and American GIs were thrown into turmoil in 1995 after two marines and a sailor allegedly kidnapped and raped a 12-year-old girl.

The Special Rapporteur's report underlines the importance of education to sensitise the public about the special horrors of rape, and of sensitivity training for the police and hospital staff who work with victims.

Within Marriage

In many countries sexual assault by a husband on his wife is not considered to be a crime: a wife is expected to submit. It is thus very difficult in practice for a woman to prove that sexual assault has occurred unless she can demonstrate serious injury.

The report of the Special Rapporteur noted that light sentences in sexual assault cases send the wrong message to perpetrators and to the public at large: that female sexual victimisation is unimportant.

Sexual harassment in the workplace is a growing concern for women. Employers abuse their authority to seek sexual favours from their female co-workers or subordinates, sometimes promising promotions or other forms of career advancement or simply creating an untenable and hostile work environment. Women who refuse to give in to such unwanted sexual advances often run the risk of anything from demotion to dismissal.

But in recent years more women have been coming forward to report such practices—some taking their cases to court.

In her report, the Special Rapporteur stressed that sexual harassment constitutes a form of sex discrimination. "It not only degrades the woman," the report noted, "but reinforces and reflects the idea of non-professionalism on the part of women workers, who are consequently regarded as less able to perform their duties than their male colleagues."

Flesh Trade

Many women are forced into prostitution either by their parents, husbands or boyfriends—or as a result of the difficult economic and social conditions in which they find themselves. They are also lured into prostitution, sometimes by 'mail-order bride' agencies that promise to find them a husband or a job in a foreign country. As a result, they very often find themselves illegally confined in brothels in slavery-like conditions where they are physically abused and their passports withheld.

Most women initially victimised by sexual traffickers have little inkling of what awaits them. They generally get a very small percentage of what the customer pays to the pimp or the brothel owner. Once they are caught up in the system there is practically no way out, and they find themselves in a very vulnerable situation.

Since prostitution is illegal in many countries, it is difficult for prostitutes to come forward and ask for protection if they become victims of rape or want to escape from brothels. Customers, on the other hand, are rarely the object of penal laws. In Thailand, prostitutes who complain to the police are often arrested and sent back to the brothels upon payment of a fine. The extent of trafficking in women and girl children has reached alarming proportions, especially in Asian countries.

Many women and girl children are trafficked across borders, often with the complicity of border guards.' In one incident, five young prostitutes burned to death in a brothel fire because they had been chained to their beds. At the same time, sex tours of developing countries are a well-organised industry in several European and other industrialised countries.

The Special Rapporteur has called on governments to take action to protect young girls from being recruited as prostitutes and to closely monitor recruiting agencies.

Female migrant workers typically leave their countries for better living conditions and better pay – but the real benefits accrue to both the host countries and the countries of origin. For home countries, money sent home by migrant workers is an important source of hard currency, while receiving countries are able to find workers for low-paying jobs that might otherwise go unfilled.

But migrant workers themselves fare badly, and sometimes tragically. Many become virtual slaves, subject to abuse and rape by their employers. In the Middle East and Persian Gulf region, there are an estimated 1.2 million women, mainly Asians, who are employed as domestic servants. According to the independent human rights group 'Middle East Watch,' female migrant workers in Kuwait often suffer beatings and sexual assaults at the hands of their employers.

The police are often of little help. In many cases, women who report being raped by their employers are sent back to the employer – or are even assaulted at the police station.

Working conditions are often appalling, and employers

prevent women from escaping by seizing their passports or identity papers.

The report of the Special Rapporteur draws attention to the fact that there are many international instruments that can be used to prevent abuse against migrant women and suggests some measures to protect the human rights of migrant women.

Glamourising Degradation

Another concern highlighted in the Special Rapporteur's report is pornography, which represents a form of violence against women that "glamorises the degradation and maltreatment of women and asserts their subordinate function as mere receptacles for male lust."

Violence against women by the very people who are supposed to protect them—members of the law enforcement and criminal justice systems—is widespread.

Women are physically or verbally abused; they also suffer sexual and physical torture. According to Amnesty International, thousands of women held in custody are routinely raped in police detention centres worldwide. The report of the Special Rapporteur underlines the necessity for States to prosecute those accused of abusing women while in detention and to hold them accountable for their actions.

Rape has been widely used as a weapon of war whenever armed conflicts arise between different parties. It has been used all over the world: in Chiapas, Mexico, in Rwanda, in Kuwait, in Haiti, in Colombia.

Women and girl children are frequently victims of gang rape committed by soldiers from all sides of a conflict. Such acts are done mainly to trample the dignity of the victims. Rape has been used to reinforce the policy of ethnic cleansing in the war that has been tearing apart the former Yugoslavia.

The so-called 'comfort women'—young girls of colonised or occupied countries who became sexual slaves to Japanese soldiers during the Second World War—have dramatised the problem in a historical context. Many of these women are now coming forward and demanding compensation for their suffering from Japanese authorities. "Such rape is the symbolic rape of the community, the destruction of the fundamental elements of a society and culture – the ultimate humiliation of the male enemy," the report by the Special Rapporteur noted. It stressed the need to hold the perpetrators of such crimes fully accountable.

Women and children form the great majority of refugee populations all over the world and are especially vulnerable to violence and exploitation. In refugee camps, they are raped and abused by military and immigration personnel, bandit groups, male refugees and rival ethnic groups. They are also forced into prostitution.

In her report, the Special Rapporteur proposes the following measures to be taken for the protection of women and girls in refugee camps: improvement of security, deployment of trained female officers at all points of the refugees' journey, participation of women in organisational structures of the camps and prosecution of government and military personnel responsible for abuse against refugee women.

In recent years some countries have taken significant steps towards improving laws relating to violence against women. For example :

- In July 1991, Mexico revised its rape law in several important ways. A provision was eliminated that allowed a man who raped a minor to avoid prosecution if he agreed to marry her. Now judges are required to hand down a decision regarding access to an abortion within five working days.
- On 9 June 1994, the Organisation of American States adopted the Inter-American Convention to Prevent, Punish and Eradicate Violence against Women (also called Convention of Belam do Para), a new international instrument that recognises all gender-based violence as an abuse of human rights. This

Convention provides an individual right of petition and a right for nongovernmental organisations to lodge complaints with the Inter-American Commission of Human Rights.

- In Australia, a National Committee on Violence against Women was established to coordinate the development of policy, legislation and law enforcement at the national level as well as community education on violence against women.
- In 1991, the government of Canada announced a new four-year Family Violence Initiative intended to mobilise community action, strengthen Canada's legal framework, establish services on Indian reserves develop resources to help victims and stop offenders, and provide housing for abused women and children.
- In Turkey, a Ministry of State for Women was established whose main goals are, among others, to promote women's rights and strengthen their role in economic, social, political and cultural life. Legal measures are being adopted towards the elimination of violence against women. The establishment of special courts to deal with violence is envisaged. Psychological treatment for abused women is also planned, along with the establishment of women's shelters around the country. Specially trained female police officers could provide assistance to victims of violence.
- In Burkina Faso, a strong advertising campaign by the government as well as television and radio programmes on the unhealthy practice of genital mutilation were launched to educate and raise public awareness about the dangerous consequences of such an 'operation'. A National Anti-Excision Committee was established in 1990 by the present head of State. Today, the practice of genital

mutilation has been eliminated in some villages of Burkina Faso. In others, there has been an incredible drop in the number of girls excised: only 10 per cent of the girls are excised compared to 100 per cent 10 years ago.

– Some countries have introduced police units specially trained for dealing with spousal assault. In Brazil, specific police stations have been designated to deal with women's issues, including domestic violence. These police stations are staffed entirely by women.

These examples illustrate some steps taken at the national level towards the eradication of violence against women. Combating and eradicating this scourge require enhanced and concerted efforts to protect women at the local, national and international levels.

States have tended to adopt a passive attitude when confronted by cases of violations of women's rights by private actors. Most laws fail to protect victims or to punish perpetrators. Passing laws to criminalise violence against women is an important way to redefine the limits of acceptable behaviour. States should ensure that national legislation, once adopted, does not go unenforced. State responsibility is clearly underlined in Article 4 of the Declaration on the Elimination of Violence against Women, which stipulates that "States should exercise due diligence to prevent, investigate and, in accordance with national legislation, punish acts of violence against women, whether those acts are perpetrated by the State or by private persons."

Any approach designed to combat violence must be twofold, addressing the root causes of the problem and treating its manifestations. Society at large, including judges and police officers, must be educated to change the social attitudes and beliefs that encourage male violence.

The meaning of gender and sexuality and the balance of power between women and men at all levels of society must be reviewed. Combating violence against women requires challenging the way that gender roles and power relations are articulated in society. In many countries women have a low status. They are considered as inferior and there is a strong belief that men are superior to them and even own them.

Changing people's attitude and mentality towards women will take a long time—at least a generation, many believe, and perhaps longer. Nevertheless, raising awareness of the issue of violence against women, and educating boys and men to view women as valuable partners in life, in the development of a society and in the attainment of peace are just as important as taking legal steps to protect women's human rights.

It is also important in order to prevent violence that non-violent means be used to resolve conflict between all members of society. Breaking the cycle of abuse will require concerted collaboration and action between governmental and non-governmental actors, including educators, health-care authorities, legislators, the judiciary and the mass media.

Every One's Responsibility

The human rights of women and girl child are an inalienable, integral and indivisible part of universal human rights. The full and equal participation of women in political, civil, economic, social and cultural life, at the national, regional and international levels, and the eradication of all forms of discrimination on grounds of sex are priority objectives of the international community. (The Vienna Declaration and Programme of Action, Part 1, Para 18).

THIRTEEN

Kids' Rights

Children's victimization in its different expressions is a constant feature of practically all societies. It is common belief that childhood as currently understood is a relatively recent creation. In the old Roman days, the life of the young subjects was strictly monitored. Roman citizens were under the authority of a tutor upto puberty, which was deemed to occur at 14 for males and 12 for females. The period before puberty was divided into two parts.

During infancy, that is to say upto the age of seven, the child was incapable of reason and could perform no legal act. Thereafter, the *pupillus* was granted a limited capacity, in other words it could acquire rights but it was not entitled to alienate them, nor to incur duties. There would follow a long period in which a young Roman would be regarded as a minor and as such subjected to *cura-minorum*, only at the age of 25 would it acquire full legal status, yet always under the *partria-potestas* or father's authority which would be lost for its entire life. The juristic concept that child being legal person is entitled to the protection of law, developed during the last two centuries, following industrialisation and the emergence of women's rights.

The advent of industrial revolution brought about the enactment of child labour laws some of them dating back to the first half of 19th century. The progressive liberation of women changed the familys' pattern of power and as a result paternal authority lost absolute decisional power over the children.

International Law for Children

The first conventions indirectly protecting children began in the late 19th and early 20th centuries in the international arena. Geneva Convention IV and the additional protocols incorporate and expand many of the principles contained in the Hague Conventions and specifically provided for the protection of the children. Articles 14, and 24 of the Geneva Convention IV and 76, 77 and 78 of Protocol Article 50 of the Geneva Convention IV affords general protection of children as well as protects children in occupied territories.

The Force Labour Conventions of 1930 and the Abolition of Forced Labour Convention of 1957, require State parties to suppress and abolish force child labour imposed by either the State or by the private individual and organisations. In 1959 Declaration, "Soft Law" documents enunciate general principles and entitlements for the care and protection of children. It is mainly concerned with economic, social and cultural rights. Any Convention on the Rights of the child must be read within the framework of the International Bill of Human Rights, composed of the 1948 Declaration and the 1966 International Covenant on Economic, Social and Cultural Rights (ICESCR) and International Covenant on Civil and Political Rights (ICCPR) with its optional protocol. Another factor of the utmost importance to the cause of children's protection comes from Article 35 which requires state parties to take all appropriate measures to prevent the abduction, the sale of or traffic in children for any purpose or in any form. The 1979 Convention on the Elimination of all forms of Discrimination Against Women insofar as it singles out a second group of individuals who deserve special protection.

The Convention is divided into three main sections:

- Preamble,
- The Substantive Articles (Part 1; Articles 1-41), and
- The Implementation provision (Parts II & III, Articles 42 to 54).

However, the beneficiaries of the Convention are

Children. Article I clarifies that, "a child means every human being below the age of 18 years unless under the law applicable to the child, majority is attained earlier." The Convention covers a variety of aspects and does this more or less satisfactorily. Among the happiest provisions Article 3 deserves a mention. It states that, "in all actions concerning children the best interests of the child shall be a primary consideration".

Child abuse and neglect have been defined as, "The portion of harm to the child that results from human action or inaction, this is prescribed proximate and preventable. Child abuse is active, and neglect passive maltreatment. There are three main causes of child suffering; war, poverty and social disruption. They all have a common denominator which is the economic impulse that rules on the rules societies.

The 1989 UNICEF report on the conditions of children in the world reveals that during the 80s in the 37 poorest countries there has been a cut of 50 per cent on health expenditure and of 25 per cent on education. As a result, the average weight of these children has lessened and the proportion of children between 6 and 11 years attending school is falling. Separation from family, community and the routines of normal life can be devastating to the children. An idea that may find its realization through the future Conventions on Right of the Child is that of stigmatizing as unlawful forms of neglect that result in an implicit denial of a positive right enshrined by the law. For instance, it would be illegal to employ a child in a job which would prevent it from attending school, thus affecting its right to education.

Convention on the Rights

With regard to child's health care, a necessary warning needs to be issued, to meet these ends, on 20th November, 1989, the United Nations General Assembly has adopted by unanimity the Convention on the Rights of the Child which entered into force on 2nd September, 1990. The expression is so wide a consensus upon the opportunity of establishing a binding legal instrument for the global protection of children is the goal of an increased awareness concerning the many problems that affect children worldwide. The final affirmation of children's rights, which would ensure the world a prosperous future, can be achieved only through international cooperation, that is to say the sound implementation of the rights to development.

A Landmark

The Convention on the Rights of the Child was adopted by the General Assembly of the United Nations by its resolution 44/25 of 20 November 1989.

This was the end of a process which had begun with the preparations for the 1979 International Year of the Child. That year, discussions started on a draft convention submitted by the Government of Poland.

Children had been discussed before by the international community. Declarations on the rights of the child had been adopted by both the League of Nations (1924) and the United Nations (1959). Also, specific provisions concerning children had been incorporated in a number of human rights and humanitarian law treaties. Nevertheless, some States argued that there was a need for a comprehensive statement on children's rights which would be binding under international law.

That view was influenced by reports of grave injustices suffered by children: high infant mortality, deficient health care, limited opportunities for basic education. There were also alarming accounts of children being abused and exploited as prostitutes or in harmful jobs, of children in prison or in other difficult circumstances, and of children as refugees and victims of armed conflict.

The drafting of the Convention took place in a working group set up by the United Nations Commission on Human Rights. Government delegates formed the core of the drafting group, but representatives of United Nations bodies and specialised agencies, including the Office of the United Nations

High Commissioner for Refugees (UNHCR), the International Labour Organisation (ILO), the United Nations Children's Fund (UNICEF) and the World Health Organisation (WHO), as well as a number of non-governmental organisations, took part in the deliberations. The original draft submitted by the Polish government was extensively amended and expanded through the long discussions.

The unanimous adoption of the Convention by the General Assembly paved the way for the next stage: ratifications by States and the setting up of a monitoring committee. Within less than a year, by September 1990, 20 States had legally endorsed the Convention, which thereby entered into force.

In the same month, the World Summit for Children was held in New York on the initiative of UNICEF and six States (Canada, Egypt, Mali, Mexico, Pakistan and Sweden). The Summit encouraged all States to ratify the Convention. By the end of 1990, 57 had done so, thereby becoming States parties. In 1993, the World Conference on Human Rights held at Vienna declared that the goal was universal ratification by the end of 1995. By 31 December 1995, no less than 185 countries had indeed ratified the Convention. This number is unprecedented in the field of human rights.

Forward-Looking Principles

The Convention on the Rights of the Child has the same meaning for people in all parts of the world. While laying down common standards, the Convention takes into account the different cultural, social, economic and political realities of individual States so that each State may seek its own means to implement the rights common to all.

There are four general principles enshrined in the Convention. These are meant to help with the interpretation of the Convention as a whole and thereby guide national programmes of implementation. The four principles are formulated, in particular, in articles 2, 3, 6 and 12.

Non-discrimination (Art. 2): States parties must ensure that all children within their jurisdiction enjoy their rights. No child should suffer discrimination. This applies to every child, "irrespective of the child's or his or her parent's or legal guardian's race, colour, sex, language, religion, political or other opinion, national, ethnic or social origin, property, disability, birth or other status."

The essential message is equality of opportunity. Girls should be given the same opportunities as boys. Refugee children, children of foreign origin, children of indigenous or minority groups should have the same rights as all others. Children with disabilities should be given the same opportunity to enjoy an adequate standard of living.

Best Interests of the Child (Art. 3): When the authorities of a State take decisions which affect children, the best interests of children must be a primary consideration. This principle relates to decisions by courts of law, administrative authorities, legislative bodies and both public and private social-welfare institutions. This is, of course, a fundamental message of the Convention, the implementation of which is a major challenge.

The Right to Life, Survival and Development (Art. 6): The right-to-life article includes formulations about the right to survival and to development, which should be ensured 'to the maximum extent possible'. The term 'development' in this context should be interpreted in a broad sense, adding a qualitative dimension: not only physical health is intended, but also mental, emotional, cognitive, social and cultural development.

The Views of the Child (Art 12): Children should be free to have opinions in all matters affecting them, and those views should be given due weight 'in accordance with the age and maturity of the child'. The underlying idea is that children have the right to be heard and to have their views taken seriously, including in any judicial or administrative proceedings affecting them.

Salient Features of the Convention

Every child has the inherent right to life, and States shall ensure to the maximum child survival and development.

Every child has the right to a name and nationality from birth.

Children shall not be separated from their parents, except by competent authorities for their well-being.

States shall facilitate reunification of families by permitting travel into, or out of, their territories.

Parents have the primary responsibility for a child's upbringing, but States shall provide them with appropriate assistance and develop child-care institutions.

States shall protect children from physical or mental harm and neglect, including sexual abuse or exploitation.

States shall provide parentless children with suitable alternative care. The adoption process shall be carefully regulated and international agreements should be sought to provide safeguards and assure legal validity if and when adoptive parents intend to move a child from his or her country of birth.

Disabled children shall have the right to special treatment, education and care.

Children are entitled to the highest attainable standard of health. States shall ensure that health care is provided to all children, placing emphasis on preventive measures, health education and reduction of infant mortality.

Primary education shall be free and compulsory. Discipline in schools shall respect the child's dignity. Education should prepare the child for life in a spirit of understanding, peace and tolerance.

Children shall have time to rest and play and equal opportunities for cultural and artistic activities.

States shall protect children from economic exploitation and from work that may interfere with their education or be harmful to their health or wellbeing.

States shall protect children from the illegal use of drugs and involvement in drug production or trafficking.

All efforts shall be made to eliminate the abduction and trafficking of children.

Capital punishment or life imprisonment shall not be imposed for crimes committed before the age of 18.

Children in detention shall be separated from adults; they must not be tortured or suffer cruel or degrading treatment.

No child under 15 shall take any part in hostilities; children exposed to armed conflict shall receive special protection.

Children of minority and indigenous populations shall freely enjoy their own culture, religion and language.

Children who have suffered mistreatment, neglect or exploitation shall receive appropriate treatment or training for recovery and rehabilitation.

Children involved in infringements of the penal law shall be treated in a way that promotes their sense of dignity and worth and aims at reintegrating them into society.

States shall make the rights set out in the Convention widely known to both adults and children.

Purposeful Monitoring

A number of international human rights bodies contribute to improving respect for the rights of the child in their particular areas of competence. In addition to the Commission on Human Rights, the Sub-Commission on Prevention of Discrimination and Protection of Minorities and its Working Group on Contemporary Forms of Slavery, which deals with aspects of the exploitation and mistreatment of children. Relevant international human rights bodies include the following:

(i) Human Rights Committee;
(ii) Committee on Economic, Social and Cultural Rights;
(iii) Committee on the Elimination of Racial Discrimination;
(iv) Committee on the Elimination of Discrimination against Women;

(v) Committee against Torture.

These five committees are commonly referred to as treaty bodies, since they were established to monitor the implementation of particular United Nations human rights treaties by States which have ratified or acceded to the instruments in question. The creation of the Committee on the Rights of the Child, established under Article 43 of the Convention, reinforced the activities of these bodies on behalf of children.

Rights Committee

In early 1991, a meeting of representatives of States parties to the Convention on the Rights of the Child was convened for the first election to its monitoring body: the Committee on the Rights of the Child. Some 40 candidates had been nominated for the 10 seats. The experts elected on this first occasion came from Barbados, Brazil, Burkina Faso, Egypt, Peru, the Philippines, Portugal, the former Soviet Union, Sweden and Zimbabwe. Six were women, four men. They represented a variety of professional backgrounds, including human rights and international law, juvenile justice, social work, medicine, journalism and governmental and non-governmental work.

The Committee on the Rights of the Child currently holds three sessions a year, each of four weeks' duration. The last week is always reserved for preparation of the next session. The Committee is serviced by the United Nations Centre for Human Rights in Geneva.

Under Article 44 of the Convention, State parties accept the duty to submit regular reports to the Committee on the steps they have taken to put the Convention into effect and on progress in the enjoyment of children's rights in their territories. First implementation reports are to be submitted within two years of ratification of or accession to the Convention and thereafter every five years. The first initial reports were due in September 1992. More than 70 State reports had reached the Committee by December 1995.

At its first session, in October 1991, the Committee adopted guidelines to help States parties writing and structuring their initial reports. Governments are recommended to prepare their reports according to these guidelines, which stress that the report should indicate 'factors and difficulties' encountered by the State in the implementation of the Convention—in other words, that it should be problem-oriented and self-critical. States are also asked to specify 'implementation priorities' and 'specific goals for the future'. Relevant legal texts and statistical data are to be submitted with the report.

In establishing its procedures, the Committee has emphasised the importance of a constructive dialogue with government representatives. In this context, it has also made clear that it seeks close cooperation with relevant United Nations bodies and specialised agencies, as well as with other competent bodies, including non-governmental organisations.

The Procedure

A working group of the Committee meets prior to each of its sessions for a preliminary examination of reports received from States parties, and to prepare the Committee's discussions with the representatives of reporting States. In addition to State reports, the working group considers information provided by other human rights treaty bodies. The Committee also receives information from mechanisms established by the Commission on Human Rights to investigate human rights problems in specific countries or on thematic issues, for example the Special Rapporteurs on torture, on extrajudicial, summary or arbitrary executions, and on violence against women. A key partner in this context is the Special Rapporteur on the sale of children, child prostitution and child pornography.

Studies on Innovation

A procedural innovation was introduced by the Committee in January 1993 when it recommended to the General Assembly that it request the Secretary-General to undertake a study on the protection of children in armed conflicts. This request was the result of a full-day 'general discussion' on the subject organised by the Committee in 1992, in which United Nations bodies and non-governmental organisations were invited to participate.

General discussions have since been held on economic exploitation of children, on the rights of the child in the family context, on the rights of the girl child, and on juvenile justice. Such thematic discussions are held about once a year and may lead to requests for studies, but can also serve as a basis for work on interpreting the articles of the Convention.

United Nations bodies and specialised agencies may take part in the deliberations of the working group and provide information. On the basis of written information received from relevant nongovernmental organisations, the Committee has also often invited such organisations to take part in the preparatory meetings on State reports.

The end result of the pre-sessional working group's discussion on a State report is a 'list of issues'. This list, which gives a preliminary indication of the issues which the Committee considers to be priorities for discussion, is sent to the government concerned with an invitation to participate in a forthcoming plenary session of the Committee at which its report will be considered. The government is invited to respond to the issues in writing, before the session.

This approach gives governments the opportunity better to prepare themselves for the discussion with the Committee. Other points not included in the list of issues may emerge during the discussion, which is one reason why the Committee prefers to discuss with high level officials, such as ministers or deputy ministers, rather than with representatives who lack the authority to make decisions.

Discussions with States parties are concrete and detailed, and tend to deal with both results and processes. Although all Committee members usually take part in the deliberations, in most cases two members take the lead on each country as 'rapporteurs'.

At the very end of the process, the Committee adopts 'concluding observations', which are a statement on its consideration of a State's report. Concluding observations are meant to be widely publicised in the State party and to serve as the basis for a national debate on how to improve the enforcement of the provisions of the Convention. They therefore constitute an essential document: governments are expected to implement the recommendations contained therein.

Notes are taken at the meetings of the Committee. The United Nations publishes both press releases on the discussions and more detailed summary records of the proceedings. The Committee encourages the publication of the State party's report, the summary records and the concluding observations on each country as a consolidated document. Some governments whose reports have already been discussed have undertaken to do so.

The whole process of discussion of States parties' reports is designed to promote public debate. The Committee's discussions are normally open to the public; only the preparatory discussions of the pre-sessional working group and the drafting of the Committee's concluding observations are conducted in private. Likewise, it is important that the national reporting procedure be open and transparent; the Committee encourages such an approach.

The reporting procedure is constructive and oriented towards international cooperation and exchange of information. The aim is to define problems and discuss what corrective measures should be taken. The Committee can also transmit requests for assistance to the specialised United Nations bodies and agencies, including UNHCR, ILO, UNICEF, WHO, the United Nations Educational, Scientific and Cultural Organisation (UNESCO) and other competent bodies.

There is no procedure outlined in the Convention for individual complaints from children or their representatives. The Committee may, however, request "further information relevant to the implementation of the Convention" (art. 44, para. 4). Such additional information may be requested from Governments if, for instance, there are indications of serious problems.

General Measures of Implementation

In drafting its reporting guidelines for States, the Committee on the Rights of the Child placed emphasis on concrete implementation measures which would make a reality of the principles and provisions of the Convention. More specifically, the Committee paid special attention to necessary reforms within the spirit of the Convention and procedures for constant scrutiny of progress.

Under Article 4 of the Convention, States parties are required to undertake all appropriate legislative, administrative and other measures to implement the Convention. With regard to economic, social and cultural rights, they must "undertake such measures to the maximum extent of their available resources and, where needed, within the framework of international cooperation."

An early step in the implementation process is for a State party to review its legislation and ensure that laws are consistent with the Convention. For instance, laws are needed for the protection of children against exploitation, in both the formal and informal labour market, and to ensure free and compulsory primary education.

Mechanisms may be introduced at the national and local levels to coordinate policies and monitor the implementation of the Convention, including through an ombudsman's office. The political decision-making process is important. What procedures are there to ensure that children's affairs are taken seriously in all relevant governmental structures, as well as in both the parliament and local assemblies? Are there opportunities for children themselves and their representatives to make themselves heard?

The gathering of reliable and relevant information on the situation of children is another important step to be taken.

With precise data, discussions regarding remedies will be better informed and focused. Improvement of the capacity of the national statistical office can therefore be an essential contribution to the implementation of the Convention.

Other means of genuine realisation of the principles and rights enshrined in the Convention are education and training of personnel working with children, such as nursery school and other teachers, child psychologists, paediatricians and other health personnel, the police and other law enforcement personnel, social workers and others. A broader awareness and knowledge of the Convention among people at large can also serve as a basis for implementation. It is an obligation under the Convention (art. 42) for States parties to disseminate such information—to both children and adults—in understandable languages. States' reports on implementation must also be made 'widely available to the public' (Art. 44, para. 6).

What is meant by the wording that States should implement economic, social and cultural rights "to the maximum extent of their available resources" (Art. 4). How does the Convention relate to financial constraints?

The Convention recognises that some of. the more costly reforms cannot take place overnight. It specifies, for instance, that the rights to health care (Art. 24) and education (Art. 28) may be achieved 'progressively'. It also makes it clear that there is an international duty to assist other States in their efforts to protect children's rights—although each State party always has its own obligations. Rich or poor, a State must allocate the maximum extent of its available resources for the implementation of the Convention: priority should be given to children.

Donor countries are encouraged to review their development cooperation programmes in the light of the Convention. At the same time, developing countries may identify a need for international cooperation in their reports on their implementation of the Convention.

Suggestions

The Convention on the Rights of the Child and the Committee on the Rights of the Child attach special importance to international cooperation and assistance as ways of achieving the effective protection of children's rights. Article 45 (b) authorises the Committee to transmit to the relevant agencies and bodies any reports from States parties that contain a request or indicate a need for technical advice or assistance, along with the Committee's observations and suggestions. The Committee often makes recommendations for technical cooperation in its concluding observations addressed to States parties as an outcome of the reporting dialogue.

The United Nations High Commissioner for Human Rights, whose mandate includes the enhancement of international cooperation for the promotion and protection of all human rights, is providing assistance in this regard and encourages governments to respond favourably to the Committee's recommendations.

General Guidelines

> General guidelines regarding the form and contents of initial reports to be submitted by States parties under Article 44, paragraph 1 (a), of the Convention on the Rights of the Child.

Introduction

1. Article 44, paragraph 1, of the Convention on the Rights of the Child provides that:

> "States parties undertake to submit to the Committee, through the Secretary-General of the United Nations, reports on the measures they have adopted which give effect to the rights recognised herein and on the progress made on the enjoyment of those rights:

"(a) Within two years of the entry into force of the Convention for the State Party concerned;

"(b) Thereafter every five years.".

2. Article 44 of the Convention further provides, in paragraph 2, that reports submitted to the Committee on the Rights of the Child shall indicate factors and difficulties, if any, affecting the degree of fulfilment of the obligations under the Convention and shall also contain sufficient information to provide the Committee with a comprehensive understanding of the implementation of the Convention in the country concerned.
3. The Committee believes that the process of preparing a report for submission to the Committee offers an important occasion for conducting a comprehensive review of the various measures undertaken to harmonise national law and policy with the Convention and to monitor progress made in the enjoyment of the rights set forth in the Convention. Additionally, the process should be one that encourages and facilitates popular participation and public scrutiny of government policies.
4. The Committee considers that the reporting process entails an ongoing reaffirmation by States parties of their commitment to respect and ensure observance of the rights set forth in the Convention and serves as the essential vehicle for the establishment of a meaningful dialogue between the States parties and the Committee.
5. The general part of States parties' reports, relating to matters that are of interest to monitoring bodies under various international human rights instruments, should be prepared in accordance with the "Consolidated guidelines for the initial part of the reports of States parties", as contained in document HRI/1991/1. The present guidelines, which were adopted by the Committee on the Rights of the Child at its 22nd meeting, held on 15 October 1991, should be followed in the preparation of the initial reports of States parties

relating to the implementation of the Convention on the Rights of the Child.

6. The Committee intends to formulate guidelines for the preparation of periodic reports that are to be submitted pursuant to Article 44, paragraph l(b), of the Convention in due course.
7. Reports should be accompanied by copies of the principal legislative and other texts as well as detailed statistical information and indicators referred to therein, which will be made available to members of the Committee. It should be noted, however, that for reasons of economy they will not be translated or reproduced for general distribution. It is desirable, therefore, that when a text is not actually quoted in or annexed to the report itself, the report should contain sufficient information to be understood without reference to those texts.
8. The provisions of the Convention have been grouped under different sections, equal importance being attached to all the rights recognised by the Convention.

Measures of Implementation

9. Under this Section, States parties are requested to provide relevant information pursuant to Article 4 of the Convention, including information on:
   (a) The measures taken to harmonise national law and policy with the provisions of the Convention;
   (b) Existing or planned mechanisms at the national or local level for coordinating policies relating to children and for monitoring the implementation of the Convention.
10. In addition. States parties are requested to describe the measures that have been taken or are foreseen, pursuant to Article 42 of the Convention, to make the principles and provisions of the Convention widely known, by appropriate and active means, to adults and children alike.

11. States parties are also requested to describe those measures undertaken or foreseen, pursuant to Article 44, paragraph 6, of the Convention, to make their reports widely available to the public at large in their own countries.

II. Definition of Child

12. Under this section States parties are requested to provide relevant information, pursuant to article one of the Convention, concerning the definition of a child under their laws and regulations. In particular, States parties are requested to provide information on the age of attainment of majority and on the legal minimum ages established for various purposes, including legal or medical counselling without parental consent, end of compulsory education, part-time employment, full-time employment, hazardous employment, sexual consent, marriage, voluntary enlistment into the armed forces, conscription into the armed forces, voluntarily giving testimony in court, criminal liability, deprivation of liberty, imprisonment and consumption of alcohol or other controlled substances.

III. General Principles

13. Relevant information, including the principal legislative, judicial, administrative or other measures in force or foreseen, factors and difficulties encountered and progress achieved in implementing the provisions of the Convention, and implementation priorities and specific goals for the future, should be provided in respect of :
    (a) Non-discrimination (Art. 2);
    (b) Best interests of the child (Art. 3);
    (c) The right to life, survival and development (Art. 6);
    (d) Respect for the views of the child (Art. 12).
14. In addition, States parties are encouraged to provide relevant information on the application of these principles in the implementation of Articles listed elsewhere in these guidelines.

IV. Civil Rights and the Freedoms

15. States parties are requested to provide relevant information, including the principal legislative, judicial, administrative or other measures in force; factors and difficulties encountered and progress achieved in implementing the relevant provisions of the Convention; and implementation priorities and specific goals for the future, in respect of:
    - (a) Name and nationality (Art. 7);
    - (b) Preservation of identity (Art. 8);
    - (c) Freedom of expression (Art. 13);
    - (d) Access to appropriate information (Art. 17);
    - (e) Freedom of thought, conscience and religion (Art. 14);
    - (f) Freedom of association and of peaceful assembly (Art. 15);
    - (g) Protection of privacy (Art. 16);
    - (h) The right not to be subjected to torture or other cruel, inhuman or degrading treatment or punishment (Art. 37 (a)).

V. Family Environment and Alternative Care

16. Under this section, States parties are requested to provide relevant information, including the principal legislative, judicial, administrative or other measures in force, particularly how the principles of the "best interests of the child" and "respect for the views of the child" are reflected therein; factors and difficulties encountered and progress achieved in implementing the relevant provisions of the Convention; and implementation priorities and specific goals for the future, in respect of:
    - (a) Parental guidance (Art. 5);
    - (b) Parental responsibilities (Art. 18, paras. 1 and 2);
    - (c) Separation from parents (Art. 9);
    - (d) Family reunification (Art. 10);
    - (e) Recovery of maintenance for the child (Art. 27, para. 4);
    - (f) Children deprived of a family environment (Art. 20);

(g) Adoption (Art. 21);
(h) Illicit transfer and non-return (Art. 11);
(i) Abuse and neglect (Art. 19), including physical and psychological recovery and social reintegration (Art. 39);
(j) Periodic review of placement (Art. 25).

17. In addition, States parties are requested to provide information on the numbers of children per year within the reporting period in each of the following groups, disaggregated by age group, sex, ethnic or national background and rural or urban environment: homeless children, abused or neglected children taken into protective custody, children placed in foster care, children placed in institutional care, children placed through domestic adoption, children entering the country through intercountry adoption procedures and children leaving the country through inter-country adoption procedures.
18. States parties are encouraged to provide additional relevant statistical information and indicators relating to children covered in this section.

VI. Basic Health Welfare

19. Under this section, States parties are requested to provide relevant information, including the principal legislative, judicial, administrative or other measures in force; the institutional infrastructure for implementing policy in this area, particularly monitoring strategies and mechanisms; and factors and difficulties encountered and progress achieved in implementing the relevant provisions of the Convention, in respect of :

(a) Survival and development (Art. 6, para. 2);
(b) Disabled children (Art. 23);
(c) Health and health services (Art. 24);
(d) Social security and child-care services and facilities (Art. 26 and Art. 18);
(e) Standard of living (Art. 27, paras. 1-3).

20. In addition to information provided under paragraph 9 (b) of these guidelines, States parties are requested to specify the nature and extent of cooperation with local and national organisations of a governmental or non-governmental nature, such as institutions of social workers, concerning the implementation of this area of the Convention. States parties are encouraged to provide additional relevant statistical information and indicators relating to children covered in this section.

VII. Education, Leisure and Culture Activities

21. Under this section States parties are requested to provide relevant information, including the principal legislative, judicial, administrative or other measures in force; the institutional infrastructure for implementing policy in this area, particularly monitoring strategies and mechanisms; and factors and difficulties encountered and progress achieved in implementing the relevant provisions of the Convention, in respect of:
    (a) Education, including vocational training and guidance (Art. 28);
    (b) Aims of education (Art. 29);
    (c) Leisure, recreation and cultural activities (Art. 31).
22. In addition to information provided under paragraph 9 (b) of these guidelines, States parties are requested to specify the nature and extent of cooperation with local and national organisations of a governmental or non-governmental nature, such as institutions of social workers, concerning the implementation of this area of the Convention. States parties are encouraged to provide additional relevant statistical information and indicators relating to children covered in this section.

VIII. Special Protection Measures

23. Under this section, States parties are requested to provide relevant information, including the principal legislative,

judicial, administrative or other measures in force; factors and difficulties encountered and progress achieved in implementing the relevant provisions of the Convention; and implementation priorities and specific goals for the future, in respect of:

(a) Children in situations of emergency:
   (i) Refugee children (Art. 22);
   (ii) Children in armed conflicts (Art. 38), including physical and psychological recovery and social reintegration (Art. 39);

(b) Children in conflict with the law:
   (i) The administration of juvenile justice (Art. 40);
   (ii) Children deprived of their liberty, including any form of detention, imprisonment or placement in custodial settings (Art. 37 (b), (c) and (d);
   (iii) The sentencing of juveniles, in particular the prohibition of capital punishment and life imprisonment (Art. 37 (a));
   (iv) Physical and psychological recovery and social reintegration (Art. 39);

(c) Children in situations of exploitation, including physical and psychological recovery and social reintegration (Art. 39):
   (i) Economic exploitation, including child labour (Art. 32);
   (ii) Drug abuse (Art. 33);
   (iii) Sexual exploitation and sexual abuse (Art. 34);
   (iv) Other forms of exploitation (Art. 36);
   (v) Sale, trafficking and abduction (Art. 35);

(d) Children belonging to a minority or an indigenous group (Art. 30). indigenous group (Art. 30).

24. Additionally, States parties are encouraged to provide specific statistical information and indicators relevant to the children covered by paragraph 23.

FOURTEEN

Rights of the Deprived

Everyone cherishes good health and long life. Health and human happiness go together. That is why, perhaps, right to health is regarded as one of the basic human rights. But on the other hand, human life, sometimes, is marred by the ravages of natural disaster, birth and accidents, causing disability of one kind or the other to many people. No doubt, the incidence of disability is the most catastrophic situation inflicted by the forces of nature on human beings, yet it does not, in any way, take away the inalienable rights of deprived people. The movement for the rights of disabled persons has grown out of the realization that they are firstly human beings. Any discrimination between the disabled and the able-bodied tantamounts to the naked violation of the human rights of the disabled persons.

The dimensions of the incidence of disability at the global level are managingly glaring at the future of mankind. Though, several steps have been taken in this regard, yet their outcome has shown little change in the situation. An attempt is made here to focus on the prevalence of the incidence of disability and the impact of the world-wide campaign for the prevention of disability and rehabilitation of the disabled on the rights of the disabled. The disabled, like others, are social beings. They have similar hopes, aspirations and rights as their fellowmen. Yet man focuses his attention on their disabilities rather than potentialities. Consequently, the disabled have been socially and economically marginalized and denied opportunities to seek self-development. The problems arising out of disability are varied and complex, but most of the problems encountered by the disabled stem from prejudices and ignorance on the part of the so-called able-bodied persons.

The concept of disability is directly linked with the societal attitudes towards disabled persons. Since the societal attitude towards the disabled has undergone change through different stages of social evolution, the concept of disability has also changed accordingly. The traditional societal attitude towards the disabled was one of pity, sympathy and charity. The disabled were considered as incapable of leading independent and productive lives.

Accordingly, the persons with a physical defect of some kind or the other were, for centuries, termed as 'crippled'. The world 'crippled' and its synonyms imply some sort of social stigma. It also refers to a state of helplessness. Under the traditional perception of disability, an important element of the welfare of the disabled – recognition and respect of human dignity and self-esteem of the disabled person – was completely missing.

A marked shift in the societal attitude towards the disabled was noticed in the second quarter of the twentieth century. As a result of several scientific and social advancements, an entirely new concept of welfare with regard to the disabled has emerged which is responsible, on the one hand, for the gradual awakening of the society towards the rights of the disabled and on the other hand, for the creation of a new consciousness among the disabled themselves towards their rights and obligations. The new approach for the welfare of the disabled is directed at the socioeconomic integration of the disabled in the mainstream of active social life. Therefore, the use of such words as 'disabled' and 'handicapped' is advocated, because they seem to take an objective view of disability.

Very often, the terms like 'disabled', 'physically handicapped', 'impaired' and 'crippled' are used almost synonymously. It is necessary to make distinction between these different terms. The term 'disabled' or 'disability' refers to a solution wherein the functional capabilities are either lost or reduced considerably due to impairment. Contrary to this, 'handicap' is a value judgement passed by others about an impaired, disabled person. It is not necessary that disability may become handicap under all circumstances. It becomes handicap, only when it causes interference with the individual's expectations, job performance or relationship with others. The term 'impairment' refers to any deviation from the normal which leads to defective structure, function, organization, or development of the whole or any part of individual's faculties. Thus, the term 'disabled' appears mere appropriate with its broad based meaning.

Besides these terminological problems, the concept of disability faces another kind of problem, i.e. the lack of any well-conceived definition of 'disability'. This problem is due to the fact that different countries follow different criteria to define disability. So much so that the scholars and international bodies have also adopted various approaches to the study of the disability. These approaches may be categorized as, medical approach, psychological approach, economic-vocational approach and socio-political approach.

The medical approach emphasizes on the physical functioning and its whole orientation is individual centred. The World Health Organization (WHO) is its best representative example. The second approach lays stress on the psychological aspect of disability. It aims at making the disabled self-reliant, The economic-vocational approach is concerned with the vocational limitations of the disabled and it is directed towards the vocational rehabilitation of the disabled. The International Labour Organization (hereafter ILO) is the most ardent proponent of this approach. The socio-political approach regards disability as a by-product of interaction between individual and environment. Contrary to the medical approach, it holds the failure of structured social environment responsible for disability instead of personal disorders or deficiencies.

It, therefore, emphasizes on the need for strengthened laws to combat discrimination against the disabled. All the above approaches take a narrow view of disability and confine themselves to only one aspect of disability. From the holistic viewpoint, the definition of the term 'disability' as given by the United Nations, seems to be quite exhaustive in its meaning. There are different types of disability, namely, (i) visually disabled; (ii) hearing disability (deafness), (iii) speech disability (dumbness); (iv) mental retardness, and (v) orthopaedic disability. All these types of disabled are covered in the definition of the term 'disabled' as given by the United Nations.

Another perplexing dimension of the problem of disability is the colossal magnitude of the problem. Though, at the global level, it is difficult to provide accurate data on the incidence of disability, however, the ever growing population of the disabled in the world is a matter of grave concern to all. According to one UN estimate," more than 500 million people in the world are physically or mentally disabled. The population of the disabled increases every year by some 15 million as a result of war, accident, malnutrition and diseases, which means a country like Afghanistan is added to the disabled population every year. If this trend continues, then the figure may surpass 700 million mark by 2000 A.D. Out of the total disabled population, women account for above one-third of it, but if female disabled children are included in this calculation, then the total female population with disability would be around 250 million which comes to about 5 per cent of the world population.

The overall plight of disabled persons in both the developing and developed countries presents a gloomy picture. While in developing societies, disability is basically caused by poverty and malnutrition, on the other hand, in developed societies, it is linked with aging and accidents. That is why, in developing countries, mostly children are victims of disability, whereas elder persons and industrial workers, for the most part, affected by disability in the developed countries. The situation of disabled women is more distressing. They are subjected to dual discrimination—firstly, due to their feminine gender and secondly, due to disability. Thus the dimensions of disability are enormous and it needs to be fought on all fronts with concerted, persistent and bold efforts.

Until the first quarter of the twentieth century, disability was regarded as life long dependence and despondency, misery and squalor. Consequently, hardly any efforts for its prevention were initiated at that time. However, international concern for the improvement of public health and prevention of diseases was manifested in various health related provisions of the League of Nations.

The first international initiative with regard to the rehabilitation of the disabled came from the ILO which came into being in 1919 as an autonomous body associated with the League of Nations. As back as 1920 for the first time, the ILO turned its attention towards the employment problems of the disabled persons. Since then, the rights of the disabled lie at the very heart of its mission. A major part of the ILO activities for the rehabilitation of the disabled consists of the adoption of international labour standards in the form of various recommendations, conventions and resolutions. The most recent among them include Vocational Rehabilitation and Employment (Disabled Persons) Convention, 1983 (no. 159) and Recommendation, 1983 (no. 168). These instruments are very significant in the sense that they contain useful guidelines on methods and measures for widening the employment opportunities for the disabled. Thus, the ILO has played an instrumental role in the field of vocational rehabilitation of the disabled.

With the inception of the United Nations (UN), the campaign for disability prevention and rehabilitation gained world wide currency. The incorporation of the human rights provisions in the Charter of the United Nations and the adoption of the Universal Declaration of Human Rights, followed by the two covenants, manifest the resolve of the international community to fight the menance of disability. The United Nations together with other specialized agencies have been working towards the goals set in different instruments. The United Nations, through its various resolutions and declarations, had laid down international norms, standards and guidelines concerning the rights of the disabled persons. A number of specialised agencies, such as, the International Labour Organization (11.0); the United Nations Educational, Scientific Cultural Organization (UNESCO), The World Health Organization (WHO), the United Nations International Children Emergency Fund (UNICEF), have oriented their activities towards the disability prevention and rehabilitation programme within the scope of their organizations. In addition, other international bodies associated with the rehabilitation programmes for the disabled include: the United Nations Development Programme (UNDP), the Food Agricultural Organization (FAO), the United Nations Industrial Development Organization (UNIDO) and the Office of the United Nations High Commission for Refugees (UNCHR), etc. Besides these, there are many other non-governmental bodies engaged in the rehabilitation task.

As of now, no international body is specifically assigned with the responsibility of implementation of the United Nations' recommendations and various other instruments. The most important reason behind it is that the global concern for the integration of the disabled has yet not been articulated in the legally binding conventions. The United Nations' activities in this regard have been, so far, confined to the adoption of resolutions and declarations. However, the Sub-Commission on the Prevention of Discrimination and Protection of Minorities is the most important body dealing with the violation of the rights of the disabled persons.

In brief, it may be said that the international bodies may only provide guidelines and set norms for the promotion of the rights of the disabled persons, but the main task of integrating and rehabilitating them rests with the member states. Unless the disabled are assigned the status of equality in these societies, the promotion of their rights shall remain a mere myth.

Rehabilitation is the most strategic weapon to combat the menance of disability. There are two perceptions of rehabilitations. One is medical perception which views rehabilitation as assisting all those medical measures which expedite recovery in the physical sense, whereas according to the other view, rehabilitation means the restoration of the disabled to the fullest physical, mental, social, vocational and economic usefulness of which he/she is capable. In other words, rehabilitation is a goal oriented programme which aims at enabling an impaired person to reach an optimum mental, physical or social functional level.

The rehabilitation process, thus, involves basically three aspects. These aspects are: physical rehabilitation, vocational rehabilitation and psycho-social integration. All three aspects are interlinked:

Measures for Rehabilitation

It is the first and most important aspect of the whole process of rehabilitation. It is directed towards the improvement of the functional loss caused by disability. Physical rehabilitation involves two phases, namely, prevention of disability and restoration of the disabled.

Measures for Prevention

Prevention is better than cure. Most of the disabilities are preventable if adequate precautionary and educative measures are taken against its outbreak. There are numerous ways of disability prevention. Some of these attack the cause of disease directly (for instance, vaccination and inoculation); while the others deal with it indirectly, such as, community education, early detection, genetic counselling, etc. The whole scheme of disability prevention comprises following steps.

Immunization is one of the most powerful and effective

means of disability prevention. The diseases like polio, measles, tetanus, whooping cough, diptheria, neo-natal and tuberculosis are responsible for the growing incidence of disability, especially in the developing countries. Immunization against these diseases, though, a challenging task, but the promise held is even greater. The World Health Organization (WHO), as a part of its global efforts, launched the Expanded Programme on Immunization (EPI) in 1974. As a result of this programme, two-thirds of the children in the developing world have been covered by vaccines and approximately two million lives are being saved each year. The Rotary International, a non-governmental organization, is also busy with its polio-immunization programme. In fact, the elimination of all these diseases constitutes a major contribution to the prevention of in fact any childhood disability.

Certain types of disability are linked with malnutrition. There are primarily four nutritional disorders in the developing countries which lead to widespread impairment, and disability. These are (i) protein-energy malnutrition (PEM), (ii) endemic goitre, (iii) xerophthalmia leading to blindness, and (iv) nutritional anaemia. There is a paucity of precise data on the people affected by malnutrition, but most of them are centred in the underdeveloped countries and the developing countries.

Pre-natal, peri-natal and post-natal care as well as obstetric practices used at the time of child birth are also related to the disability causes, especially in the developing countries where it is found that inappropriate obstetric practices and improper neo-natal care lead to neurological impairments. Lack of immunization of pregnant mothers render the new borns more susceptible to all communicable diseases resulting in various conditions. All this can be successfully prevented by taking recourse to the immunization of pregnant mothers and observance of elementary hygiene.

Accidents and Hereditary Defects are two causes of disability and are the least controllable factors. Accidents are usually of two kinds—industrial and traffic. Industrial accidents are more common in the developed countries, whereas the developing countries are mainly in the grip of traffic accidents. There are other causes of accidents also as, fall, slip, explosion, animal and insect bites, etc. In the case of hereditary defects, endogamous marriages are responsible for genetic disorders. The hereditary defects may be prevented only if the disorder is a dominant one, but not if the disorder is necessible.

Restoration of the Disabled means that every medical, surgical and auxiliary services should be used to reduce the impact of disability. There is a co-relation between restoration and the vocational rehabilitation. Restoration, eventually, helps in the vocational rehabilitation of the disabled. The process of physical rehabilitation involves adequate training, evaluation of the working capacity of the individual and remedial gymnastics and prosthetics.

Vocational rehabilitation may he defined as a service necessary to render a disabled person fit to engage in remunerative occupation. The end product of vocational rehabilitation is resettlement of the disabled into gainful economic life. Work or employment has a psychological, social and economic value for the disabled and it instills a feeling of self-confidence in them. But, in actual practice, the successful placement of the disabled is affected by several factors, such as, attitude of the community, the attitude of the disabled towards disability and job-availability for them.

If a community accepts the potentialities of the disabled, the placement of the disabled becomes easy. But employers usually rationalize their feelings on economic grounds. They argue that disability reduces productivity and so, is an economic liability or that the disabled are prone to accidents and if injured at work, the employers become liable to employ them.

- The vocational rehabilitation of the disabled is co-terminus with his own self-perception. In any community where the disabled have been over protected by their families, or have been given a negative role by the community, it may be quite difficult to convince him of the benefits of vocational rehabilitation.

– Severe unemployment or underemployment creates the greatest obstacle to the placement of the disabled. In such a situation, it is necessary to concentrate on a few selected groups for vocational rehabilitation. The agriculture based community may offer good prospects of their placement in industrial enterprises, provided they are properly skilled in the job. Much can be accomplished by educating the public about the capabilities of the disabled.

Psycho-Social Integration of the disabled is the most crucial stage in the process of rehabilitation. The physical and vocational rehabilitation cannot achieve the desired results, unless the disabled may feel themselves psychologically integrated and the society is willing to accept them as productive members.

Disability brings in its wake so many adjustment problems, the disabled has to bear a double burden of handicaps—'social handicap' in addition to his 'specific handicap'. Rehabilitation encompasses the whole process of adjustment and readjustment of the disabled in various spheres of life. The disabled faces quite many adjustment problems of different nature which may be categorized thus.

The disabled faces a great deal of uncertainty in his life due to permanent structural and functional disorders of his body. He needs to assure himself whether he would be able to move around in the outside world. According to psychologists, the self-concept is a determining factor in the personality development of the disabled individual. It determines not only his own perception, but also of others towards his disability. Therefore, it is imperative that the self concept should be reconciled.

The feeling of insecurity, both physical and emotional, is

greater in a disabled person than in any other able-bodied person. The perpetuation of false notions about sex and disability in the minds of common men deprives the disabled person of his right to lead a married life. This causes a deep mental agony in him. Besides, some other factors such as, physical discomfort, aversion, ridicule and scorn of the able-bodied, escalate emotional problems in him Love and affection give them emotional satisfaction and helps in his psycho-social integration.

Family is the most important agent of socialization of the disabled. The impact of disability is closely interlinked with the adequacy or inadequacy of the parental attitude. If the parents view the disability of their child as calamity, the disabled child also thinks likewise. Therefore, the parents and family members should objectively accept the limitations potentials of their disabled child.

In spite of the wise scope of rehabilitation strategy to combat the incidence of disability, it has failed to deliver the desired goods. The reason is that due to the cumulative effect of several factors, the pace of rehabilitation process is hampered. These factors are: poverty, ignorance and illiteracy, neglect of public health, lack of commitment on the part of planners and statesmen, lack of political and administrative will and social barriers. Besides these, the manpower problem and problems concerning technology need some elaboration.

The problem of manpower is a great stumbling block in the way of the proper placement of the disabled. The functioning of rehabilitation institutions in the developing countries affords a good example of it. In most of these countries, the last few decades have witnessed high specialization of rehabilitation manpower which has culminated in the creation of too many new professional groups and sub-groups. This is because more than one experts are generally involved in the treatment of one disabled individual. Needless to say that 'the team work' is a must in the rehabilitation process. But experience shows that it has very often led to the decline in the efficiency of utilisation of the viable manpower. In fact, the need for rehabilitation is so great that it cannot be properly met by specialists alone. Unless each country introduces basic task concerning rehabilitation in the training curricular of doctors, nurses, social workers, teachers and others, any solution of such manpower problem cannot be imagined.

In recent years, there has been a rapid development of rehabilitation technology. Much more is known today regarding exercise and other active forms of training for the disabled. But the development of technical aids and devices cannot yield the desired results, unless the disabled are adequately trained in their use.

The problem arising out of the incidence of disability are varied and complex. It is gratifying to note that as of now, the question of disability prevention and rehabilitation is receiving due consideration at different levels. Yet, several measures initiated by national and international agencies for the disability prevention have resulted in limited success. The fact that the world or organisation is merely a voluntary association of sovereign states rather than a supra-national body, is the most obstructive limitation in this regard.

While considering some constructive steps for the promotion of the rights of disabled persons and their rehabilitation as well as integration into the mainstream of socio-economic life, this fact must be taken into account that the problem of disability is a mere syndrome; the root causes are inherent in mass poverty, social segregation and illiteracy. Therefore, the only permanent solution of disability problem could be their psycho-social and economic integration and proper placement which would enable them to stand on their own with dignity and decency. With this objective in mind, following suggestions are offered:

(1) Education can go a long way in creating an awareness among the people about the basic causes of disability, its prevention prospects and

rehabilitation. It may also prove an effective weapon in eradicating the dogmatic fears attached to disability.

(2) The development of community based rehabilitation services is another step necessary to expedite the integration of the disabled. It also entails the balanced development of community based services in both urban and rural areas. It should be based on an appraisal of the most appropriate forms of service delivery to assist the disabled in accommodating to the life of their social milieu.

(3) The development of technical aids and devices may be another significant step in the physical rehabilitation of the disabled. Steps should be initiated in each country to allow the disabled to have financial and physical access to technical aids and devices.

(4) Rehabilitation technique should be simplified and made more economical.

(5) Disability prevention and rehabilitation should be incorporated as an integral and high priority component of national socio-economic policies and development plans. Action in these fields should be recognized as legitimate targets for development assistance.

(6) Allocation of financial resources for rehabilitation of the disabled should be enhanced by all countries to give boost to existing educational, medical, social and vocational systems.

(7) Society should realize that the disabled are not second class citizens. Disability does not deprive them of their liberty and equality of opportunity. Social structure should be revamped in such a way so as to facilitate their full participation in the socio-economic and political life.

(8) Manpower should be mobilized with efficient and

dedicated rehabilitation experts and sincere and committed government officials to hasten the pace of rehabilitation.

(9) Public opinion should be educated to protest against any discriminatory policy adopted by the government. The people must be vigilant against any violation of human rights. If any such violation takes place, this should be forthwith brought to the notice of local authorities.

(10) In order to prevent any atrocity and violation of the rights of the disabled, special cells and courts should be set up to monitor such Incidents.

(11) Non-governmental organizations and voluntary agencies have a significant role to play in this field. Legislative measures and efforts at official level alone cannot be effective in solving this challenging problem.

(12) The last but not the least important thing is that a general consciousness should be created at grass-root level against the incidence of disability.

To conclude, it may be said that the global problems of disability are of such a colossal magnitude that as of now, any worthwhile effort to meet the challenge does not seem to be in sight. However, there is enough scope for optimism and let us hope for the day when, with all necessary changes in social perceptions and with greater opportunities for the development available, the disabled would feel that they are no longer disabled.

FIFTEEN

In the New Millennium

Fukuyama's conceit (I mean it in both senses) that the triumph of Western liberalism has stopped the clock of change—has put an end to history—is already waning. We may reflect that human rights themselves have played a sacrificial role in this process, for the demise of the regimes of Eastern Europe was accelerated by a megaphone rhetoric of human rights from States, including our own, with an embarrassing capacity for overlooking human rights abuses among their own allies and clients and even within their own frontiers. The message between the lines has been that human rights are a commodity like any other, capable of being traded for political or economic advantage, and the rhetoric little more than the conduct of politics by other means.

This is not, however, a complaint about the politicisation of human rights. They are by nature political, for they seek to condition how States treat individuals. The reason why it is we who feel able to lecture others about them is that human rights are historically and ideologically the property of the liberal democracies of the West. In their received and accepted form, whether one takes the European Convention or the Universal Declaration as the example, they enshrine values which are universal neither in time nor in place. They are in essence the enlightenment's values of possessive individualism, derived from the historic paradigm, which has shaped our world, of the conscious human actor whose natural enemy is the State—a necessary evil—and in whose maximum personal liberty lies the maximum benefit for society. To accept, as we can and should, that this view is rooted in time and place is not to consign it to the bin of relativism, for the same has been and will continue to be true of all historic proclamations of self-evident and universal truths. (The two most self-evident truths of life on this planet are after all that the earth is flat and that the sun goes round it.) The truth that all men are created equal was far from self-evident to the slaves owned by some of the men who proclaimed it at the dawn of American republicanism. That free speech or family life is today a fundamental individual right is by no means self-evident in a good number of the contemporary world's States, where history and conditions have made it apparent that they are primarily the State's business; and it is entirely conceivable that the States of Western Europe may during the coming century recast their thinking about family life and the right of the incurably or expensively ill to life itself as social and economic pressures be are down on ethics and theology. Who will then be right: our grandchildren or us?

In Time and Place

It is perfectly possible to recognise the localisation of ideas in time and place and to assert that they are none the worse for it; indeed, that ideas which pretend to universality are historical delusions. To do so, however, carries two corollaries. One is that as times change our premises and assumptions about the content of fundamental rights will change. Secondly, what is made of currently accepted rights in each country and each generation by its courts and adjudicators is itself a function of time and place. (Law spends its life stretched on the rack between certainty and adaptability, sometimes groaning audibly but mostly maintaining the stoical appearance or steady uniformity which public confidence demands.) But lest the mask become the face, it is important that new generations of lawyers should become actively curious about why the certainties of the law themselves change constantly. How and why is it that the same American Constitution in 1896 legitimated racial segregation in public services and then in 1954 forbade it? How does it come about that not dissimilar abortion laws have in recent years been struck down by Canada's Supreme Court as too restrictive and by Germany's Constitutional Court as too permissive? On our own patch, how did it come to be self-evident to the Court of Appeal in 1925 that it was perfectly all right for an education authority to sack married women teachers on the ground that their duties lay at home or, in 1948, that it was perfectly all right for Wednesbury Corporation to use its cinema licensing powers to stop young people going to the pictures on Sunday?

Not one of these decisions, each of them affecting what we would recognise now as fundamental human rights, is intelligible today except by situating the reasoning of the deciding court in its peculiar time and place; and the same will, I hope, be true of the decisions handed down by this judicial generation—for it would be only in an ossified and retrograde society that the laws of one generation were good enough for the next. Precedent, far from becoming redundant, takes on an organic role in this scheme of things—not perhaps in the grand Tennysonian image of freedom slowly broadening down in a kind of Fabian long march to happiness, but a centuries-long culture of reasoning and principle which ebbs and flows, so that, for example, the charge of contempt of court made on behalf of a Zairian asylum-seeker against the holder of one of the three great offices of State, the Home Secretary, could found upon Sir Edward Coke's assertion of the sovereignty of the courts in the face of the Crown's prerogatives and upon Wilkes's recovery of punitive damages from an earlier Home Secretary, Lord Halifax, for the unlawful issue of a general warrant. A former jobbing electrician who became a distinguished teacher of law once told me that in both jobs he had found the most useful part of his equipment to be a well-filled box of junk; and while I would not put the great cases I have been referring to in that class, an eclectic mind is not a bad asset in a modern lawyer.

The ministerial contempt case illustrates, too, the way in

which modern public law has carried forward a culture of judicial assertiveness to compensate for, and in places repair, dysfunctions in the democratic process. It is a remarkable fact that a judiciary which has taken a public battering in recent years over miscarriages of criminal justice has in the same period earned large public approbation for its willingness to prevent and correct abuses of governmental power. When the history of modern judicial review is written, it will recount how the coming of the adult franchise through the two great nineteenth century Reform Acts was matched by the introduction of the Northgate Trevelyan civil service. This replaced ministers' placement with an intellectual and administrative elite from the same schools, universities and clubs as the judges themselves, and encouraged the judiciary to retreat from its prickly Victorian invigoration of the executive into a passivity. This passivity by the 1950s, had allowed executive and local government an unprecedented measure of unchallenged power, to the extent that even the administrative tribunals set up to adjudicate between citizen and State were treated as instruments of departmental policy. It will also, I hope, observe how the subsequent reassertion of judicial oversight of government which has been the achievement of the 1970s and 1980s in this country has been replicated all over the common law world as judiciaries have moved to fill lacunae of legitimacy in the functioning of democratic polities—a process of which the Pergau Dam decision can stand as a sharp recent illustration. The historian's conclusion may well be that the last three decades of the twentieth century have seen a judicial refashioning, with popular support sufficient to mute political opposition to it, of our organic constitution. If so, its consequence is that we have today both in this country and in those with which it shares aspects of its political and judicial culture a new and still emerging constitutional paradigm. This is no longer of Dicey's supreme parliament to whose will the rule of law must finally bend, but of a bi-polar sovereignty of the Crown in Parliament and the Crown in its courts, to each of which the Crown's ministers are answerable — politically to Parliament, legally to the courts. That the government of the day has no separate sovereignty in this paradigm is both axiomatic and a reminder of the sharpest of all the lessons of eastern Europe: that it is when State is collapsed into party that democracy flounders.

Primacy of Democracy

To assume a jurisdiction of this kind is of course to assume, without having argued it, the primacy of democracy. It is therefore worth remembering how temporary and vulnerable the desirable sense of democracy is. A term of abuse synonymous with mob rule in Burke's vocabulary, its contemporary feel-good usage finds its origin in America, where from its first known modern use in the Rhode Island Constitution of 1641 it became a vehicle of challenge to the colonial power in the hands of Hamilton and his contemporaries and in due course a vehicle of challenge in this country in the hands of the Chartists and their successors to the rotten boroughs and aristocratic oligarchies which electoral reform was eventually to sweep away. But although the power of the world has become such that there is barely a regime anywhere in the world which has not sought during the twentieth century to characterise itself as democratic, there is nothing which determines that the notion of democracy as the higher-order law beneath which constitutions must operate is there for all time. If anything, history should lead us to expect the converse; but apart from watching phlegmatically as the great oxymoron of the nineteenth century, the nation States, fissiparate and super States now arm the world's poor nations to kill each other, we cannot peer very far into that darkness.

For these and other reasons I have trouble with the concept of a higher-order of law as the basis of human rights adjudication. To postulate such a law is to attract all the theological problems which attend any argument from a first cause and which can ultimately only be answered by an act of faith. (It may be in the end that a society's consensus about its basic values is an act of faith, but my own preference is to reason, as Hobbes or Bentham might have done, that it is society itself which is given and which poses certain overriding needs for its own existence.) While shared perceptions of what those needs are change as societies change, there are moral and practical continuities—of which the democratic principle is one—which can be powerfully represented as fundamental values, at least within the temporal and social horizons of each society. This relatively modest foundation for the legitimacy of human rights has perhaps the virtue that, without reducing all discourse to incoherent subjectivity, it recognises that a single 'right' outcome to every issue is attainable, if at all, only locally and temporarily, and that just as the only universal truth is that there are no universal truths, true objectivity may well consist in recognising the reality of history and of change. When the future Chief Justice Hughes of the US said eighty years ago, "The Constitution is what the judges say it is", he was speaking of all rights instruments at all times, and to a realist concerned with human rights he was offering not despair but hope.

This will be thought perverse by many whose views I respect and who point to what happens when the judges are put in the driving seat in order to show the that way constitutional madness lies. They point, among many other examples, to the record of the Privy Council as a constitutional court composed chiefly of English judges, veering between indefensible interference with democratic decisions (for example with the legislation by which Canada was trying to replicate Roosevelt's New Deal, and which the Privy Council actually wrecked because Canada could deploy no equivalent of Roosevelt's threat to pack the Supreme Court), and indefensible abstention in the face of illiberal and oppressive conduct by Commonwealth regimes. They point too, to the outcomes of a series of cases from Northern Ireland decided in the House of Lords and in the European Commission and Court of Human Rights, in which principle seems to have taken second place to expediency and the lesson of Liverside v. Anderson to have been forgotten. These critics are opposed, however, by a respected school of rights discourse which holds that once fundamental human rights are articulated and set down, to attack them for their outcomes is to substitute venality for principle and to drag rights adjudication in the political mud.

Historical Assumptions

For reasons which I have touched on, I have little sympathy with this critique: it not only makes historical assumptions about the primacy and universality of currently accepted principles of political and social conduct, but assumes the neutrality of adjudication and at worst ascribes rogue decisions to rogue judges. It is equally plain, nevertheless, as the end of the century approaches that the argument for a bill of rights for the United Kingdom is being won by its proponents, and that the off-the-shelf solution of incorporation of the European Convention heads the list of possible measures if only on the practical ground that adherence to a set of standards enforceable on the State by an international tribunal but not by its own citizens in its own courts makes no sense at all. Moreover, the House of Lords has now recognised that our constitution knows such a thing as a fundamental law—the European Communities Act 1972—capable of overriding subsequent primary legislation if the courts find the two to be in conflict; so self-evident in fact was the doctrine that the House in Factortame (No. 2) found it unnecessary to articulate it before giving it effect.

As to the shape of a UK bill of rights I shall have a little more to say; but my present argument is that our agenda for the twenty-first century is not necessarily confined to a choice between a rights instrument interpreted for better or for worse by a judiciary with a long record of illiberal adjudication, and rejection of any rights instrument in favour of parliamentary government. Certainly, the better government becomes, the less scope there will be before judicial review of it: it is not mere piety to say that the aim of the nominated judges is to work themselves out of a job. But for the foreseeable future we have a problem, shared in large part with other developed democracies: how to ensure that as a docility we are governed within a law which has internalised the notion of fundamental human rights. If posing it this way means adopting the rule of law, like democracy, as a higher-order principle, we likewise have the social consensus, which alone—and without the need of a leap of faith— can accord it that primacy. And if in our own society the rule of law is to mean much, it must at least mean that it is the obligation of the courts to articulate and uphold the ground rules of ethical social existence which we dignify as fundamental human rights, temporary and local though they are in the grand scheme of things.

Principle of Outcomes

The largely unexplored avenue to this end, and the one I want to explore, is what I will perversely call the principle of outcomes. In common with the critics of a bill of rights I believe that in a democracy people have every right to scrutinise and appraise not merely the integrity of the judicial process but what it actually delivers. It is one thing, however difficult, to explain to the public that a directed acquittal because of an improperly extracted confession seeks to preserve the integrity of legal process as a greater good than the conviction of a possibly guilty individual without due process; it is another to try to justify, by reference to the legal principles which undoubtedly explain them, the kinds of award made in major libel actions. There is nothing wrong with the argument that if this is the due result there is something wrong with the principles or the processes that have produced it.

Refusing to accept the objectionable outcome alongside the welcome one is not simply allowing predilection to triumph over principle: it is to recognise that outcome—the result we want—is symbiotic with principle, because it is only for their concrete effect that we reconsider principles worth having and fighting over. If I thought there were any self-evident truths I would rank this high among them. Take the right to life, qualified as it ordinarily is in favour of limited inroads made into it by law. No rights instrument I know of tells you whether capital punishment is compatible with this fundamental right, but nobody suggests that for this reason the right is not worth articulating or that courts cannot adjudicate on it. It is simply that argument about the content of the right cannot be conducted in purely overrun principally legal terms, and the answers given by constitutional courts are inevitably and rightly a function of that large debate.

The new transitional Constitution of South Africa, a country which till recently led the world in the rate of judicial executions, accords the right to life and permits derogation to any extent which is reasonable and justifiable in an open and democratic society, but not so as to negate the essential content of the right in question. The first case in the list of the new Constitutional Court has been a challenge to the constitutionality of the death penalty. Its judgement, whichever way it goes, will resolve an issue which politicians had consciously decided was better left to the courts, even if (as one suspects) the prohibition on derogations which negate the essential content of the right makes the outcome fairly certain. The Canadian Charter of Rights and Freedoms puts it very differently: "Everyone has the right to life . . . and the right not to be deprived thereof except in accordance with the principles of fundamental justice", but the words are capable of giving rise to much the same debate. In tomorrow's world the role which courts have had to accept as society's arbiter and conscience is a role capable of embracing issues of this kind without forfeiting the epithet judicial. It is not a new role; it was the English courts which, however reluctantly, grasped the nettle that legislators would not touch and declared slavery—at least on these shores—illegal; although it is a fine irony that the famous phrase of Lord Stowell in the case of the Slave Grace in 1827, that the air of England was too pure for a slave to breathe, appears to have originated in a sixteenth-century decision of the Court of Star Chamber, which had used the same metaphor in depriving an Englishman of his imported slave. But to say that the courts are likely to continue to discharge this role, whether under the name of public policy or of human right adjudication, tells us little about how and by what standards they will do it.

Common Law Judiciary

Until recently it was to Canada that we could most usefully look from this country for a prognostication of how a common law judiciary might be expected to interpret and apply a modern rights instrument. These messages have been mixed: it has become apparent that the big battalions are getting an unfair share of Canadian rights adjudications; but there have been many decisions to cheer up liberal thinkers. But it is in Australia that the real problem has recently been highlighted: its High Court has reached into the bowels of the country's now elderly Constitution and extracted certain modern human rights—a process that outcome watchers might applaud; but it has proceeded in one case to apply them to an effect which, seen from this side of the globe, looks so partial as to justify every fear the outcome watchers have expressed. In the first of two cases decided on the same day in 1992, a statute which criminalised criticism, justified or not, of members of the Industrial Relations Commission was struck down as creating a fetter on free speech out of all proportion to the permissible objective. In the second, the court struck down a statutory provision which, in order to stop the loading of the dice in elections in favour of candidates or parties with wealthy supporters who bought television advertising time and used it to promote them, provided for free airtime for all parties and allowed full and free journalistic coverage, but banned other broadcast political advertising in the run-up to elections. The reasoning in the second case went like this: the Australian Constitution of 1900 contains no bill of rights and gives the courts no express power to review primary legislation; but it is predicated on the primacy of representative government, which in turn depends on the full and free communication of ideas; so that any legislation which obstructs the fullest desired flow of opinion in the electoral process is unconstitutional. In Australia too the Constitution appears to be what the judges say it is, and these two decisions and their more recent successors have serious implications.

First, they illustrate vividly the trend in the free-market democracies for the courts, with a great measure of popular support, to keep government within the law by—if necessary—strong and innovative measures. In the UK we are already some way down the road of legislative review, and legislation may well carry us the rest of the way by the end of the century. Whether it does so by entrenchment, giving a power to strike down legislation on human rights grounds as well as European Union ones, or by infiltration along the lines of the New Zealand Bill of Rights Act 1990, may not matter very much—at least if we can expect in the latter event to emulate the approach to outcomes adopted by Sir Robin Cooke in a recent leading case. He said: "It is necessary to be alert in New Zealand to the danger that both the courts and parliament at times may, or at least be asked to give, lip service to human rights in high-sounding language, but little or no real service in terms of actual decision." And he went on to hold that there was now a cause of action for breach of the Bill of Rights Act, basing himself—to be fair—on a 1979 decision of the Privy Council.

Secondly, however, the cases illustrate the fickleness of outcomes. Speaking for myself as a citizen I applaud the first and deplore the second. The first cuts down an indefensible protection of public figures from civilised criticism. But the second adopts, it seems to me, a very particular and partisan view of what free speech is: because it demands a free flow of ideas, the court holds that to accord a hearing to ideas in proportion to the wealth of those who hold them is not only a democratic course but the only democratic course; and in doing so it assumes a symmetry which simply does not exist between freedom of speech and freedom of information. In Britain where we have lived all our lives with Representation of the People Acts predicated (despite judicial inroads) on a financially limited and level playing field for all contenders, and with a complete prohibition on political advertising on television, the fallacy is more readily seen. In the United States, by contrast, the Australian decision is prefigured by a long history of legislative attempts to stop wealth buying seats, frustrated every time by a Supreme Court with both eyes fixed mesmerically on the First Amendment, and with results that are well known in terms of the wealth needed to run for office. The Australian decision certainly makes it harder to defend the fitness of the courts to undertake constitutional adjudication on human rights issues, for the High Court of Australia has taken to be self-evident and universal views which many would regard as partial and highly contentious in a democracy.

What's to be Done?

What then is to be done? The answer, whether we like it or not, is in large part being determined for us. The courts of these and other countries—India prominent among them—are by now engaged on a broad highway of constitutional adjudication along which issues of fundamental rights relentlessly present themselves. In this country, as I have outlined, the modern growth of public law and the internationalisation of our jurisprudence have moved adjudication towards a new catholicity of subject-matter and a greater preparedness to intervene to right wrongs in the polity. The only choice in this situation—and it is a choice which the judiciary can make for itself but which Parliament can no longer realistically make for 'it—is to retreat from rights adjudication into the long sleep of Wednesbury and before, or to develop the role with which we are now becoming familiar and to continue to move in the direction of a rights culture compatible with constitutional adjudication in a democracy. With all its pitfalls, the latter looks to be the only worthwhile choice. There is no means of standing still, but neither is there any virtue in proceeding down the path of constitutional and human rights adjudication without taking very careful stock indeed of where it might lead us. This is why it is to outcomes as much as to principles that we need to look for the future, recognising that even then the future will one day be the past and its decision be seen, like ours, to be creatures of a dialectic of time, place and principle. It is also why there is nothing unprincipled in arguing from outcomes.

The first and most important lesson that experience is teaching us is that human rights can be treated as commodities and, like commodities, appropriated by those who have the means to do so. I began by mentioning this on the international plane, but it is equally true domestically, and the free speech issue provides perhaps the sharpest illustration of how and why. The splendour of American First Amendment jurisprudence sets a standard, which nobody can ignore: the marketplace of ideas, the heresy that grows into orthodoxy. It is between the glories of the First Amendment and the horrors of a Ministry of Truth that the region of debate lies, for all societies place a restraint at some point on who can say what. Time and again in recent years it has been the free speech issue which has come banging at the court's door, asking it to open up, in the name of fundamental human rights— in this country from the Sunday Times thalidomide case to the Sinn Fein broadcasting ban, in Australia in the television broadcasting case and a number which have followed it. I do not for a moment contest the right of any of them to do so, nor the vast importance of the Miltonic freedom, and I might privately applaud what each plaintiff or applicant was setting out to achieve. But if I ask myself: why of all the human rights issues there are, should it be the issue of free speech which is constantly at the head of the queue for rights adjudication? The answer is very clear: it is because for the mass media free speech is a valuable commodity and litigation a worthwhile investment in it.

This in itself in no way negates the importance of the issue, for there is no law against doing well in the process of doing good; but it throws up a series of further issues which either a future rights instrument or the courts are going to have to address. For example, freedom to speak includes freedom to keep silent. In relation to the State, this is one thing – though not a thing beyond the reach of our law if we are prepared to take freedom of information seriously. For a transitional corporation on which hundreds of millions of people depend for their information about the world, it is another: the power to suppress information, of which we should firmly deny the State control, is a power possessed by the media corporations. Does human rights theory then have anything to say about a transitional media corporation which, in order to secure satellite TV rights for China, agrees not to transmit BBC broadcasts because they have a standard of objectivity which the Chinese government dislikes? Is it perhaps a corollary of the right to speak freely that others have a right to listen freely, and not merely to hear what those who control the media think they should hear? If so, who is to articulate it and on whose behalf? Are human rights there for corporations or for people? Are they a form of property or a constraint on power? If freedom to speak is a right, does it carry correlative obligations towards those who wish to hear? Above all, by what possible test of democracy or of equality before the law is it possible to pose a State, which maintains a high standard of public service broadcasting, as the unique natural enemy of individual liberty, and a media corporation possessing far greater communication resources than any State, as a disempowered candidate for freedom from State interference with its right of free expression? And where in this grand contest does the intended human beneficiary of the dialogue sit? However the problem is posed, it is as impossible to discuss principles divorced from outcomes as it is outcomes divorced from principles: if the reception of news and information at large is a principle which matters, the operative matrix in which the principle is to be cast cannot matter less.

If then, without abandoning principle, we are to escape the cold wind of history, which blows, sooner or later on higher-order laws and self-evident truths, it is to our present epoch's consensus about society's ground rules that we have to turn. To admit this is to admit, as perhaps we should, that different societies will agree on different ground rules, and to accept accordingly that we have both a right to review and recast our standards and an obligation to make the case for the adoption of them by others rather than continue to assert loftily that ours, being self-evident, are the only acceptable ones. It certainly denies us any moral right to preach to others what we do not practise ourselves.

Controlling Power

One of the keynotes of our epoch was struck by the Civil War radical John Warn who, writing in 1649, looked for 'a spirit of understanding big with freedom and having a single respect to people's rights' (a phrase 150 years ahead of its time). Wan contended that justice was anterior to law and postulated as the prime function of law 'the protection of the poor against the might'. One of the principles we have derived from the upheavals of the seventeenth and eighteenth centuries is the primacy of democracy, but it is a principle which carries with it a baggage of inchoate assumptions—free speech according to means is only one of them—which are capable of subverting the principle itself. Both in enacting our own rights instruments for the future and in applying them by adjudication it is important to understand that such principles are not self-implementing and that in their application they can readily be hijacked by those who already possess the greatest power in society. It is only by being rigorous, as Warr was, about a second such ground rule or principle, substantive equality before the law, that it becomes feasible to set about fireproofing the juridical elements of life in a democracy and to be serious about preventing the appropriation of legal rights and democratic processes for private or partial ends. There is a potential tension, in other words, between the principle of democratic government and the principle of equality before the law. If human rights theory has an urgent job in the coming years it is to turn this tension from its present destructive motion towards a creative balance between the individual whom democracy offers to empower and the sources and the repositories of power, both within and outside the apparatus of State, which a democracy has both to licence and to control.

This is why a rights instrument for the new century needs to address in its terms the imbalances and appropriations of power which threaten the values—possibly even the meaning:—of democracy; and it is equally why a judiciary charged with upholding the rule of law in a democracy has in making its adjudications to address the same questions. To take a modest example, in the US an enacted right of reply has been struck down as an unconstitutional interference with freedom of expression—conceiving the freedom, therefore, as a form of property—and an informal right of reply is resisted here for the same reason. In an attempt to meet this problem, an ANC draft of South Africa's transitional constitution proposed to provide: There shall be freedom of thought, speech, expression and opinion, including a free press, which shall respect the right to reply.

The last clause of the formulation was omitted from the final document, but the issue remains a real one and the Constitutional court may one day be asked to decide, since the legislature has declined to do so, what responsibilities are bound up with this and other human rights.

The New Millennium Agenda

If then we are to anticipate a continuing debate about outcomes, these too can and should be debated in terms of principle, focused now by experience on the more complicated subtext, which every rights instrument silently carries. To say that the courts are not fit to absorb and respond acceptably to such a debate is to assume both too much and too little; too much because our judicial culture has historically pretended to be insulated from public debate and so has always had to disguise its social and ethical judgements as value-free adjudications; and too little because our capacity for open and intelligent response to the wider issues of human rights is as a consequence largely unexplored: it is a language in which we are not entirely illiterate but are certainly dyslexic, and in which with remedial help we can probably do a great deal better. The tale told in Canada that a Supreme Court judge, debating an early Charter case (Canada, Charter of Rights and Freedoms) and told by his clerk that Dworkin has written something on the point, said 'Who's Dworkin?', while apocryphal, can stand as a parable of the expansion of a common law universe under the impulse of rights adjudication—for many of today's Charter decisions have a degree of legal literacy and an intellectual catholicity which our courts have so far been able (I am thinking principally of the Tony Bland case) to touch only briefly.

I hope that in constitutional adjudication, which is what our public law cases are, we shall be moving in the not too distant future toward the reception of Amicus and Brandeis briefs—the kind that were desperately lacking in the Gillick case. To do so will help us to escape the pincers which at the moment are closing on us: the pressures, which cannot be wholly resisted, towards omnicompetent adjudication, and the want of any corresponding expansion in the data and culture with and within which we carry it out. There are no guarantees that better educated the courts will get everything right, but to be sent as history is sending us on a voyage without modern navigational aids and supplies is to experience the worst of both worlds, the old and the new. My argument is that we should assemble the equipment and go on.

If, as is almost inevitable, this voyage is going increasingly to take us into the deep water of fundamental rights, this is a culture which English lawyers are going to have to acquire and absorb. To rest, as our courts sometimes do, on the laurels of having been the first to articulate a number of the freedoms the world now takes for granted is not really enough, not least because the content of these rights has at present to be subordinated giving the courts a currently watertight defence for illiberal decisions. But where, in John Mortimer's metaphor, we have so far survived by 'clinging to the wreckage', rights adjudication under a fundamental law of some description is going to mean that we have to learn to swim. This much is uncontentious. What may be more contentious is the proposition that the waters in which we shall be swimming are shark-infested and that our human rights armoury at present gives us little protection against the predators.

The notion that the prime function of human rights and indeed the rule of law is to protect the weak against the strong is not mere sentimentality. It is the child of an era of history in which equality of treatment and opportunity has become perceived—as it is not perceived in societies based on status—as an unqualified good, and of a significant recognition that you do not achieve equality by proclaiming it but only by levelling up from the inherited or systemic inequalities which make some social actors too weak to make use of their rights and others strong enough to stifle their aspirations. The deconstruction of the State as provider as well as entrepreneur is now a world-wide phenomenon; but because power in every society on this planet is and perhaps always will be unequally distributed, every society today has a problem not just with Leviathan, against whom contemporary rights instruments continue to be directed, but with Jaws. It is going to be the task of those who write and those who implement the human rights instruments of the next generation to build on the jurisprudence of substantive race and gender equality which has been one of the real achievements of this generation, so as to distinguish between the strong and the weak as claimants of fundamental rights and to avoid what one writer has characterised as a culture in which self-respect and human dignity depend upon being in a position to make strident, querulous and adversarial claims.

I have not embarked on the vexed questions of group rights as against individual rights or of social and economic rights as fundamental human rights. As to the first, it seems to me that the dichotomy of individual and group involves at least in part a false antithesis, for as individuals we are defined by our relationships with others, and which social cadre is to be the context of an individual's rights is itself a function of the rights debate; so that the Inuit women comes by political choice to have rights as a Canadian citizen which deny the relationships of an aboriginal culture recognised but not entrenched by the Charter of Rights and Freedoms. Nor have I entered the debate about whether the right to shelter or to work can or should rank as a human right, for these are in my view questions to be answered by social consensus from time to time, not by definition *a priori* and certainly not by derivation from some higher law. Simply observe that the right not to suffer racial or sexual discrimination, which we now take as axiomatic, was entirely foreign—except perhaps as an aspiration—to the thinking of our grandparents' generation; that rights to education or to justice could only have been treated as self-evident in their time—which is our time—by societies that could afford to provide them; that the right to an unpolluted environment which the Indian High Court has in recent years extracted from the constitutional right to life depends less on what a society can afford than on what it cannot afford; and that it is not easy to see how in any humane society a right to shelter and food deserves any less regard than the right to life.

The path I hope we shall follow in this country is therefore not simply that of the European Convention with its inevitable historical limitations, but that of a juridical culture which does not imagine that the poorest citizen is made equal to the richest corporation simply by according both the same rights; which does not co-opt the powerless into the opposition of the powerful to the State; which perceives the role of power in determining who gets to drink first and longest at the well; and which understands above all that in every society fundamental human rights, to be real, have to steer towards outcomes which invert those inequalities of power that mock the principle of equality before the law.

SIXTEEN

Analytical Note

Virtually everything encompassed by the notion of 'human right' is the subject of controversy. The controversies of relevance here are not those associated with enforcing compliance to human right law, or with the execution of foreign policy options allegedly dedicated to the protection of human rights—these are important topics but they are not the concern of this chapter. Instead its theme emerges from the fact that the idea that individuals have, or should have, 'rights' is itself contentious, and the idea that rights could be attached to individuals by virtue solely of their common humanity is particularly subject to penetrating criticism. That such criticisms exist is commonplace, but what is less well established in the international relations discourse on human rights is the fact that virtually all the current arguments have a very long pedigree—indeed, are associated with positions that have been argued over for centuries within the canon of Western political theory. It is particularly important to stress that this is so, because so much of the current discourse on rights assumes that the conceptual problems thrown up by the notion are peculiarly the product of particular late twentieth century problems—the so-called problem of cultural relativism which, allegedly, has been generated by the globalisation of the international system.

This is a partial misapprehension, while it is indeed the case that the particular forms the contemporary dilemmas on human rights trade are in part shaped by the problem of 'difference' and modern contextualist notions of ethic, there is a deeper sense in which the key elements of these dilemmas have been present since the beginnings of the discourse. It is a mistake, and moreover a mistake with serious political implications in terms of intercultural on the present. Without a sense of the past of these dilemmas it would be easy to conclude, mistakenly, that the only serious difficulties associated with human rights thinking are generated by the unacceptable practices of alien others.

The concern to dispel this notion dictates the shape of this chapter, which falls into two main parts. In the first part, the conceptual difficulties with the discourse of human rights will be examined; the conclusion will be that rights only make sense in the context of a particular kind of society—an 'ethical community', to use the language of contemporary communitarian thought—and what this entails will be briefly elaborated. The second, shorter part traces the implications of this position for the international protection of human rights and the characteristic agenda of late twentieth century thinking on the subject.

Before moving to this agenda, there is one important preliminary that must be addressed. This chapter is subtitled "A Critique", and this is a polite, academic way of saying that in what follows the idea that there are universal human rights will be attacked, and attacked quite forcebly. Decent opinion—no irony intended—finds this distressing. Human rights activists are liable to respond in a pained way to this kind of discourse; they are in the firing line, sometimes literally, and, understandably enough, they resent carping from academics who write of these matters from the safety of their studies in Western universities. This is a serious criticism but one that misses the point, and, ultimately, can lead to a counter-productive refusal to acknowledge important difficulties faced by human rights activists. Along, probably, with the majority of readers, the present writer would be glad to live in a world in which liberal, Western freedoms and rights were enjoyed by everyone, but one of the obstacles to achievement of such a world is created by the unwillingness of some human rights activists to admit that the cause they espouse is liberal and Western. By adhering to the fiction of a universal grounding rights independent of the particular kind of societies are characteristically found, such advocates place themselves in a false position, and, perhaps paradoxically, weaken the credibility of their stand. In short, any violator of human dignity and decency who believes that this chapter provides a sanction for his or her activities is profoundly mistaken—and any rights activist who feels undermined had, equally, misunderstood the argument. These points will be readdressed in the conclusion to this chapter.

Liberal Position

Since the late eighteenth century it has become commonplace in liberal societies to assert that individuals possess rights to liberty, the secure possession of property, the exercise of freedom of speech, and so on. That these rights are inalienable and unconditional, and that the primary function of the government is to protect these rights—indeed that political obligation rests on the extent to which governments at least try to do this. This position is the burden of such seminal documents as the American Declaration of Independence of 1776 and the French Declaration of the Rights of Man and of the Citizen of 1789, and twentieth-century liberalism and progressivism. The language of rights has facilitated the establishment of some of the freest, safest and most civilised societies known to history. On the basis of this record, the liberal position, in the second half of the twentieth century, has been extracted from its original association with particular kinds of societies and turned into a template against which all regimes are to be judged. This universalism was, perhaps, always implicit; it is now explicit. The contemporary human rights regime is in general, and, for the most part, in detail, simply a contemporary, internationalised and universalised, version of the liberal position on rights.

The thesis argued here is that the liberal position on

rights is now and always has been incoherent and confused and that the undoubted success of 'liberal' societies over the last two hundred years is not, at root, traceable to their individualistic rights-oriented features. Before suggesting to what it is attributable, it is necessary to spend some time on the philosophical and conceptual problems surrounding the discourse of rights, because, as suggested above, these problems are particularly pertinent when it comes to the international dimension of rights, and it is important to stress that they are not generated by some new set of circumstances, such as the problem of other cultures.

The American legal philosopher Wesley Hofeld produced the standard classification of rights in a work of 1919 in which he distinguished among rights as claims, as liberties, as powers and as immunities (although in his view the only true rights were claim-rights, because only here were correlative duties clearly identifiable). The key point here is that each of these categories makes sense only in the context of some kind of legal system. Thus, a contract which establishes specific claim rights and duties presupposes a context in which it is agreed that contracts ought to be observed. Likewise, liberties, powers and immunities are ultimately notions, which make sense only against the background of a system of law. However, this tells us nothing about the kind of law that is involved, and, historically, two quite different kinds of law have been invoked in rights discourse.

Positive and Natural Laws

On one hand there is positive law—the kind of law enforced, we hope, by institutions such as the police and the judiciary. On this count I, as a citizen of a democratic country, can, in principle, enforce my claim-rights through the civil or, in some circumstances, the criminal courts; I am at liberty to dress as I please within the limits laid down by public order legislation; I am empowered to vote if over eighteen and not peer of the realm of insane; and I am immune to criminal prosecution if under the age often. I possess these rights because such is the law of the land, whether the statute law enacted by Parliament, or the common-law heritage of the freeborn English (and Welsh but not Scottish) man (or woman). The history of these rights can be traced back to the alleged customs of our (notional) Saxon forebears and a long list of statutory instruments that conventionally begins with the Magna Carta of 1215. Whether or not these rights are adequate or easy to enforce is, of course, debatable; the key point is that they are the rights of a specific group of people. There is no sense in which they are, or could be, universal or human rights.

To establish human rights, a different kind of law is necessary; some version of natural law. The most developed version of natural law was established in the Middle Ages by Catholic Schoolmen, philosophers and jurists. One of their most distinguished modern successors has described the idea of natural law as being based on the existence of: (i) A set of basic practical principles which indicate the basic forms of human flourishing as goods to be pursued and realised, and which are in one way or another used by everyone who considers what to do; (ii) a set of basic methodological requirements of practical reasonableness....which distinguish sound from unsound practical thinking, and which, when brought to bear provide the criteria [which enable us] to formulate; and (iii) a set of general moral standards.

Rights—whether claims, liberties, powers or immunities—are based on these general moral standards, as are the duties, which accompany these rights. Crucially, these standards are general, which is to say that they are not limited in application to the inhabitants of any particular jurisdiction or legal system or to any race, creed or civilisation. There may be additional rights and duties associated with Christian acceptance of Revelation but some general moral standards are common and binding on all people (and peoples).

The specific content of the natural law of the Schoolmen was challenged by social contract theorists such as Hobbies and Lock in the seventeenth century, and many later versions of the idea are further away from the substance of the original, as is the case, for example, with Alan Donagan's notion of common morality. Nonetheless, it seems that some idea of natural law must underlie all genuinely universal approaches to human rights. If human beings have rights by virtue of their common humanity it can only be because there are some 'general moral standards' that are universal in application; these standards must, in principle, be discernible by everyone, and, therefore, less obviously but still necessarily, refer back to some kind of common notion of human flourishing. These are the characteristics of natural law thinking and thus natural law is the basic foundation for rights discourse other than positive law.

Natural law and positive law each have advantage and disadvantages as foundations for rights. Rights associated with positive law are associated with particular jurisdictions and thus are not, as such, human rights—but on the other hand ontological status is secure. If I am asked why I consider myself to have particular rights as a citizen of the United Kingdom. I can, most of the time, point to specific pieces of legislation or to common-law judgements to support my case. A citizen of the United States can—probably with a greater chance of success—point to the Bill of Rights and Supreme Court decisions, Germans to the Grundgesetz of the Federal Republic, and so on. The problem here, of course, is that the 'and so on' stands for a relatively short list of countries where the rule of law applies and thus where the rights to be found in constitutional documents have actual forces. Those who live in countries where this is not the case can find little solace in a view of rights which makes them the product of positive law, and this is particularly unfortunate since it is clearly the case that it is in precisely those countries where the rule of law is absent that individuals are most likely to suffer the sort of oppressions that rights are designed to rectify.

The great merit of naturalist approaches is that they

provide a basis for a claim to possess rights which is not so unhelpfully restrictive. If one has rights solely by virtue of one's humanity, the fact that one happens to be the citizen of a tyrannical regime, while still deeply regrettable, no longer leaves one without intellectual resources, because the heart of a natural law perspective is precisely the assertion of universal right against local custom. Potentially, natural law provides the basis for a powerful critique of existing social institutions in a way that positive law does not and cannot. Rights established by positive law may be critical in the sense that they may allow one to argue that a particular social institution is not working in the way that it ought to, but they are less useful when, as is too often the case, a social institution is working exactly as intended, but the intention is itself oppressive. Positive legal rights provide no basis for an argument that the whole way of life of the society in which they exist may be oppressive, because, by definition, they are based on the way of life. To exercise a critique at this level it is necessary to bring to bear the natural law position that general moral standards exist independently of the particular law of any particular society.

But what are these 'general moral standards'? What is their ontological status? There are, broadly, two possibilities here, each of which is unsatisfactory. On the one hand, these standards might be derived from actual practice, on the argument that all functioning societies need to have some kinds of rules which, for example, define property rights, or regulate sexual conduct, and that from these some kind of lowest common denominator can be discerned. There are two problems with this position. First, such a lowest common denominator is likely to be vacuous because customs vary considerably and any formula designed to cover all the possibilities is likely to end up devoid of real content. Secondly, and more importantly, if general moral standards are defined in this way they lose their critical cutting edge—it ceases to be possible to use such standards to criticise existing practices if the former are defined in terms of the latter. The whole point of the exercise is to produce an account of rights which is discriminatory in a way that this kind of minimalist code cannot be at best, the occasional, obviously deviant regime—Hitler's Germany, Pol Pot's Cambodia, Amin's Uganda—might be 'caught' by these criteria but, almost by definition, no longstanding system of injustice could be recognised as such by an argument that takes longevity as a sign of virtue. A common morality which is actually common to all societies is an uncritical notion.

The alternative is that general standards might be derived without reference to any particular societies by the use of 'practical reason'—reasoning from the basic forms of human flourishing by applying the critical edge to the notion because there is no definitional reason why actual practices will always correspond to the demands of practical reason. But then a new problem emerges, namely, that of explaining why local practices do vary, that is why practical reason seems to produce different results in different places and at different times. To take an example much in the thoughts of contemporary Catholics who argue in this way, if practical reason tells us that abortion is contrary to natural law, why is it that so many societies now and in the past have sanctioned the practice? Finnis and his colleagues would clearly refuse to accept that contemporary American legal reasoning—and the widespread popular support for the product of this reasoning—meets the standards of practical reasonableness, but it is difficult to see why this denial should be convincing. Natural law theorists claim only to privilege the products of practical reason devoted to human flourishing but the claim that the operation of such reason leads always and everywhere to the same result seems to be contradicted by the fact to value-pluralism.

The argument that 'we' (or at least those of us who are Catholic natural lawyers) are more intelligent or more moral than those who reach a different conclusion are, clearly will not do. The most plausible way out of this difficulty is not to suggest such a personal validation of the product of one's own thought, but to argue that practical reason is defective and likely to produce the wrong result unless situated within an authoritative tradition. In this way individuals are no longer reliant on their own resources; they can bring to bear the practical reasonableness of generations of thinkers as though it were their own. However, this clearly changes the nature of the argument and weakens the claim that general moral standards can be generated in this way. If it is the tradition itself that is the justification for a particular practice, the potential for universalism claims goes by the board, or at least, is severely damaged.

Thus far, this discussion has centred on the universalistic and particularistic dimensions of rights discourse, but there is a further feature of this discourse that deserves, rather briefer attention, namely, the potential absolutism of the notion of right. In Dworkin's famous formulation, rights are often seen as 'trumps'—cards which automatically win tricks—that is, as considerations overriding all other considerations. It is easy to see how, on this account, rights could exist in opposition to the common good—indeed, the very point of having a right is precisely to be protected from someone else's notion of the common good. Rights absolutists may further reject the notion that there could be a 'common good' in the first place. This position is the origin of the insult and necessary rivalry between utilitarian and rights theorists, a rivalry that dates back to Jeremy Bentham's fulminations against the idea that there are natural rights. It has become common in modern debate to suggest that the problem with utilitarianism is that it does not take seriously the fact that individuals are distinct from one another and have their own projects. Conversely, one might argue that the orients take this distinction too seriously. This is the position of a diverse range of modern thinkers from Brian Barry and Robert Good on the one hand, to Amitai Etzioni and Jean Bethke Elshtain on the other. The absolutism of rights claims can be a menace to civilised society, as the inability of the American public authorities to control the ownership of firearms in the United States illustrates quite vividly. Even in a less extreme case, it is not clear that the free-speech absolutists who defend all forms of expression in First Amendment terms are not acting against the public interest.

What is interesting about this critique is that it is particularly relevant to positive law accounts of rights. One of the important features of natural law thinking is that it relates rights to other features of the human condition, the requirements of human flourishing, and therefore it is hospitable to a distinction between those rights which are absolute and those which may be overridden in the public interest or common good. Positive law approaches find it difficult to make such a distinction. Each item in the American Bill of Rights has the same legal status, whether pointing to case where an absolute claim perhaps ought be made, for example, barring cruel or unusual punishment, or where policy considerations might in some circumstances legitimate a restriction, perhaps regarding free speech, or where, as it happens, the right in question is positively harmful to common good, most obviously the right to bear arms. It is not a necessary feature of positive law that it has to have this absolute quality—for example, the Canadian equivalent of the Bill of Rights has an override clause—but many supporters of rights would argue that absolutism is a desirable feature, and criticise Canada's law on exactly this point.

Again, there is a genuine dilemma here. If rights are thought of as trumps, as absolutes to be defended in all circumstances, then it is very likely that some of these circumstances will involve the violation of an obvious public interest. However, if rights are thought of as.less than absolute, as simply one set of considerations to take into account when deciding on the tightness or otherwise of action, then the protective power of rights simply withers away, the debates over 'hate speech' in the United States revolve exactly around this dilemma. On the face of it, defending speech that offends public standards of good behaviour and incites anti-social attitudes would seem perverse, and yet if free speech is a meaningful notion it must apply to 'offensive' speech, since no one tries to ban any other kind.

Position Re-examined

To summarise the story so far, 'rights' are trick, slippery things, and rights discourse is a minefield, where each conceptual step risks a detonation and self-destruction; moreover, this is so even without introducing complications allegedly generated by cultural relativism. And yet, very little of all this comes through in the liberal position on rights outlined at the start of this chapter. There is a clear disassociation between, on the one hand, the conceptual failings and, on the other, the rhetorical appeal of rights discourse. If it is indeed the case that societies built upon the liberal position on rights have been successful in providing a context within which people can live civilised lives, ought we to be concerned with the philosophical niceties?

It is now, perhaps belatedly, that the thesis of this chapter can be stated more fully. It is that liberal societies of the last 150-200 years have indeed been the freest and most generally congenial societies known to history, but not because they have been constructed on the basis of rights; their success has been based on features within them that pointed towards a different, less individualist, context for political action. It was because of the existence of this context, because these societies were, in certain respects, ethical communities, that rights were widely honoured and respected; a successful rights-based politics is parasitic on features of the polity that have nothing to do with rights—indeed, which may even be inimical to rights thinking. For this reason, the philosophical niceties referred to above are important; it is implausible to think that rights can be extracted from liberal polities, decontextualised and applied as a package world-wide. This is not simply because internationals value pluralism; it is decontextualisation that is critical, whether international or domestic. However, the international dimension of rights will be the subject of the second section of this chapter, and the final part of this section is devoted to an elaboration of the meaning of an ethical community.

Ethical Community

The term 'ethical community' rightly had strong Hegelian overtones and the position in general is indeed characterised by a kind of coarse, demythologised Hegelianism – coarse and demythologised because it is usually presented without the reliance on Geist that Hegel himself would have regarded as crucial. If we read the philosophy of Rights as a free-standing text rather than as a work which is embedded in Hegel's system, it is not too difficult to extract the elements of a model of an ethical community, elements which have been employed explicitly or implicitly by later communitarians. This community has three institutional elements, or moments – the family, civil society and the State – the role of these institutions being to 'constitute' individuality, that is, to construct the kind of individual that liberal rights-based thought takes as given. Briefly, the role of the ethical family is to provide an environment within which the individual can develop a sense of self-esteem, where regard is unconditional, based on love rather than achievement. Civil society provides a contest where the individual differentiates him or herself from other individuals, making his or her way in the world, rubbing along with other people and acting in a context where law and government are seen as external forces; here we have the kind of atomised, self-interested individuals who are usually held to need rights to protect them from over-mighty rulers. Finally, we have the State, the location where these individuals come to see their competitors as fellow citizens, and to realise that the laws that bind them are self-made. Here the 'rule of law' ceases to be an external phenomenon but comes to be seen as the product of one's will.

This conception of a political community does provide a context within which rights.can operate, but it is not a context which is always compatible with the liberal position on rights. The rights of the individual are of great significance in 'civil society'; it is in this realm that the power of the State appears to the individual as an externalised force from the operation of which they require the protection of rights. The State itself cannot be limited by rights in this way; the substantial unity represented by the State 'possesses' the highest right in relation to individuals, whose highest duty is to be members of the State. Rights may exist but 'rights absolutism' cannot be a problem here. The idea that the rights of the individual are subject to the will of the collective is precisely what the liberal position is designed to avoid, but the reason that this need not be seen as a serious problem is that the communitarian position is not designed to work with any individual under all circumstances—on the contrary, what is being presented here is a package in which the kind of individuals who make up the community are not a more or less random collection of people who happen to inhabit a particular territory at a particular time, but rather a group of people who are simultaneously the creators of community and created by it. The 'rights' that they assign each other are not the manifestation of a general moral code or the product of universal practical reason— nor are they simply the product of a political bargain; rather, they are more like reminders that the community gives itself as to what it takes to be proper conduct. They are enforceable against the administration government—the police and the corporation as Hegel would put it—but not against the State as such, that is the State in its role as the expression of a higher unity.

Only a strictly limited sense of universal or human rights can be drawn out of this. The approach is universalistic in the sense that it is Hostile to any kind of racial discrimination—'A human being counts as such because he [sic] is a human being—but it is only particular kinds of community that are ethical, and it is only within such communities that rights are or can be situated. Cross-communal or intertemporal judgements on ethics miss the point. To criticise, say Athenian slavery because it does not correspond to our understanding of the nature of human equality makes no sense because this understanding was not available to Athenians. Slavery is incompatible with the modern, rational, ethical State but it was not incompatible with the Athenianpolis. Any particular practice has to be contextualised. However, this does not mean that all contexts are morally equal. There is a role for moral absolutes in this schema, but the role is in terms of historical development—the unfolding of Greekpolis. The modern State represents a higher morality than the Greek polis—and, of course, than contemporary regimes that are not rational or ethical. But, notwithstanding this point, Sitten (ethics) are more important than Moralitat (morality) in the actual life of the community.

Has all this any real purchase? That is to say, is an 'ethical community' simply an intellectual construct or has it any real-world reference point? It is very clear that there are not now, nor have there ever been, ethical communities in any full sense of the term. Indeed, it seems to me equally clear that for Hegel and many (most?) of his successors the model was intended to be critical. His account of what an ethical, rational community would look like can be seen as providing an ideal against which existing societies can be measured, and found wanting. But there is also a teleological element here— the thrust of the argument is that the modern world, modernity if you like, has within it tendencies that make this kind of society desirable and, perhaps, approachable. The rational, ethical community is the answer to the question: 'How can we live rational, ethical lives in societies characterised by mass membership, an extended and complex and responsible government? This is as important a question today as it has ever been, and the answer Hegel gave to it remains highly relevant.

What is more, it is arguable that insofar as liberal societies have been successful over the last two centuries, it has been because they have been constructed as approximations to the communitarian model rather than because of their dependence on rights-based individualism. This is the thesis of the communitarian movement in contemporary politics. The United States functioned as a community when it had a strong family structure and an active civil society to go with its constitutional arrangements; in recent years, however, the former institutions have gone into decline and, as a partial response, the constitutional framework has grown in significance. Americans have more and more rights, but less and less of a society within which to exercise them. In the past, American individualism was embedded in a non-individualist structure; this is now fading, rights stand alone, and American society is in deep trouble. Similar sorts of stories could be told elsewhere. In Britain, for example, a deferential and traditional notion of community gave real meaning to the idea of rights, even though the rights themselves were poorly articulate within the legal system. As the old order fades away, attempts are made to situate rights within a new, more formal, context; unless the structures that might support such rights are rebuilt—on different foundation—this strategy is unlikely to succeed. Similarly, contemporary Russians and East-central Europeans are learning that snippily importing systems of rights without the institutions of civil society to support them is no recipe for a good polity.

Obviously there is much more that should be said about all this, but for the purpose of this chapter enough has been said to clarify the basic thesis. The next step is to relate these ideas to the international context, or, rather, to show that this step has already been taken, because all the resources that are needed to examine the international dimension are already present in the analysis.

International Regime

International human rights legislation can be traced back to the nineteenth century but the modern regime really begins in the aftermath of the second World War. The Universal

Declaration of Human Rights, adopted by the UN General Assembly in 1948, was a direct response to the atrocities of the war; it set an important precedent as the first attempt by the international community to set out what were, if taken seriously, quite strict limits on the range of variation of internal regimes that was to be tolerated. It has been followed by a raft of legislation, regional and global, such that now it is no exaggeration to suffuse that virtually all areas of the domestic structure of states are covered by some kind of international standard setting. For the most part the standards in question are those of the liberal position set out at the state of the first section of this chapter. Although the Universal Declaration specifically recognised that the individual was entailed to 'the economic, social and cultural rights indispensable for his [sic] dignity and the free development of his personality' and this approach has become extended in later statements of so-called second-generation (economic and social) and third-generation (rights of peoples) etc., it remains the case that the first-generation (political, liberty) rights of the individual remain at the heart of the Declaration.

It is clear that although the human rights regime is never elaborate in the demands it makes upon States, it influences the conduct of States in their treatment of their own nationals. It may be that the international protection of human rights has become a 'settled norm' of international society in the sense that States virtually never acknowledge they are deliberately breaking internationally established standards, but tribute that vice pays to virtue can be little comfort to those who would prefer actual compliance to verbal assent. It is not too difficult to identify reasons for the failure of the regime, nor to see how these reasons relate to the difficulties with the nation.

There are obviously problems connected to compliance and enforcement of international human rights, which are related to the legal system within which these rights are embedded. International human rights legislation purports to create positive law in the same way that, say, the US Bill of

Rights creates positive law, but it is clear that in practice this is not the case. With the exception of the 1950 European Convention for the Protection of Human Rights and Fundamental Freedoms, international human fights legislation has not involved the creation of effective enforcement machinery, for the obvious reason that not enough of the States involved wished to see human rights law enforced; indeed, even some States with a record of general respect for human rights have been unwilling to accept international supervision and have hedged around their ratifications of international agreements with extensive formal reservations – true of, for example, the United States and the United Kingdom.

The result of these factors has been that enforcement of human rights by the international community is determined, in practice, by the foreign-policy imperatives of the major powers, on the whole, these imperatives give a relatively low priority to issues of human rights. During the Cold War, violations of human rights by the army went unpunished because of its power, while violations by friends were excused or justified on essentially strategic-diplomatic grounds. Even now that the Cold War is over, commercial and financial considerations frequently get in the way of a high-priority, even-handed policy on human rights. That this is so may be deplorable, but it ought not to be surprising; the international legal system remains premised on the idea of sovereignty, international obligation remains dependent on particular sovereign wills, and within such a system it is implausible that States will actually allow their external policy to be guided consistently by an impartial concern for human rights – which is not to say that policy will always be determined by power and interest, rather that a systematic commitment to higher goals is always liable to be 'tainted with contingency'.

One response to this might be to try to transcend these limits by moving beyond the 'anarchical society', beyond, that is, a legal system based on sovereignty. Apart from the obvious practical difficulties here (all it requires is 'the consent of

Europe, and a few similar trifles' as Frederick the Great put it in another, not-dissimilar context) this project runs up against the difficulties with 'universalist' accounts of rights outlined in the first section of this chapter. The present sovereignty-based international order allows for different and potentially competing accounts of the Good; this contradicts the idea of universal human rights which, in the full package as developed since 1945, is based on one particular conception of the Good. If this contradiction is to be removed by the elimination of difference, then there had better be good reasons why rights-based individualism should be privileged in this way—and the burden of the first section of this chapter was that there is no such good reason, at least none that it would be unreasonable for those committed to another account of the Good to reject. It was argued there that the universal claims of natural law cannot be sustained, and that the argument from the consequences of rights individualism, namely, that societies where rights are established are more successful than those are where they are not, misunderstands the nature of the success of 'liberal' societies.

It is important that the relationship between this chain of reasoning and the issue of international 'multiculturalism', relativism and contextualism be clearly understood. It clearly is the case that in the post-colonial late-twentieth-century world; different countries have different notions of what are the appropriate rights— if any—for their inhabitants. In parts of East Asia authoritarian regimes justify restrictions on individual liberty in the interests of economic development and, on their account, in accordance with local custom. Islamic regimes do not recognise certain rights regarded as crucial in Western liberal societies—the right to change one's religion being an obvious case in point. It is difficult to see how notions of human equality could be consistent with a caste system, or with social arrangements that privilege the family rather than the individual. In many respects these differences are greater than those to be found within Western societies over the last two centuries; but the diversity that does exist within the West is such as to undermine naturalist accounts of what it is to be human without adding in these extra difficulties. Moreover, on many issues, the relevant divide in the modern world is not between the West and the Rest; Catholic natural lawyers may well find they have more in common with their Islamic counterparts on many social (and especially sexual) issues than they have with secularists, Western or Eastern, while an issue such as the corporal punishment handed out to minor offenders in Singapore reveals a solid wedge of support in some Western quarters – for the authoritarian capitalist mores of East Asia. The absence of consensus in the modern world is not simply the product of differences between the major world cultures – the fault lines run within as well as between cultures.

Contextualism and Judgement

Does all this mean that we are committed to a relativist, contextualist approach which refuses to make judgements, which is obliged to accept that whatever practices exist and are long-standing are immune to criticism? Not necessarily; as is demonstrated by the presence of deep splits and arguments within our own culture(s), it is possible to criticise existing practices without reference to universal norms. What is important from this perspective is that social criticism should rest on conceptions of the good which relate to the contexts in which life is lived rather than that they should rest on 'general moral standards' applicable to all humanity. As Michael Walzer has demonstrated so capably, this kind of criticism is not a hypothetical possibility but an actuality, his 'company of critics' have engaged in critical interpretations of the shared moral understandings of their own societies without reference to transcendent norms or universal standards. The key issue is whether this kind of social criticism can also be exercised beyond the community, in realms where, apparently, moral understandings are not shared.

Walzer's own account of this problem is attractive, but

not, in the end, satisfactory. He argues for the notion that some kind of 'thin' moral code can be identified, which is not in itself sufficiently rich to live by, but which has sufficient purchase to allow us to make some kinds of judgements. Thus, when the citizens of Prague take to the streets waving placards with 'Truth' and 'Justice' written on them, we may not know exactly what they mean by these terms but we are still capable of catching their drift. This seems to be right, but, as suggested above when examining lowest-common-denominator accounts of natural law, it is often the case that the devil is in the detail and broad-based categories may not get us very far. A thin moral code may enable us to identify a number of obvious evils, human wrongs on a large scale, but this is not necessarily where the most important debates are focused. Establishing that, say, genocide is to be condemned is highly desirable, but most international human rights issues involve rather less clear-cut cases.

Perhaps a better way into this issue could be found through the example of Athenian slavery alluded to above. The point made there was that it was not possible to criticise the Athenians for the practice of slavery because their form of life did not include the sort of concepts that would make sense of this criticism; social criticism must employ the material to hand, and the ideas of individual worth, autonomy and personhood that make slavery intolerable today were not part of the moral vocabulary—whether thick or thin—of classical Greece. So far the argument is potentially relativist, but where the Hegelian position moves beyond relativism is in its willingness to say that the mores of Athenian society have been superseded by the movement of Geist. Our moral vocabulary has become enlarged—we do have the means at hand to realise that slavery is wrong and it would be culpable of us not to act upon this. It becomes possible for us to assert with confidence both that the Athenians were not necessarily wrong in condoning slavery, and that our ways in this matter are better than theirs—history has moved on and moral development has taken place. Although values cannot be judged out of context, contexts themselves can be judged: contrary to Wittgenstein, forms of life do not have to be accepted.

The Athenian example is intertemporal; Athens is separated from us by over two millennia. However, in Hegelian—and, perhaps, commonsense—terms it can be asserted that we are linked to classical Athens; it is part of our Western past. A key question is, how do these arguments play when what is at issue are cross-national, cross-cultural contexts where no such relationship is plausible? Put differently, can we find a way of recasting the discussion which does not rely on the Hegelian notion of absolute morality, of the movement of Geist? This is necessary because if Geist is taken as fact rather than as metaphor, cross-cultural judgements are as easy to make as intertemporal ones; the judgement that some cultures/societies are 'history-less', outside the scope of moral developmental schemes, and have nothing to offer the world except examples of prejudice and superstition, becomes a matter of fact rather than a judgement of value. Perhaps fortunately, albeit inconveniently, this kind of certainty is no longer available to our modern consciousness—it is not necessary to be post-modern to be sceptical about the force of this particular metanarrative. Instead, if we want to use neo-Hegelian notions in the way that they are used in this chapter we are obliged to find a language that works without the reassurance that underpinned Hegel's own work. Is such a language available?

Quite possibly not, but the writer who comes closest to providing such a moral language is Richard Rorty, a 'post-modern' who explicitly links his ideas to a demythologised Hegelianism. Predictably, he is opposed to any foundationalist accounts of rights. Rights act to 'summarise our culturally influenced intuitions about the right thing to do in various situations'; such summarising generalisations increase 'the predictability, and thus the power and efficiency, of our institutions, thereby heightening the sense of shared moral identity which brings us together in a moral community'. Since the Enlightenment, Americans and Europeans have created a 'human rights culture' in opposition to prejudices of one kind or another—racial, religious, and, more recently, misogynist and homophobic—and thereby extended the scope of this shared moral identity. This is an achievement which is both based on and reinforced by 'security'— 'conditions of life sufficiently risk-free as to make one's difference from others inessential to one's self respect, one's sense of worth'— and sympathy, the ability to put one's self in another's shoes, to perceive the other as a fellow human-being. And, it is worth stressing, it is also an achievement which is continually open to question; our sense about 'the right thing to do in various situations' is always corrigible; prejudice is never conquered once and for all, and what counts as prejudice is never a closed issue. Nonetheless, Rorty's suggestion that in the West the scope of shared moral identity has expanded in this way seems to me to be broadly accurate, and a pretty good way of putting what Hegel would have called the movement of Geist into non-foundationalist, demythologised terms.

What does this tell us about societies where these extensions of shared moral identity seem not to have taken place? What do we do, or could we do, about, for example, Bosnian Serbs who kill Bosnian Muslims because they cannot see them as fellow human beings, or, conversely, Muslim extremists who think that the death penalty is an appropriate response to apostasy (or writing a book that, allegedly, defames the Prophet)? Rorty's point is that it is futile to suggest that these people are wrong or irrational, that they have not understood that the nature of human beings is such that these are not appropriate responses. There is no such nature; there are no general moral standards that apply here. UN Declarations, Covenants and the like cut no ice, because human beings create themselves and if they have not created themselves in ways that are amenable to a human rights perspective nothing can get through to them. This does not mean we are unable to judge their conduct, but Rorty suggests that the best way to see such people is not as 'wrong' or 'irrational' but as 'deprived', deprived of the security and sympathy that has allowed us to create a culture in which rights make sense. They are in need of an environment in which they can reflect on these matters in relative safety; they are in need of a sentimental education—more accurately, it is quite likely too late to soften 'the self-satisfied hearts' of the killers and fanatics themselves; it is the next generation that is crucial to the 'progress of sentiments'. In any event, he suggests, we need to argue for and promote the extension of the human rights culture as a culture, and not as a movement that could be grounded by some form of knockdown moral reasoning.

This perspective does not solve all the problems of relativism; indeed, critics will say that Rorty's redescriptions of our moral life simply conjure away all the important issues. What it does highlight, however, is a point made at length above, namely, that rights are best seen as a by-product of a functioning ethical community and not as a phenomenon that can be taken out of this context and promoted as a universal solution to the political ills of an oppressive world. It may be that talk of a 'sentimental education' seems a woefully inadequate response to these human wrongs but it is difficult to see what other moral vocabulary is available to us once we reach the limits of an ethical community.

The argument of the first section of this concluding chapter was that the standard liberal approach to universal human rights is based on a misunderstanding. Rights have no separate ontological status; they are a byproduct of a particular kind of society, one in which the 'State' operates constitutionally under the rule of law, is separated from 'civil society' and the 'family', and in which private and public realms are, in principle, clearly demarcated. Societies in which human rights are respected are more civilised and secure than those in which they are not. Our rights are a symptom of this civilisation and security, not a cause. To overemphasise rights in isolation from their social context is counter-productive, potentially undermining the very factors, which create the context in which rights are respected. It follows from this analysis, as the second section of the chapter demonstrated, that the international regime, which attempts on a global scale to promote decontextualised human rights, is engaging in a near-impossible task. From the liberal perspective human rights are universals; from the perspective outlined above, they are associated with a particular kind of society, and to promote these rights is to promote this kind of society. Proponents of universal human rights are, in effect, proposing the delegitimation of all kinds of political regimes except those that fall within the broad category of 'liberal democracy'. Although such a delegitimation might be regarded as desirable, it is by no means clear that majority of societies world-wide are actually capable of becoming liberal societies, at least in the medium run, and it is equally unclear on what moral authority those who require them to take this step can rely. Those who take these objections to Universal human rights seriously either look to the promotion of a minimal, 'thin', moral code (Michael Walzer) or to the, admittedly nebulous, benefits of a sentimental education (Richard Rorty).

Many advocates of universal human rights will be untroubled by the critique made in this chapter. Insofar as this is because they regard the ontological grounding of rights as an ivory tower issue of no relevance to real world problems—or, at worst, relevant only in that to raise such issues is to give aid and comfort to the enemies of human dignity—they are seriously mistaken. Even judged in its own terms, the international human rights regime has not been very effective, and this is at least partly because of the blithe unwillingness of some activists to recognise that there are philosophical and cultural problems associated with their position. There are, however, more serious and thoughtful critiques of the position outlined in the bulk of this chapter, critiques that will be addressed in this concluding section.

The basic argument of these critics can be presented in a composite form as follows:

Of course, human rights are in some sense fictional, but they are valuable fictions; of course, in fact, human rights are associated with a particular way of life and cannot be taken in isolation, but this way of life is actually the way of life that most people would like to follow. The sort of objections you raise are those characteristically employed by power-holders who try to justify their privileges and bad behaviour in the name of culture and tradition. Ordinary people will have nothing to do with such arguments, the falsity of which activists in Indonesia and China, Saudi Arabia and Iran have exposed by putting their lives on the line. The international human rights regime may not be very effective but at least it gives those who would oppose tyranny some moral support and a standard to which they can appeal. We should be very careful about employing arguments, which undermine this valuable work.

This is not a position to be dismissed lightly; one element can be accepted with no difficulty, but a second is quite crucial and gets to the heart of the matter. First, it can readily be accepted that not all of those national leaders who resist the demands of the international human rights regime do so from a genuine desire to protect 'difference' and a way of life; many, perhaps most, are simply concerned to protect their own position. There is a wider problem here. Normative work in international relations needs to be able to distinguish between those non-liberal regimes which are simply criminal conspiracies and those which genuinely incorporate what Walzer would call the 'shared understandings' of a society. John Rawls attempts this task in his recent essay on 'The Law of Peoples' in which he introduces the category of a 'well-ordered' but non-liberal society; unfortunately the example he gives of a well-ordered hierarchical society is designed on such peculiar lines that it is not much use in this context. However, there is clearly an issue here, and future work on this topic is called for.

The more important point concerns the popular standing of the liberal position on universal human rights. One of the firmest of liberal beliefs is that liberal values are indeed universal, that we would all be liberals were it not for the distorting effects of ignorance on the one hand and privilege on the other. Deep-down, in our heart of hearts, we believe ourselves to be the autonomous individuals liberalism takes us to be, and thus the real wishes of the peoples of Indonesia or China, Saudi Arabia or Iran are represented by those relatively few free spirits who are active in the cause of freedom. Such is the liberal belief and the self-confident strength of this belief is one of liberalism's greatest political assets. However, in his last book, *Conditions of Liberty*, the great (liberal) scholar Ernest Gellner provides a sobering commentary on liberalism's self-confidence. Without weakening his own commitment to liberty and civil society, he acknowledges its historicist foundation. Civil society is a profoundly unusual social formation in which political, coercive power is concentrated but balanced by a separate set of independent institutions focused on the economy. This kind of society is associated with economic growth and scientific-industrial society generally, but in the late twentieth century limits to growth are emerging, and, in any event, industrial success is being experienced by societies which do not value an independent civil society. Most societies have valued order above either economic growth or political liberty and so have most people—civil societies are rare entities which will do well to preserve themselves from their internal and external enemies. It is an illusion to think that the truth that Gellner finds in liberal thought has, he argues, in itself any power, and the Enlightenment belief that a social order without coercion and falsehood is possible is equally illusory. As he puts it, any culture is a systematic prejudgement; the miracle of civil society is that, for once, and in exceptional circumstances, the prejudgement was made milder and flexible, and yet order was maintained. Repeating this miracle is always going to be difficult.

Gellner presents from within a liberal perspective an account of the achievement of civil society, and thus of individual human rights, that is in some ways rather more pessimistic about the possibility for generalising the model than the neo-Hegelian account presented above. And so he is cited here not in support of the thesis argued in the bulk of the chapter, but as an antidote to the sometimes facile optimism of liberals less well versed than him in the history of human societies—and that means virtually all other liberals. Let his be the final words:

> But what point is there in vaunting our values, and condemning the commitment of others to absolutist transcendentalism or demanding communlism? They are what they are, and we are what we are: if we were them we would have their values, and if they were us, they would have ours. I am not a relativist— the existence of a culture-transcending truth seems to me the most important single fact about the human condition, and indeed one of.the bases of Civil Society, for it made possible that cognitive growth and the denial of absolutism on which it is based. But all the same, preaching across cultural boundaries seems to me in most circumstances a fairly pointless exercise.

Bibliography

Books and Journals

Aiyer, Sir Sivaswamy, *Evolution of Hindu Moral Ideals*, (Calcutta University Press, 1935).

Alston, *'Human Rights and Basic Needs'*.

Antonio Cassese, *'The Self-Deterrnrrrntiorr of 1'eoplrs', in Louis Henkin led.)*, The International Bill of Rights (New York, Columbia University Press, 1981).

Antony G.N. Flew, *'Wants or Needs; Choices or C mmands', in Fitzgerald, Human Needs and Politics.*

Asborn Eide, *"Hrrnram Riohts in World Society"*, Oslo. 1977.

Basu, M. *Introdttction to the Indian Constihrtiott*, Rejhi Publishing House, New Delhi, 1960.

Bell Whitaker, *The Biharis in Bangladesh* (London: Minority Rights Group, 1982).

Bhagwati, P.N. *Human Rights in the Criminal Justice System*, Indian Bar Review, 1985.

Caur K.D, *"Poor Victims of Uses and Abuses of Criminal Law and Process in India"*, Journal of the Indian Law Institute, (New Delhi), vol. 35.

Carter, J. L. Inaugural Address, 1977, quoted in, David P. Forsythe, *"Human Rights and World Politics"*. University of Nebraska Press, 1983.

Chimni B.S. *"The Legal Conditions of Refugees in India"* journal of Refugee Studies, Vol. 7.

Durga Das Basu, *Human Rights in Constitution*, L.azu Practice Hall of India, Private Ltd. New Delhi, 1994.

Found Ajami, *'Human Rights and World Order Politics'*, Alternatives, (1978).

Frank E. Krenz, "*The Refugee as a Subject of International Law*", International and Comp. Law Quarterly, 1966.

Habermas, J. "*What is Llnizcersal Pragmatics?,*" in Communication and the Evolution of Society, (traps. T. McCarthy, 1979).

Henkin, "*Human Rights and 'Domestic Jurisdiction,"'* in Buergenthal, ed., Human Rights, International Law, and the Helsinki Accord 21, (1977).

Jois, M.R., *Human Rights and Indian Value* (National Council of Teacher Education), Revised Edition, New Delhi, 1998.

Kalim Bahadur (eds.) *Domestic Conflicts in South Asia* (South Asia Publishers, New Delhi, 1986).

Kanan Gahrana, "*Human Rights: A Conceptual Perspective*", Indian Journal of International Law, Vol. 29, Nos. 3 and 4, July-Dec. 1989.

Kemp, R. "*Planning, Public Hearings, the Politics of Discourse,*" in J. Forester, Critical Theory and Public Life (1985).

Kenneth E. Boulding, '*The Shadow of the Stationary State*', Daedalus, (1974).

Manfred Woelilcke, "*Environmental Refugees*", (Economic and Political Weekly).

Muklierji, Partha Nath, "*The Great Migration of 1971*".

Murthy, T.S., *Assam: The Difficult Years,* Himalayan Books, New Delhi, 1983).

Myres S. Mc. Dongal, Harold D. Lasswell and Lung-Chu Cheri, *Human Rights and World Public Order,* 1986.

Myron Weiner, *Sons of the Soil: Migration and Ethnic Conflict in India,* (Prineton, New Jersy: Princeton University Press, 1978).

Myron Weiner, *Rejected Peoples and Unwanted MigrantsThe Impact of Migration of the Politics and Security of South Asia* (1991).

Nagendra Singh, *India and International Law,* (1969).

Nagendar Singh, *Human Rights and International Community* S. Chand & Co., New Delhi, 1969.

Narayanswamy M. R., *Tigers of Lanka: Front Boys to Guerrillas* (Konark Publishers, New Delhi, 1995).

Richard Falk, *'Comparative Protection of Human Rights in Capitalist and Socialist Third World Countries'*, Universal Human Rights, (1979).

Roberta Cohen, *"Human Rights Diplomacy: The Carter Administration and the Southern Cone,"* Human Rights Quarterly (May 1982).

Rose, *War and Secession: Pakistan, India and the Creation of Bangladesh* (Berkeley University of California Press, 1990).

Sadruddin Aga Khan, *"Legal Problems Relating to Refugees and Displaced Persons"*, Recueil Des Courts, Collected Courses of the Hague Academy of International Law, 1976.

Saxena, J.N. *"Problems of Refugees in the Developing Countries and the Need for International Burden Sharing"*, International Law in Transition, Essays in Memory of Judge Nageendra Singh, Lancers, New Delhi, 1992.

Saxena J.N., *"Legal Status of Refugees: Indian Position"*, Indian Journal of Int. Law, Vol. 26, No. 3 & 4, 1986.

Seervai H., *Constitutional Law of India* (N.M. Tnpathi & Co., Bombay, 1967).

Shama Sastri R., *Kautilya's Arthasastra* (Mysore: Raghuveer Press, 1951).

Singh, Amrik, *"Human Rights and the Rule of Law"*, Mainstream, Vol. XXXIII No. 22.

Singh M.P., *"Position of Aliems in Indian Law"* Heidelberg Colloquim, September 1985.

Sri Aurobindo, The Foundations of Indian Culture, (New York: Sri Aurobindo Library, 1953).

Thomas Buergenthal, *International Human Rights in a Nutshell* (Minnesota: West Publ. Co., 1988).

Tom J. Farer (ed.), *Towards a Humanitarian Diplomacy: A Primer for Policy* (New York, New York University Press, 1980).

Trikamial R. Desai, *The Indian Easements Act*, IIth ed. (C. C. Vora, Ahmedabad, 1956).

Urmila Phadmis, *Ethnicity and Nation-Building in South Asia* (Sage, New Delhi, 1990).

Weis, P., *'The International Status of Refugees and Stateless Persons,'* Journal du droit international, (1956).

Treaties

1919 Covenant of the League of Nations.

1919 Treaty of Versailles.

1926 Convention to Suppress the Slave Trade and Slavery.

1945 Charter of the International Military Tribunal at Nuremburg.

1945 United Nations Charter.

1948 Convention on the Prevention and Punishment of the Crime of Genocide.

1948 Statute of the International Labour Organization.

1948 Charter of the Organization of American States.

1949 Statute of the Council of Europe.

1950 European Convention on Human Rights and Fundamental Freedoms.

1956 Supplementary Convention on the Abolition of Slavery.

1961 European Social Charter.

1966 International Convention on the Elimination of All Forms of Racial Discrimination.

1966 International Covenant on Economic and Social Rights.

1966 International Covenant on Civil and Political Rights.

1969 Vienna Convention on the Law of Treaties.

1969 American Convention on Human Rights (Pact of San Jose).

1973 International Convention on the Suppression and Punishment of the Crime of Apartheid.

1979 Convention on the Elimination of All Forms of Discrimination Against Women.

1981 African Charter on Human and Peoples Right (Banjul Charter).

1984 UN Convention Against Torture and other Cruel, Inhuman or Degrading Treatment.

1987 The European Convention for the Prevention of Torture and Inhuman or Degrading Treatment or Punishment.

1989 UN Convention on the Rights of the Child.

1989 Protocol to the American Convention on Human Rights Pact of San Salvador.

Index